Organizing Age

Organizing Age

Stephen Fineman

UNIVERSITY PRESS

OXFORD
UNIVERSITY PRESS

Great Clarendon Street, Oxford OX2 6DP

Oxford University Press is a department of the University of Oxford.
It furthers the University's objective of excellence in research, scholarship,
and education by publishing worldwide in

Oxford New York

Auckland Cape Town Dar es Salaam Hong Kong Karachi
Kuala Lumpur Madrid Melbourne Mexico City Nairobi
New Delhi Shanghai Taipei Toronto

With offices in

Argentina Austria Brazil Chile Czech Republic France Greece
Guatemala Hungary Italy Japan Poland Portugal Singapore
South Korea Switzerland Thailand Turkey Ukraine Vietnam

Oxford is a registered trade mark of Oxford University Press
in the UK and in certain other countries

Published in the United States
by Oxford University Press Inc., New York

British Library Cataloguing in Publication Data
Data available

Library of Congress Cataloging in Publication Data
Data available

Typeset by SPI Publisher Services, Pondicherry, India
Printed in Great Britain
on acid-free paper by
MPG Books Group, Bodmin and King's Lynn

ISBN 978–0–19–957804–7 (Hbk.)
 978–0–19–957805–4 (Pbk.)

1 3 5 7 9 10 8 6 4 2

For Trudy

Preface

This is a book about age, or more precisely, how age is constructed. How does age insinuate itself into organizations, into institutions and into the meanings we make for ourselves and others?

I see age as a powerful master of social discourse, and a remarkable one given its taken-for-grantedness. It is a window on how we are. In focusing on age, we encounter a wide lexicon, such as infant, child, teenager, youth, elderly, old, senior, generation, aged, and pensioner. These are important social markers, indicators of position and status, and of where one is in a lifecourse. Thus, my interest is beyond age as just a number or correlate: it is with the way age is organized, politicized, regulated, used, abused, stereotyped, celebrated, stigmatized, struggled with, managed, and commodified.

I have written this book primarily as an accessible introduction to a fascinating field that crosses many disciplinary boundaries. It exposes the interpersonal and social games we play with age, and the extensive industry that has been built around age. I have lent considerably on social scientific literature, but first-hand accounts and popular representations all play a key part. I raise questions throughout the book—some of which I attempt to answer, others I am more hesitant about.

This book would not have happened without the encouragement of David Musson of Oxford University Press, and the patience and professionalism of Emma Lambert. I am grateful for Anna Fineman's help, while the book would have been a lesser product without the cogent feedback from Yiannis Gabriel and Carol Grossman. My thanks to you all.

Stephen Fineman

Contents

List of Figures

List of Tables

List of Boxes

1 Why Age?

BOX 1.1 MAKING NEWS

Business big shot: Richard Burrows, former Bank of Ireland governor

Moving from banking to tobacco does not, on the face of it, look an obvious career move—but Richard Burrows, a former governor of the Bank of Ireland (BoI) who is likely to be confirmed as the new chairman of British American Tobacco (BAT) this week, is better qualified to do the job than first appearances suggest [. . .].

Mr Burrows, 63, qualified as a chartered accountant before he joined Irish Distillers, best-known for Jameson Irish whiskey, at the age of 25. Within a year, he was managing director of the Old Bushmills Distillery, becoming chief executive of the entire business at the age of 32. [. . .] Sales quadrupled between 1989 and 2005, thanks partly to a long-running advertising campaign, which carried the famous tagline: 'The Smoother the Irish.'

No sympathy for drink-drive teenager

Gabriella Edmonson, the teenage driver who killed her friend after a drunken night out, has no excuse [. . .].

Gabriella Edmonson pleaded guilty to drink-driving 'My car, my rules . . . !' These four, glib words sum up the casual arrogance of a certain type of gilded youth, and they will haunt Gabriella Edmonson for ever.

Given the tragedy she caused, she deserves no less. The 17-year-old was one-and-a-half times over the drink-drive limit when she insisted on driving home from a nightclub in the early hours. [. . .]. One of her passengers, Grace Hadman, also 17, was dead; another, Joe Robinson, was critically injured.

Couple enjoy same holiday for 50 years

Michael Hirst, 79, and his wife Mary, 76, enjoyed their first trip to Malta so much that they have spent their holidays at the same hotel in the same resort for the last 50 years.

The couple, from Harefield, Middlesex, have been back and forth to the Hotel Phoenicia in Valleta, Malta, since 1959. Their holiday photographs chart the changes, as the structure of the building, pool, sun loungers and even the view from the balcony alters over time.

Their daughter Sarah, 47, shown as a little girl during the '60s and as a teenager in the '70s, now visits the island herself with her husband Richard, and children Lara, 12, and Giles, 8.

I picked these contrasting reports pretty much at random from the UK's *Times* and *Telegraph* newspapers.[1] The accounts are both ordinary and extraordinary. Ordinary in that, in style, they are much like the vast number of reports that display the journalist's craft: sharp portrayals of people and events that define or dramatize 'news', designed for rapid reading. Extraordinary in that each embeds a locater of meaning that we very much take for granted: age. To put it another way, what would it matter if we did not know that Richard Burrows in the first report was now 63, and was originally a chief executive at 32? Or that we were unaware that Gabriella Edmondson was a teenager of 17 when she killed her passenger, also 17? Or, in the last story, that we were ignorant of the precise ages of Mr and Mrs Hurst and their family members?

The texts would be coherent if we edited out the ages but, journalistic conventions apart, they would lack a bundle of associations that now come with chronological age. Even in this small sample, a clutch of age-related characterizations or caricatures is evident, such as: a particular age profile that validates the corporate 'high flyer' (first story); the fecklessness and recklessness of youth (second story); the benign charm and conservatism of the elderly, reproduced in and by their offspring (last story). The inclusion of age acts as a cipher or shorthand for socially constructed images—sentiments, stereotypes, expectations, prejudices—of what 'goes with' a person who is of a certain age in a certain setting. It attests to the potency of age as a shaper and divider of perceptions of others and of ourselves.

Chronological age is well infused into the cultural fabric and rituals of most societies. There are specific ages to be celebrated, others to feel anxious about or resisted. In the West, each decade 'reached' represents another significant notch in the lifecourse—for good or ill. Particular ages bestow certain eligibilities, social rights or privileges—such as for schooling, paid work, voting, driving, marriage, financial credit, social security, or pensions. Age is a political device (and a fairly crude one) for social structuring, and says something about one's position or status in society. It underpins the way state agencies distribute their services, according to whether one falls into the category of 'infant', 'child', 'adolescent', 'teenager', 'adult', 'middle aged', 'senior citizen', or 'elderly'.

Peering at cultures through an age lens reveals much preoccupation with chronologizing. We may accept this as simply a fact and go on to examine how age as a 'given' correlates with what we do or how we are (e.g. our health, abilities, preferences, performance). Alternatively—and this is my purpose in this book—we can ask why age has been socially constructed in the way it has. Why has it become such a master discourse, often a surreptitious backcloth to social divisions and key decisions in organizations, especially in the workplace? What are the moral and management implications of age grading on how our lives are shaped and how we shape our lives?

Age norms, although somewhat shaken in our postmodern times, still define what is proper or desirable conduct. They indicate expected levels of emotional and cognitive development, for 'young' and 'old' alike. Age norms demarcate the ineligible from the eligible, the promotable from the unpromotable, the proper from the improper, the clever from the dull, the odd from the eccentric, and the healthy from the sick. Many are converted into instruments of social policy: they are institutionalized. They are also convenient carriers of stereotypes. As enacted, chronological age, in these terms, is laden with political and moral import, reflecting particular contexts and times.

The implications of such a perspective are far from trivial. They expose age as a malleable resource that can be used or abused by those who manage or control others, framing our everyday assumptions as well as specific organizational practices, such as human resource management. Age is a potent organizer of our lifespace and power accrues to those who are able to shape age cultures and control the age agenda. The meanings of age categories such as infancy, childhood, youth, adulthood, and old age, are fluid, and depend on cultural and political circumstances. Age designations, accordingly, cannot be neutral or 'just a number': they compress and impress ways of feeling, thinking, and understanding about a person, issue, organization, or society. They seep into our identities, sometimes as pleasant infusions, other times as sharp erosions. Some can feel patently unfair or unjust and trigger resistance. As noted by Lawrence (1996), our feelings about age 'are saturated with ambivalence... Age is ordinary but holds intimate information about our lives, which makes it and everything we learn about it exceedingly personal, relevant, and potentially threatening' (21).

In this chapter, and those that follow, I develop these thoughts further. As the title of the book suggests, I am most concerned with how age operates within the everyday fabric of organizations. But I cannot divorce organizations from their societal and cultural context, where the 'organizing' of age is rooted: societal boundaries are porous. The academic material I draw on is widespread and multi-disciplinary: psychological, medical, sociological, social historical, organizational, gerontological, and management. There is no shortage of research of a positivist nature that takes age as a variable to associate with, or predict, some personal, organizational, career, or societal outcome, a stream of inquiry that has a long history. Some of this work has been helpful, but less so than critical ageing studies and critical gerontology— most of which is informed by a fairly small cadre of researchers. It is here that much of the qualitative, social constructionist work has taken place. Other sources I have used include popular literature (magazines, newspapers), television and websites, all absolutely key in defining some of the wider cultural images of age and ageing. Finally, wherever possible, I introduce 'live' illustrations, personal testimonies drawn from my own and others' fieldwork.

Historical constructions of age

Ancient depictions of the lifespan did not tally the years in annual sequence but tended to favour broad, but definitive, 'ages'. That is, life divided into a small number of distinct periods (Covey, 1989). They were to be found in writings of the time and accessible to the wider, often illiterate, populace through art and folk wisdoms—although how influential they were on actual behaviour is arguable (Aries, 1962; Burrow, 1986). An early rendition has been attributed to Solon. Solon was an Athenian statesman of some influence around 638–558 BC (Ehrenberg, 1973). His *Elegy of the Ages* combined social, cultural, and biological observations into ten ages (Cokayne, 2003). The first four concerned physical development from infancy to early maturity. Social obligations, such as marriage and children, defined the next age. In the sixth age, full maturity was achieved along with the first signs of physical deterioration. Language skills were at their best in the seventh and eight ages, while decline accelerated markedly in the final two ages, a gloomy prospect according to Solon:

He can still do much in his ninth period, but there is a weakening in his ability to think and speak. But it if he completes the ten ages of seven years each, full measure, death, when it comes, can no longer come too soon. (Cokayne, 2003: 60)

Solon's influence can, perhaps, be detected in a later, early fourteenth century, liturgical manuscript, *The Wheel of the Ten Ages of Man*. It symbolizes the ever circularity of the human condition in God's eyes. Christ's head is at the centre of the 'wheel', from which radiates ten spokes that end in finely painted scenes depicting various phases of 'infancy', 'youth', 'age', and 'decrepitude' (Bradley, 1920).

Though ten was the favoured division in these examples, early thought was mixed as to how many ages there were—three, four, six, seven, or more. However, the most popular numbers were far from arbitrary. They tended to reflect existing cultural knowledge, beliefs, or folklore, some inspired by the rhythms of growth and decay in nature. For example, three ages were common in the sixth century, associated with the biblical three wise men—one as youth, one as middle age, and one old age (Covey, 1989). A triadic division is also portrayed, vividly, in Hans Baldung Grien's sixteenth-century painting, *The Ages of Man and Death* (Figure 1.1). A grotesque figure of Death holds an hourglass showing the sands of time running out. He links arms with an old

Figure 1.1 The Ages of Man and Death (Grien, 1510). Permission kindly granted by Museo del Prado

woman looking askance, while also overshadowing an infant and young woman—the other two ages.

Four ages—childhood, youth, middle age and old age—were in evidence in the Middle Ages, associated with the four seasons, the four elements (earth, air, fire and water), and the four 'bodily humours'—black bile, yellow bile, phlegm, and blood—about which there was much curiosity (Dove, 1986). Major works of art also portrayed four ages, such as Anthony van Dyke's *Four Ages of Man*, and a similarly named series by the French painter Nicolas Lancret.

However, from the twelfth century, the number seven held particular significance. Seven was the number of virtues. There were also seven vices and seven planets (Burrow, 1986). Seven ages followed suit, dramatized by Shakespeare in *As You Like It*: the 'mewling and puking' infant; the 'whining schoolboy'; the 'lover sighing like a furnace'; the 'soldier full of strange oaths, quick in quarrel'; 'the justice in fair round belly'; the 'lean and slillper'd pantaloon with spectacles on nose'; and finally, cataclysmically, 'mere oblivion, sans teeth, sans eyes, sans taste, sans everything' (Shakespeare, 2000).

The different ages were anchors for meaning, solace, and anxiety. They gave a picture of life as predictable and fixed and ordered in times that were anything but, and where illness or death could occur at any time (Burrow, 1986; Covey, 1989). As templates for age-related behaviour they could be somewhat idiosyncratic or contradictory. For example, the final ages were often regarded as times of marginalization and decay (e.g. pictures of individuals bent with crutches and canes). But other images were morally toned, depicting the old as greedy and avaricious—a salutary warning to those in, or approaching, the later stages of life. Yet still others portrayed advancing years as a positive period, where spiritual strength was fortified by meditation, reflection, and contemplation.

Getting organized with age

> *Buried 19 July 1762 Thomas Knaggs, son of Thomas tailor of Byers Green and Elizabeth, age 13, drowned, double fees.*[2]

This early entry in an English parish register reflects the beginnings of a formal, chronologized culture. Recorded dates and age were becoming an important organizing principle (Kohli, 1986). Parish priests in seventeenth and eighteenth-century England were required to record births, marriages, and burials. After successive legal amendments, the parish register was a reasonably secure depository for birth dates, ages of marital partners, and age of death (Ashton, 2006). It provided population information for a state bent on levying taxes, regulating inheritances, and enforcing its moral agenda—such as preventing 'forbidden' marriages.

In early renditions of the register, even when the precise age of death was not recorded, the chronology of burial was a convenient instrument for taxation. Burial fees were, in effect, an immediate local tax, but the state intervened more directly in 1678 when it required all corpses to be buried in a wool shroud—in order to boost the crucial wool trade. Sworn entries to this effect had to be made in the parish register, with a £5 punishment (a substantial sum at the time) for non-compliance (Rivoli, 2005). One Northamptonshire entry, for a deceased of some means, read as follows:

Affidavit was brought from a neighbouring minister that the aforesaid Frances Pickering was shrowded only in a winding sheet made of the Fleece of a good Fat Mutton.[3]

Only those too poor to afford a woollen shroud were exempt. Their entries were marked 'naked' in the register befitting their state of burial, although it was customary to confer some decorum by covering their body with hay or flowers (Olsen, 1999).

The legal niceties of age in the parish registers were significant social-economic inventions yet, in everyday life, notions of age were still vague or irrelevant. As Aries (1962) wryly notes:

A man of the sixteenth or the seventeenth century would be astonished at the exigencies with regard to civil status to which we submit quite naturally. As soon as our children start to talk, we teach them the name, their age and their parents' name. We are extremely proud when little Paul, asked how old he is, replies correctly that he is two and a half... Little Paul will give his age at school; he will soon be Paul _____ of Form _____. (15)

Should Aries' man have lived in late sixteenth-century England, his identity in his village would have been unlikely to have been defined by coordinates of his birth. More significant was his occupation (his 'byname'), his physical characteristics, or his original place of provenance. So a baker could be Jeremy Baker or, if he were short or red-haired, Jeremy Little, or Jeremy Red, or if he came from Bristol, Jeremy Bristol (Laning, 2000).

In pre-industrial times, age was not a differentiator of who did or did not work in the fields. Farm work required the efforts of all family members where physical strength, experience, and sometimes gender divided the work to be done—but not age. In urban settings, family members also blended in exercising their crafts, such as boot and shoe making, baking, blacksmithy, butchery, and carpentry (Chudacoff, 1989). A form of apprenticeship was key to on-the-job learning and, when there was no natural or willing heir, the apprenticeship could be extended to those outside of the immediate family. In Europe, the conditions of apprenticeship eventually came under state purview. A key piece of legislation in England was the 1562 Statue of Artificers which set out age parameters: all householders over 24 could take apprentices for at least seven years, and apprentices themselves needed to be 24 or older when had they completed their term (Wallis, 2008). The starting age was not regulated, but was typically mid teens (though 'teenager' is a modern, 1950s', construct).

The behaviour of covenanted apprentices has received a mixed press. Charles Dickens' *The Lazy Tour of Two Idle Apprentices* reinforced a none-too-complimentary image of apprentices. Contractually, they were expected to be obedient, industrious, and orderly, and not to waste their master's time or goods. But, unsurprisingly, not all apprentices were so inclined. Disputes could sometimes be rancorous and reached the courts for settlement.[4] Some writers, though, such as Wallis (2008), suggest that the image of the recalcitrant apprentice has been much overstated:

First, it is clear that regarding apprentices as callow youths, of little worth to a business until instructed, is misguided for most of our period.

In early modern England, apprentices were generally bound in their mid-to-late teens. From the outset, they could be set to a variety of unskilled yet necessary tasks, such as cleaning, carrying, deliveries, shop watching, and simple preparatory or processing jobs. They might also have some useful skills. Most would have been engaged in productive work in the household or their parents' workshop, farm, or shop for years prior to entering service, giving them the chance to acquire skills that would later be useful to their new master.   (846–847)

Increasing age consciousness

Societal age-consciousness accelerated markedly with the increasing pace of modernization and its emblematic factory system. The level of operator skill was minimal and certainly did not require long apprenticeship. Young workers and children were now machine minders, some drawn cheaply from the ranks of parish-pauper children (Rose, 1989). Older workers found that their accumulated skills and knowledge were not valued in a system that privileged peak stamina and quick reflexes. They were squeezed out, so narrowing the age range of employees. In America, employers began to populate factories with cheap, young, immigrant labour—leaving behind 'distinct categories of unemployed teenagers and elderly men' (Chudacoff, 1989: 19).

In the early nineteenth century the state extended its regulatory arm to child labour. For example, the UK Factories Act of 1802 stipulated that children under 9 could not work and had to be enrolled in elementary schools funded by the factory owners. Children between 9 and 13 could work a maximum eight hours. In 1843, on the other side of the Atlantic, the first American state child-labour law was enacted in Massachusetts. It stipulated that children under 15, working in factories, should attend school for at least three months a year.

Age consciousness was to become a taken-for-granted feature of daily life as it, and time, entered everyday discourse. Both would become axiomatic to how the state allocated its resources for education, military membership, health, and social care: an institutionalization of purpose that would 'trickle down to the minds of individuals as they set and strive for developmental goals, thereby serving to create and constrain options, and to organize and link life experiences over time' (Settersten, 2003: 84). The new and widespread availability of the clock or timepiece was an especially important feature of modern capitalism and bureaucratic efficiency, virtually absent from pre-industrial societies. Now people, production and services could be 'on time', 'ahead of time', or 'behind time' (Rodgers, 1979; Chudacoff, 1989).

Age and the modern state are deeply intertwined. Since the mid nineteenth century the population census has employed age as a key metric for the planning of health, social, educational, and housing services. The census's viability, though, presumes a population that is reasonably accessible, and also sufficiently knowledgeable to accurately report its age. Both issues have proved problematic for census takers. In the UK, for instance, there are signs that, after 2011, the traditional census may be coming to an end. The population has become so mobile and fluid that it has proven difficult to take a reliable snapshot. Meanwhile, census enumerators in some poorer countries face the challenge of people not knowing their age. In parts of India, for example, enumerators for the 2010 Indian census (who visited over 630,000 villages and 5,000 cities), used a calendar of local events to help individuals position themselves in time.[5] The events ranged from India's independence in 1947 to the country's cricket triumph over the West Indies in 1983. Without an age entry, an identity smart card could not be issued, complicating tax collection as well as an individual's access to social benefits.

Age comes of age

The social sciences have employed various schemes and metaphors to characterizes the structure of age and ageing, some not unlike early 'ages'. Most prominent are 'the life cycle', 'seasons of life', 'life span' and 'the lifecourse'. Often these terms are used interchangeably, rarely with consensual precision. But together they constitute an important conceptual backcloth to our understanding of age and the chapters to come.

CYCLES AND SEASONS

Life as a 'cycle' assumes—like ages—a progression of age-related changes over time, each with invariant characteristics. For some prominent authors, such as Erikson (1959), the cycle reflects 'inescapable strivings' from infancy to old age. Erikson was heavily influenced by evolutionary theory and the biological programming of ageing. He proposed an eight-stage cycle: infant, toddler, preschool, childhood, adolescent, young adulthood, middle adulthood, and senior. Each stage presents particular psychosocial hurdles or crises for the individual to surmount, such as developing trust in infancy, addressing role confusion in adolescence, and dealing with despair in the senior years.

Daniel Levinson's popular *Seasons of Man's Life* (Levinson, 1979) parallels Erikson's cycle in many respects, but focuses more on adult (male) transitional stages and the demands of family and work. Levinson's four 'seasonal cycles' include preadulthood, early adulthood, middle adulthood, and late adulthood. In building his model, Levinson takes some of the accepted concerns of his time as key staging points, such as 'adults hope that life begins at 40—but the great anxiety is that it ends there'; 'the dreams we have are so compelling that not short of total success satisfies'. In many ways, Levinson's work captures the ups and downs of the traditional 'achieving' male, located in a stable economy and equally stable family. The image has been a cultural touchstone of striving in modern America, and has had a marked influence over how we have defined the meaning of age, achievement and career in modern capitalism. Let us examine this in a little more detail.

ENTER THE CORPORATE CAREER

The advent of the corporation in the early and mid twentieth century created a prototypical career/life cycle for men comprising education (youth), work (adulthood), and retirement (old age). Chronological age served the modern bureaucratic corporation well, providing order and calculability to those who passed through it (Kohli, 1986). Promotion and wage or salary would be age related, and time served was a definite asset, implying both loyalty and accumulated knowledge.

Hard work and 'a career' expressed the American Dream of a better, richer, and happier life, available to all regardless of social background or class (Cullen, 2004) Conspicuous consumption and materiality were its celebrated trademarks (see Figure 1.2). And as organizations and the state inscribed ages into their rules on employment, pay, social security and retirement, the 'normal' hierarchical, stepwise, male, career became institutionalized. It shaped how people thought and felt about their own position, adequacy and crises on life's 'ladder'.

But the reality was that The Dream, for many, remained just that. Nevertheless, even when unrealized, its aspirational grip remained intact. Moen and Roehling (2005: 3) explain:

Although this lifestyle worked for some, it was never a reality for poor women and men, those on the fringes of the labor market. Still, the breadwinner/homemaker family became the icon of the American Dream. 'Success' for men entailed a career that enabled their wives to stay at home. Although not all families in the 1950s could afford this version of the good life, even those on the outside looking in—poor

Figure 1.2 The American Dream. Permission kindly granted by Plan59

families, immigrant families, divorced or single parents – aspired to this breadwinner/ home-maker lifestyle, replete with house in the suburbs and a car in the carport, if not the garage.

Age effects are frequently gendered. Young women wanting to enter the workforce in the 1950s confronted deeply ingrained obstacles comprising 'facts' about how women 'are'. These 'truths' became internalized and, in turn, institutionalized. They included assumptions about difference in ability between the genders (e.g. women are weaker and in need of protection), and the inappropriateness of employing single women of 'marriageable age'. They should be at home caring for their family, an image epitomized in the magazines and advertisement of the 1950s (see Figures 1.3a, 1.3b). Men, 'by nature', were unsuited to the domestic sphere (Chodorow, 1979). It was an ideology that, in the USA, prohibited employment for married female teachers in the 1950s and, as late as 1961, excluded women from jury service because their home and family role were regarded as more important (McDonagh, 1996).

The rise of feminism and economic pressures in the late twentieth century began to dent, and ultimately reconfigure, such malestream practices. They eroded traditional beliefs about 'appropriate' work for women at different

(a)

(b)

Figure 1.3 A woman's place. . . . Permission kindly granted by The Advertising Archives

stages of their lives and, especially, the myth of the 'uniquely nurturant mother' (Barnett, 2004).

This substantive liberalization, alongside 'family friendly' employment policies, has evened out the playing field for women somewhat, underpinned now by some thirty years of equal opportunities legislation in North America, the UK, and much of Europe. In the UK, the number of men and women at work is now nearly equal, and many young woman graduates enter the professions. Meanwhile, successive surveys of both men and women across Europe and the USA record a progressive rejection of traditional gender ideologies by both men and women, especially 'that a man's job is to earn money and a woman's job is to look after the home' (Scott, 2006).

But this general picture tells only part of the story. Fine-grained studies expose a more complex reality. For example, qualitative portraits of family roles in multicultural Britain reveal that the father's role as 'financial provider and protector' is still strongly adhered to in particular communities (Hauari and Hollingworth, 2009). And for many school pupils, 'equal opportunities' have failed to dissolve a hard core of stereotypical attitudes about 'men's jobs' and 'women's jobs' (McQuaid and Bond, 2004; Gadassi and Gati, 2009), predispositions reflected in their later employment patterns. In 2004, the UK had more than twice as many women as men in secretarial, administrative, and sales positions. The reverse was the case in the skilled trades (Begum, 2004). Age and ethnicity further skew this picture. At 16, some 'two thirds of Bangladeshi and Pakistani girls and more than half of Black Caribbean girls feel they cannot apply for certain jobs because of their race, gender or faith, compared to a third of white British girls' (EOC, 2007: 9).

Pay differentials can discriminate particularly against young females. For instance, young women starting working life as apprentices in the UK earn three-quarters less than their male peers—a gender pay-gap that is reproduced across many industrial sectors and levels within Europe (Arulampalam et al., 2006). It reflects what Booth, Francesconi and Frank (2003) evocatively call 'a sticky floor', whereby men and women of similar age, background, and experience can be allotted the same pay scale or rank, but the women are appointed at the bottom of the scale, while men are placed further up. In some quarters, note Booth and colleagues, 'such a strategy can evade some discrimination laws, since the appointment rank is the same' (164).

While women's chances of joining the higher echelons of skilled and managerial occupations or government have certainly improved, they are still poor relative to men (Begum, 2004). In the UK barely 20 per cent of members of parliament are women, and even fewer are in local government (EOC, 2007). In the USA most female managers up to the age of 34 are as eager as their male counterparts to achieve superior positions in their companies, but the men consistently aim higher, and by the time women reach their 40s and 50s their aspirations decline rapidly as home and family demands compete for their attention (Hudson, 2008). The reality too is, like the UK, that very few of them actually reach the top (UCDavis, 2008).

THE LIFECOURSE—A POSTMODERN TURN

Life as a 'course', rather than predetermined cycles or seasons, admits many possible routes, turns, re-skillings, and loops. And importantly, it opens the door to the heterogeneity of age experiences at different periods of life and career. Indeed, some lifecourse theorists argue that an entrenched adherence to a traditional 'lockstep' career and its age, gender, and educational assumptions, is both divisive and retrograde:

Employers, men, women, and, frequently, even children take for granted that regular, paid work means spending five days, or forty or more hours a week on the job (a standard enacted in 1938 by the [US] Fair Labor Standards Act), that education is for children and young people, that retirement is a one-way, one time, irreversible exit, and that family-care work is women's responsibility. This sense of the career mystique as 'the ways things are' creates, perpetuates, and exacerbates inequalities. (Moen and Roehling, 2005: 23)

Lifecourse is more attuned to the 'the postmodern condition' where the structures that once provided a fairly predictable rhythm to life and its stages are now far less or have vanished altogether (Hancock and Tyler, 2001; Linstead, 2004). Organizations are flatter and leaner and less stable. Short-term goals and fast gratification have supplanted a traditionally cautious, long-term planning view of life and progress. Gender roles are more fluid and the expectations and meanings of old age are shifting as people live much longer and, often, healthier lives—at least in the developed world.

Careers under the lifecourse umbrella are more fragmented, individualized and 'protean'—the rewards dependent less on the organization and loyalty to it, and more on individuals' resourcefulness to morph into new 'employability' forms. Dechronologization underpins many of these shifts. Age-related assumptions, transitions, and boundaries are more plastic, less well-defined (Settersten, 2003). The flexible career is, amongst other things, seen as better matched to a risk economy and to major economic upheavals. Indeed, amongst the many 'certainties' that crumbled in the world recession of the 2000s', two were particular casualties: that new graduates had a fast track onto the career ladder, and the loyal experienced employees in middle age (50 plus) were especially valued. Both groups were the heaviest hit in the turndown, and only the most enterprising and adaptable people amongst them were able to find work (TAEN, 2009; Taylor et al., 2009a).

LIFESPAN'S POLITICS

Conceptually, 'lifespan' sits somewhere between life cycles and lifecourses. At its simplest, it signifies the time, normally in years, between birth and death. But the notion is richer than that. Lifespan raises questions about why there should be variations, sometimes startling, in lifespans, and the place of biological, social, and cultural explanations (Alwin and Wray, 2005; Kail and Cavanaugh, 2008). It highlights attempts to increase lifespans. It also queries the meanings of age or an age category (e.g. childhood, adolescence, old age) to people at different points of their 'span'.

History reveals some stark snapshots of the length of lifespans. The best estimates suggest the average life expectancy in early Greece was 30 years, and lower, around 25, for the hunters of that era (Achenbaum, 1998). In ancient Rome, the urban masses lived in crowded, disease-rampant conurbations. Children often predeceased their parents who, themselves, would survive no more than 20 or 30 years (Marshall and Hope, 2000). A fourteenth-century tenant landowner in England did rather better. He could live up to 50 years if he managed to evade the highly virulent Black Death (Jonker, 2003).

But we do not have to reach into the ancient past to find social conditions where survival at birth is highly precarious, and life for survivors is arduous and brief. While most developed economies currently enjoy the longevity benefits that come from good housing, healthcare, diet, and sanitation, the advantages are not evenly spread between, or indeed within, them. In the UK for example, a woman residing in Kensington and Chelsea, a wealthy area of London, can expect to live, on average, nearly 88 years—nine and a half more than her counterpart in Hartlepool some 260 miles away (Mooney, 2009).

Country comparisons make for sober reading. Table 1.1 reveals countries where the average lifespan is not dissimilar from that of ancient Rome. A cocktail of poverty, disease, deficient infrastructure, environmental degradation, conflict, and in some cases state oppression, can make survival extremely tenuous.

Swaziland occupies an unenviable position at the bottom of the table. Swaziland's veneer of urban modernization disguises deep rural poverty, droughts and its own version of Black Death, rampant AIDS, which affects some 50 per cent of 20- to 30-year-olds. It is hard to comprehend this bleak picture without an appreciation of traditional Swazi culture and its age and gender assumptions. For example, Swazi women are regarded as dependent minors, excluded by men from public meetings and subject to men's decisions on sexual and reproductive issues, including contraception. Modern contraception is seen to decrease a key source of family wealth and security: children. Children are viewed as one of the few routes to security in old age, and numbers of children and wives determine the status of Swazi men.

Table 1.1. Life Expectancies in Different Parts of the Globe[6]

Country	Both Sexes (years)
Hong Kong, SAR	82
Japan	82
Switzerland	82
Australia	81
France	81
Sweden	81
Finland	79
Germany	79
United Kingdom	79
United States	78
Yemen	61
Ghana	59
Kenya	53
Tanzania	51
South Africa	50
Burundi	49
Nigeria	47
Afghanistan	43
Zimbabwe	40
Zambia	38
Lesotho	36
Swaziland	33

Source: Population Reference Bureau, World Population 2009.

Polygamy is rife: ideal conditions for the incubation of disease (Daly, 2001; Ziyane and Ehlers, 2007). Accordingly, birth rates are high, but so is infant mortality—some 85 per 1,000 births (Phakathi, 2009).

Age norms

The notion of norms as central regulators of human conduct and expectations has been with us since the early days of sociology and social psychology. Age norms essentially operate in three, sometimes overlapping, ways. They structure institutional laws and professional regulations, they define key life transitions, and they regulate the fine grain of organizational conduct.

At the institutional level, age norms determine entry to, and exit from, schooling, employment, and the military. They underpin civic eligibilities, such as voting, marriage, alcohol consumption and pension rights (Settersten, 2003). The law is infused with age assumptions, such as on criminal responsibility, and when one is officially a child or adult. In medicine and psychology, age norms differentiate levels of health, competence, and ability. Norms of this ilk may be more or less strictly applied, depending on the cultural setting and discretionary boundaries. The legal age for marriage in India is 18, but robust informal norms and weak policing have sustained child marriage in nearly 50 per cent of cases.[7] Similarly, the legal prohibition of child employment (under 14) is widely ignored in Northern India, where it is accepted that children as young as 5 will work to provide money for their poor families[8] (see chapter 5). In the UK, 'binge drinking' has had a strong normative hold on people as young as 13, well below the legal drinking age of 18 (Coleman and Cater, 2005; Cheung et al., 2009).

As transition makers and markers, age norms are akin to a socially constructed clock. They are informal expectations about appropriate times and ages for particular achievements, roles or transitions in life, such as leaving home, entering work, getting married, becoming a parent or retirement (Neugarten and Moore, 1965; Settersten and Hagestad, 1996; Lashbrook, 2002). Age norms will also fuel expectations about particular accomplishments or activities, often with implied moral sanction or disapproval for those who are 'off time', of the sort:

> 'He's *only* 21 and they've given him a director's position—how can that
>   be right?'
> 'Oh, she's *still* trying to complete her first degree in her 40s!'
> 'You're getting on a bit to have your first baby, aren't you?'
> 'Aren't you rather old to go partying so much?'

Age stereotypes often accompany age norms, many captured in rich metaphors, such as 'wet behind the ears' and 'over the hill', and animalistic associations—'just a pup', 'can't teach an old dog new tricks', 'no spring chicken', 'mutton dressed as lamb'.

The final role of age norms is in regulating the micro order of organizational life. Norms can infiltrate all manner of organizational practices, from judgements about a candidate's suitability for a job to expectations about someone's performance at different ages and stages of their career. Age norms have been shown to define career progress, competence and seniority, where people's actual age, or age appearance, affects their perceived credibility—such as 'too young' to be a 'proper' manager/CEO/consultant physician and so forth (Lawrence, 1988; Lawrence, 2004).

In these different ways, age norms create an invisible structure that holds an organization in place. Lawrence (1996) makes this precise point by challenging some of our age expectations:

If age held no meaning, organizations might be unrecognizable. The role, power, and status structure might not change, but the ages of the people within that structure and their typical interactions would constantly violate our expectations of appropriate behavior. How would we react to being interviewed for a job by a fifteen-year old? What if the best venture capital proposal came from an eighty-year old? What if an engineering team with members in its 40s treated a marketing group in its 20s as equals? (2)

Some of Lawrence's illustrations, written over fourteen years ago, now seem less extraordinary as age-diversity has been increasing. There are influential financial experts, such as George Soros (2008), now in their 80s; there are students in their 70s, CEOs in their 20s and retirees in their 50s. But the tenor of her central message remains: the universal experience of chronological age is deeply ingrained in how we make sense of ourselves and our social worlds, such that age expectations and norms will shape what we see and do in organizations. Where organizational hierarchies are age based, as is still often the case, deference patterns are typically age normed. They delineate patterns of respect and power such that, for instance, the young new recruit would be out of place in voicing his or her opinion first in a meeting with his elders, without invitation. Cultural patterns in Japan and China have long reflected such norms—although globalized business practices are now beginning to redefine them (Selmer, 2001; Debroux, 2003).

BREACHING THE NORM

When an age norm is breached, the significance of the norm is most apparent. Our emotional reactions to such breaches may vary from mild surprise and discomfort to anger or dismay, while a self-transgression can feel distinctly embarrassing (Staller and Petta, 2001). Such emotions are vital signatures: they reveal how strongly an age norm is held and internalized, shaping the conduct of our daily affairs (Fineman, 2003).

When organizations, rather than individuals, transgress age norms, the consequences can soon become politicized—as has occurred in the fashion industry. The fashion industry has long recruited young (and ultra thin) females as models. The minimum employable age varies between countries, but ranges between 14 and 16—ages that are within, or close to, what many would consider childhood. But what if models as young as 12 were employed as 'adults' on the catwalk? In September 2007 an Australian fashion show fronted just such a model. The newspaper report in Box 1.2 captures the controversy that ensued, a tense meeting of modern and postmodern moralities.[9]

BOX 1.2 THE CHILD MODEL

Fury as 12-year-old 'model' fronts world fashion show

A 12-year-old has caused a media frenzy after she was chosen to front one of the world's largest fashion shows. Blonde-haired, blue-eyed Maddison Gabriel was picked as the official ambassador of Gold Coast Fashion Week in Australia and has also worn a number of revealing outfits for the Queensland event.

The country's Prime Minister John Howard strongly criticised the decision saying it was unacceptable. He said: 'Catapulting girls as young as 12 into something like that is outrageous.'

Mr Howard wants Australia to follow the example of Europe and ban models younger than 16 appearing on catwalks. 'There should be age limits, I mean there has to be, we do have to preserve some notion of innocence in our society,' he said.

'It doesn't matter about age, it matters that you can do the job. Modelling is all I've wanted to do since I was six—I don't think I'm too young," said Maddison.

Her mother Michelle Gabriel has defended her child's right to model and demanded an apology from the Prime Minister.

'I believe the Prime Minister is getting very doddery,' she said. 'He does not know exactly what 13- and 14-year-old girls are like. I used to vote for him. We're trying to get our teenage daughters to act older. I am so happy that I've got a daughter who has got a good head on her shoulders.'

Age norms collide here, as do emotions. On the one hand, a 12-year-old girl is regarded (by an older, male, authority) as a symbol of innocence, to be protected from lost childhood, precociousness and the sexualized capture of the catwalk. She is out of place. On the other hand, she represents the realization of the (commercialized) ambitions of pre-teenagers where appearing and 'doing' older is the norm, here encouraged and celebrated by her own family. Indeed, researches consistently point to the shifting expectations of what 'dressing your age' means and, for any age group, the imperative of not dressing too young or too old (Laurie, 1981; Klepp and Storm-Mathisen, 2005). For teenage girls there is the challenge of balancing modesty and sexiness against an upwards age-pull from the fashion industry. As a 13-year-old girl bluntly put it, 'If you don't follow fashion you wear, like, sorta, childish clothes' (2005: 323).

The fashion industry has attempted to redefine age norms for older people. To appeal to older consumers, 'mature' models have been recruited for live fashion events and fashion advertisements (Kozar and Damhorst, 2008). At first blush this appears a radical departure from the industry's long-standing accent on youth and bodily perfection, now reaching out to 'real' people getting older, 'warts 'n' all'. However, a close examination of the job descriptions for mature models (two reproduced in Box 1.3) suggests the shift in chronology is not matched by a change in the norms of appearance: youthfulness and perfection are very much still present.

BOX 1.3 OLDER MODELS WANTED

So what does it take for men and women to become mature fashion models? First and foremost, modeling agencies look for natural, attractive people. Fit, trim seniors have a better chance of breaking into modeling. You must love to be in front of the camera and not afraid to be a bit of a performer, acting out various parts as the photographer or shoot supervisor directs. While there's no one type that is sought after for senior models, in general, the agencies look for:

- Mature men and women age 40 and over
- Good skin
- Slim, toned body
- A natural beauty that shines through the camera and lights up photographs[10]

******

The [celebrity] models are healthy, driven women, mothers, who eat and work out and continue to enjoy their lives to the full. This is what the industry is endorsing and that is what makes it relevant and positive for many of the older ladies out there![11]

In reconstructing the image of the body, many of the common signs of biological ageing are selected out, while remaining ones are camouflaged with cosmetics or a digital airbrush (Ogden and Sherwood, 2008). As a provocative illustration, in 2009 *The Daily Mail,* a UK national newspaper, juxtaposed two facial photographs of celebrity fashion model Twiggy at 59: one as she appeared in a then-running cosmetics advertisement, and the other 'her more natural appearance on a trip the supermarket.'[12] The former was distinguished by its youthful appearance, free from blemishes and wrinkles.

The power of the fashion industry to define unrealistic, fantasized, body shapes has caused disquiet amongst it critics, especially given the prevalence of eating disorders and body dysmorphia (Thompson and Heinberg, 1999; Grogan, 2008). And indeed, a backlash to the digital retouching of the image of Twiggy forced its withdrawal, but not without an attempt at mitigation by the UK's advertising watchdog, the Advertising Standards Authority:[13]

[W]e considered that consumers were likely to expect a degree of glamour in images for beauty products and would therefore expect Twiggy to have been professionally styled and made-up for the photo shoot, and to have been photographed professionally.... We concluded that, in the context of an ad that featured a mature model likely to appeal to women of an older age group, the image was unlikely to have a negative impact on perceptions of body image among the target audience and was not socially irresponsible.

Lastly, in sharp contrast, some norm breaches are met with a mixture of admiration and wonder—because they resonate with a valued societal product or expertise. Child movie stars are often widely feted, as are teenage dot.com millionaires. Teenage dot.com millionaires are youngsters who are 'off time' in terms of traditional age/life stages, but very much 'on time' in a information-technologized world where rapid riches are coveted (Beroff and Adams, 2000). They are looked upon with a mixture of awe and admiration, especially by their peers. The weblogs in Box 1.4 capture the mood:

BOX 1.4 TEENAGE TRIUMPH

I think it's amazing that thanks to the internet, a school kid can become a millionaire. At 17 I'd only just finished my first ever jobs working in brick and timber yards over the summer holidays. I remember how proud my parents were that I was capable of doing a real 'mans'' job, getting up at dawn and working my ass off all day . . . I seriously think that if I were a teenager growing up now, my life would have taken a totally different path. I really doubt that I would have wanted to go to Uni, although I'm sure my parents would have forced me too, even if I was generating money online.[14]

Auctomatic sold for over 5m last week. It was co founded by two Irish teenage brothers—the Collison brothers. The two brothers aren't sole owners though, so that sum will be diluted, however Patrick is on record as saying he's now a millionaire so I'm not sure what way it was all split.

Their story helps show that ideas and work rate, when mixed together online, can explode in to multi million dollar websites. NEVER before has it been so easy to build a business and promote it. Still teenagers, these guys are now set up for life and can really enjoy themselves and pick their own career path. THAT is the life.[15]

Summation and Queries

In this chapter, we have seen the way that societies have long attempted to deal with the passage of time by constructing some form of age profile or age map. The map's shape, divisions, and contours have varied and, to this day, continue to be re-drawn. But whatever its form, it has provided a system of meaning, or narratives, by which to evaluate the present, to anticipate the future, and to reflect on what has already passed.

The number that signifies a particular age is a complex mix of ideologies, myths, norms, scientific facts, and existential fears. It encapsulates images of hope and doom, of health and sickness, of dependence and independence, of belonging and loneliness, and of progress and failure. It is a measure of how long we each inhabit this planet and, by implication, the social conditions that lengthen or shorten that period. It also is a device that defines one's employ-ability, regulates one's career, and shapes societal policies.

Age can be regarded as a master discourse that carries much of the human condition, replete with its curiosities and contradictions. Age narratives are gendered, age norms often demanding different behaviours and appearances from women than men, with different freedoms for compliance or resistance. Why, we might ask, should we be proud or ashamed about how we look for our age? How might this change? Ethnic background can also shape age norms, a fertile, or confusing mix for ethnic minorities. How might multicultural societies best respond to such distinctions?

Being classified as a child, adult, or old/senior carries with it many individual expectations and state obligations, usually taken for granted in Western settings. But what of cultures that blur, ignore, or fail to protect such divisions? How might 'age' be felt and performed when life's roles are very limited or make little concession to chronological age? And what leads to switches in age norms, such as revaluing older members, or seeing a young person's contributions as especially valid? Does this break down old hierarchies in the workplace?

2 Age Work

How do we know we are getting older? Our lifecourse is typically punctuated with rituals that mark the passing of the years, from annual birthdays to 'special' decades such as 40, 60, 70, and 80 and, in increasing frequency, 100 and beyond. The British monarch has been sending, 'on application', congratulatory messages to its centenarian citizens since 1917 (then very few), but this has now been extended to the 'one hundred and fifth birthdays and then every year thereafter'. The decade between 50 and 60 is often a sharp reminder of ageing and mortality, typically heralding the death of parents and shift to grandparental roles. But as lifespans increase and life roles became less age-bound, we can expect the years to signal ageing in different ways.

Age reminders are a regular feature of childhood, in admonishments such as 'You're far too young for that, Alice!', 'Only when you're older can you do that, James', '*Do* act your age, Gerry!', and in compliments such as 'You must be nearly 4!', 'Wow, you do that really well for a 6-year-old!' Moreover, children are soon conscious of age/body/ability comparisons as they travel through age-graded classes at school and, for a time, will be keenly aware of what proportion of a year there is left before their next birthday ('I'm 8 and three-quarters'). Many are exposed to classic children's stories which give a folklorish image, often none too complimentary, of 'old' adults—such as the evil old witch in Hansel and Gretel, Cinderella's malevolent stepmother and the abusive old lady who lived in a shoe. In 1978 Edward Ansello published his scrutiny of over 600 children's books to expose a portrayal of the elderly as problem creators, lacking in importance and jobless—but recent work by Parsons (2007) suggest a more positive shift, at least in films. She observes that popular films for Western child-audiences now show older women as heroic figures and as an important bridge between the generations

Coming-of-age ceremonies, marking the passage from child or youth to adult, are important to many religions, such as Confirmation in Christianity and Bar Mitzvah and Bat Mitzvah in Judaism. Secular comings-of-age can be seen in the 18th and 21st birthday celebrations common to the UK, Australia, and New Zealand, while Latin America's Quinceañera celebrates a 15-year-old girl's move into adulthood. Also of influence are popular economic discourses that value or devalue particular ages. Magazines in Germany, for example, have included bylines such as 'War to the old' and 'Old against young: how the old steal the future from the young' (McConatha et al., 2003: 206), while in the USA, a cover article in *New Republic* pigeonholed the affluent elderly as 'greedy geezers' (Butler, 1989).

In sum, age awareness is a major thread running throughout the lifecourse, a chronology infused with cultural meaning, ritual, and symbolism. How we frame our lives and the stories we tell about ourselves are defined by the experiences, feelings, and language produced by such age constructions. It is hard *not* to know one's age, or that one is getting older, in societies where age is persistently on the agenda.

The birthday business

The annual birthday is at once both private and public. It infuses an individual's sense of self, but also 'requires' some public acknowledgement and ritual. In work settings there are companies that have co-opted (some might say hijacked) the ritual to express their 'caring', 'bonding' philosophy, while also attempting to engineer workforce loyalty. Age celebrations are regarded as motivational fodder, to join the ranks of other managerial incentives to performance (Louise, 1985). A marketing manager outlines the nuts and bolts of one such policy.[1]

One workplace that I was in previously had the policy that people who were celebrating the birthday bought a cake in. This equalled out to be fair along the way because everyone was responsible for it and created the sharing aspect. One person from management was always there when we stopped for morning or afternoon tea break so the person was aware the company acknowledged it. This also helps solve the problem if someone really does not want to acknowledge their birthday they can still keep it quiet.

Also, I think the card idea is nice idea to get staff and management to sign. Plus if you had the CEO wish the person a happy birthday in person if practical or via phone would be a nice touch, organise in their diaries when each person is having a birthday.

As this manager notes, not everyone wants to join in. But the catch is that it is hard not to when others are, and when everyone knows that everyone has a birthday. One resister voices his worries:[2]

I work in an office of about 150 coworkers. My birthday was this past year. I did not want a big deal made of it and I told people that. I walk into work the next morning having my desk decorated, a huge food spread in the empty cube next to mine, gifts, cake, etc.

My problem is I feel I can't possibly participate in every birthday celebration at work for financial reasons and stuff. I cannot begin to tell you how many times birthday cards go around at work asking for money for birthdays and food day celebrations. My question is how do you say 'no' to giving money for EVERY birthday at work etc.? I have seen parties at work burn so many people, and I am so turned off by them any more. How do you avoid these 'obligations'?

While birthdays have become part of business, the business of birthdays has enjoyed a long history, epitomized by the greeting card industry, now a multimillion dollar enterprise. In England, birthday cards began over a century ago in order to provide an apology for being unable to do the customary face-to-face greeting (mimicked today in 'sorry I forgot your birthday' cards). In Victorian times, birthday cards were mass produced, mostly ornate and decorative. In addition to 'wishing you a happy birthday', many contained a sentimental message about the joys, hopes, and dreams that should attend the birthday person.

Birthday cards have, alongside special gifts (another commercial spin-off of birthdays), become two things. First, ephemera of an 'age' culture, something to fleetingly enjoy giving and receiving, and then forget and discard. Second, manufactured feelings, ersatz emotions. As Papson (1986) observes, 'To speak to one another through the greeting card is to speak through the greeting card industry' (100). They 'bottle' age in, now, a myriad different shapes and forms, offering the card purchaser a bewildering selection of others' (copy writers', card crafters') messages to forward to the birthday person. The seemingly inexhaustible supply of off-the-shelf messages plays upon, and reinforces, stereotypical images and clichés about age periods, such as teen-agehood, middle age, and old age. The genteel sensibility of the Victorian card is now hard to locate amongst the postmodern card rack. Oblique and not-so-oblique jokes sit alongside cards that tease, provoke, mock, shock, sexualize, debunk, or flatter. Cards in Really Good Company's range (Figure 2.1) reflect the genre:

Figure 2.1 Packaged age. Permission kindly granted by Really Good Company

And ageing

A child or adolescent will be aware that they are 'getting older', but they are unlikely to say that they are ageing, or be described so. 'Ageing' comes later in the lifecourse when we talk about others, and possibly ourselves, as 'ageing well' or 'poorly', and use phrases such as he or she 'really looks her age'— pejoratively. Culture plays a major role here, a point that social anthropologists have long been keen to make.

A cultural perspective on ageing and the very existence of 'old' as a category, competes strongly with biological views of ageing and its progressive enfeeblement. In Columbian Cuiva communities, for example, the elderly do not comprise a discrete social group and are included in all activities (Henrard, 1996). They are specially valued for their ever-accumulating knowledge of the world and the supernatural, which increases their power as they age.[3] Vestiges of the clear-headed, 'wise elder', transmitting crucial traditions and lore, are close to extinction in Western societies. Ageing now, according to Margaret Gullette, is indelibly tainted by 'a narrative of decline':

Decline is a metaphor as hard to contain as dye. Once it has tinged our expectations of the future (sensations, rewards, status, power, voice) with peril, it tends to strain our experiences, our views of others, and explanatory systems, and then our retrospective judgement.   (Gullette, 2004: 11)

In other words, ageing, especially in later life, becomes a social disease somaticized; we become what we learn to expect to become. It follows that if we could somehow, magically, turn back the clock to a period when we were less preoccupied with our 'decline', then present symptoms of illness and deficiency could reduce, if not vanish. Ellen Langer's 'counterclockwise' experiment in 1979 attempted just such a trick.

Langer and her psychologist colleagues at Harvard University recreated, in convincing detail, a microcosm of the world of twenty years earlier, 1959, in a building of that period. They invited men in their late seventies and early eighties to participate in a one-week study on 'reminiscing'. The participants were surrounded by the objects and memorabilia of the sort experienced when they were in their 50s and 60s, and they were asked to 'let yourself be just who you were in 1959' and to share with one another, relive, the then currents events. The research team created a separate control group that mimicked the experimental group in all respects except that they were asked to stay very much in the present time, and simply share their memories of 1979. Before-and-after measures included hearing, memory, grip strength, joint flexibility, gait and posture—all of which are commonly expected to decline in older age. Psychological measures included mental acuity and independent judgements of the age of the participants from photographs taken at the start and the end of the exercise.

Langer found that, on all these measures, participants improved, got 'younger', the experimental group most so. Their bodies and minds belied their chronological age and the debilities they had brought with them. In her own words: 'This study shaped not only my view of ageing but also my view of limits in a more general way for the next few decades. Over time I have come to believe less and less that biology is destiny. It is not primarily our physical selves that limit us but rather our mindset about our physical limits' (Langer, 2009: 10–11). Langer's conclusions are tantalizing and go some way in demonstrating, albeit from a contrived setting, that ageing can be a matter of we how feel we ought to feel at a particular stage of life.

DECLINE AND ANTI-DECLINE

In the industrialization of the 1900s, men in their forties and fiftiess were regarded as too old, too worn out and often unemployable (Gilleard and Higgs, 2007). The poignancy of this state of affairs is revealed in Robert and Helen Lynd's 1920s' account of life in Middletown, a small Midwest American city:

One woman spoke frankly about how youth was her family's most precious commodity. Speaking of her husband, she prophesised, 'He is forty and in about ten years now will be on the shelf...'. She added that 'We are not saving a penny but we are saving our boys'. (Lynd and Lynd, 1929: 34–35)

The parameters of decline were configured by industrial owners and their new technologies. Older people, once valued for their craft skills and experience, no longer fitted the economic calculus. Young men and women, including children, could, in Marxian terms, yield more surplus value—for a time. Upton Sinclair's social critique of the period, *The Jungle,* graphically portrays the physical demands of the production line on young male workers, drawn from his personal experiences in the Chicago livestock-processing industry:

The pace they set here, it was one that called for every faculty of a man—from the instant the first steer fell till the sounding of the noon whistle, and again from half-past twelve till heaven only knew what hour in the late afternoon or evening, there was never one instant's rest for a man, for his hand or his eye or his brain. Jurgis saw how they managed it; there were portions of the work which determined the pace of the rest, and for these they had picked men whom they paid high wages, and whom they changed frequently. You might easily pick out these pacemakers, for they worked under the eye of the bosses, and they worked like men possessed. This was called 'speeding up the gang,' and if any man could not keep up with the pace, there were hundreds outside begging to try. (Sinclair, 1906: 80–81)

Sinclair's central character, Jurgis, is a keen, fit, young man at the outset. By the end of the story he is physically broken.

Today, youthfulness still has a definite, yet more varied, hold on the labour market—which I elaborate in chapter 4. In 'non-brawn' occupations, such as investment banking, advertising, or information technology, 'not to have made it by 30' means one is downwardly mobile—too old not to have already succeeded, and too old to start. The decline narrative starts to bite early, 'lowering resistance and helping business to chisel away' (Gullette, 2004: 86). An aspirant banker airs his grievance:

At 38, I feel like a dinosaur. It seems nearly impossible to be considered for an analyst position, although entering the analyst ranks may not be the best idea, given a ripe age. I've been given advice that it may be best to get an MBA and then try and gain entry. Definitely a long road ahead.[4]

And an IT worker wrestles with his conscience:

I really don't want to be the guy who made it harder for anyone older than 30 to get funded in the web services market. But I've been thinking about all the young entrepreneurs we are seeing walk through our offices. I've been thinking about the 15 year olds who are hacking up facebook. You can't ignore it. There is something fundamental and important going on.[5]

The employment market reminds these individuals that they are ageing. But there is another market that offers antidotes: products and services that promise to camouflage, arrest, or even reverse the manifestations of ageing. They tackle the lethargies, lines, sags, bulges, droops, and wrinkles that have come to be regarded as cultural deficits and a loss of social capital. The ubiquitous, 'forever young' industry sells zest and youthfulness to those who, chronologically speaking, no longer belong to that category.

The reach and sophistication of this industry is extensive. It capitalizes on cultural fears about ageing, fears that can be more potent than any doubts about the manufacturers' claims. The phenomenon is not entirely new. We can, for example, turn to 1920s' marketing of *Phyllosan,* a tablet containing (undeclared) amounts of chlorophyll and iron that promised—amongst many other things—to 'fortify the over forties'. *Phyllosan* survived well into the 1950s when it was marketed as a palliative for the ageing housewife. The advertisement in Figure 2.2 conveys the message, reproducing the age and gender norms of the times. *Phyllosan* is presented cheerily as an essential boost for the 'over forties' housewife as she manages home and family chores for her much admiring husband—and with 'no maid' to support her.

Phyllosan predated the boom in 'anti-ageing' dietary supplements, as well as the current fashion for celebrity endorsements of products and devices that, purportedly, make one *look* younger—such as The *Tua Viso Electrostimulator,* an apparatus that 'so impressed celebrity model Kate Moss'. Its promotion material reassures the user that their youthful looks can be reclaimed: 'Your

Figure 2.2 Fortifying the over-40s. Permission kindly granted by Paul Carrington

unique facial contours and planes will gradually re-appear just like when you were years younger'.[6]

All such practices are sustained by a manufactured mix of nostalgia and age anxiety. The nostalgia is for a lost youthfulness, portrayed as comforting and rosy. It reinforces the belief that one's present, older, age is somehow less adequate, less worthy. Common adages convey the nostalgic tone: 'It's only the old who know the benefits of being young', 'I'm really feeling my age', 'Youth is wasted on the young'. Age anxiety trades on the fear of exclusion from important, age-bound rites of passage—such as a sexual partnership, a marriage, a desired job or career—because one has become, or looks, 'too old'. Canadian women, in a study by Clarke and Griffin (2008), speak of their own age anxieties:

I wish I could say that I feel at peace about ageing and that I will let things play out the way they do, but if I gave you an honest answer today, I think I'm scared because I know that essentially the world thinks old things and old people are kind of like garbage. I'm just holding my own and when I look like a piece of garbage, it's probably how I'll be treated. (9)

Youth is more attractive...young people is where there's fashion. Young people are where there's fun. I guess it's important for anybody who is not young to think they should either be young or they don't count. If you put it into a sentence—be young or you're not counted. (7)

Performing age

Age as performance is axiomatic to age work. We have, in Erving Goffman's terms, to stage our age according to the norms and cultural scripts available (Goffman, 1967). Some scripts are more public than others. Turning 40, for example, is little different in chronological or biological terms from being 39, but in 'acting decline' it is a marker of potential change in many Western societies. The 40-year-old (as is the 50-, 60-, 70-, or 80-year-old) is confronted with 'reality definers': those keen to say how the new decade should be for the birthday person, and what constitutes appropriate performance on the de-cline/rejuvenation axis. This can be anxiety provoking, a struggle to align private experiences with public pressures to 'act' an age. Laz, for example, reports an anecdote from a colleague: 'Fifteen or 20 years ago (that makes me 30–35) I was sitting on the front steps with D- and A, and one of the children came up asking for conflict resolution. I was all of a sudden struck by the fact that we were the "grown ups". I was shocked' (Laz, 1998: 101). Likewise, one of my own colleagues tells the following tale:

When I was 60 I was eligible for a senior bus pass—free travel. People said how fortunate I was. That certainly wasn't how I felt! I suddenly realized I was in the 'old' category, and the bus pass sort of symbolized it. It didn't feel right, feel *me*. Then there were the cinemas where I could now get a 'concessionary' ticket. I was loath to ask at first. Even embarrassed. What if I were challenged? I certainly didn't *feel* a 'senior citizen'—what a euphemism! It was a category I resisted. But eventually I found myself making jokes about it and even playing the 'oldie' role.

Age work is brought alive in these accounts and runs along three tracks: age as felt; chronological age, and performance age (the role behaviours associated with a chronological age). Chronological age, especially, turns out to be a poor proxy for the existential features of age, or for functional abilities and lifestyles (Henrard, 1996). We attempt to negotiate our way through these often conflicting meanings and messages, which can impact differently over time. The challenge is to create a story for ourselves that encompasses both what we feel about our age and how others, 'the world', casts us.

Subjective age does have a habit of being out of sync with chronological age, where the older we get the younger we say we feel (Barak, 2009). A survey of US citizens by the Pew Research Center (see Figure 2.3) reveals how the gap between actual age and felt age widens with increasing age: between 50 and 64 respondents felt some ten years younger than their chronological age, while those between 65 and 74 reported feeling up to 20 years younger (Taylor et al., 2009a).

In the workplace, discrepancies between chronological age and performance age can influence one's sense of efficacy and identity. It can be frustrating to be judged as younger than one really 'is' if that means that one's competence is underestimated. A self-confessed 'baby-faced' editor of a UK regional newspaper, the *Bath Chronicle,* wrestled with just such a dilemma: 'If you were to ask people around me to list my most irritating faults', he writes, 'I am pretty certain that that one thing that would crop up frequently is that I am forever banging on about the fact that I don't think I look my age' (Holliday, 2009: 41). Intriguingly, the baby-faced adult—large eyes, small nose, high forehead and small chin—may be laden with even more import than this editor suspects. In a series of experiments, Gorn et al. (2008) explored the way an image of a 'baby-faced CEO' was perceived compared to a digitally matched, 'mature-faced', one (see Figure 2.4a, b).

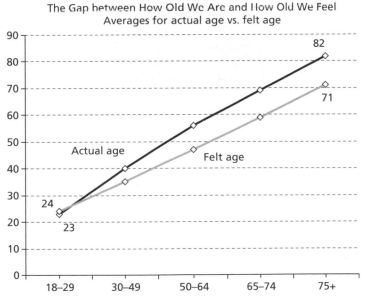

Figure 2.3 Feeling ever younger. Permission kindly granted by Pew Research Center

(a)   Baby-Faced CEO

(b)   Mature-Faced CEO

Figure 2.4 The face that fits

Source: Gorn et al., 2008. Permission kindly granted by the authors.

When shown a fictitious, but convincing, news report of the CEO's apology for unanticipated side effects of a drug his firm had released, the baby-faced CEO was judged the more honest and credible. But baby-faced honesty did not always win the day. In a linked experiment, the investigators were curious as to whether a baby-faced or mature-faced person would be preferred to replace a past CEO, but this time one suspected of 'lack of vigilance', precipitating a public relations crisis. The maturefaced individual was seen as the more competent to take over the role.

A lesson from this tale (notwithstanding its contrived methodology) is that facial characteristics that belie one's chronological age may work for or against you. It depends on the implicit personality theories that we hold: the physical age-characteristics we believe 'go with' different abilities or moral capacities (Borkenau and Ostendorf, 2006). The contrasting tales in Box 2.1 add to the point. The first is from Rachel who is in her 20s and works in an art gallery.[7] The second is from Melanie, a museum director in her 50s.[8] Both struggle to reconcile how their age, as perceived by their colleagues, fits with how they see themselves.

BOX 2.1 AGE OUT OF PLACE

Rachel's story

A few times at work I've felt people think I'm younger than I am. I'm 28 and perhaps over sensitive to this, as in a work setting I would like to appear my age and demonstrate the skills and experience which go with it. There's been a lot of hard work to get to the stage I am at, therefore I'm a bit offended to be mistaken for someone who has recently completed an undergraduate degree.

There've been two specific encounters. One was with a colleague within my team, who seemed quite shocked to learn my age, thinking me at least three years younger. Thinking about it now, three years difference doesn't actually seem very much. But since every year since my degree has been so integral to getting to this stage, that's three full years of progress missing!

Another incident was with a colleague from another department, who could not be expected to know about the work I do, but who I talk to regularly each week on the bus home. In this way I would hope to still come across as my age. But upon asking whether I lived with my family, seemed rather surprised that I lived with a boyfriend! Since partners may live together from 18 or younger, I was left wondering exactly how old she thought I was!

I do think I have a heightened sensitivity to this, and have friends who are happy to be thought younger. I suppose I may not mind so much if it weren't a work situation. It's one thing to guess an age on looks, but I feel it's different if you have had dealings with a person and they know you quite well.

I don't change my behaviour to 'correct' people's impressions, but rather try to maintain a level of professionalness. For example, there are some days when where staff will dress casually, and I've been surprised at how different people look in their jeans as opposed to their normal work clothes—not age-wise, but just that they look different. Therefore I'll never dress too casually as I want to maintain a certain image at work, and to dress too casually may make me appear less professional or younger.'

Melanie's story

I'm on the main board of directors of the museum; an equal on the board. Though I've been promoted, there's this weird thing—I'm 55 not yet 60 but over the past few years there's a very different view of me than 10 years ago. People in their 40s are viewed very differently than their mid 50s. I've been promoted for my ability to deliver, the ability to manage. Now, when I was younger I was seen as thrusting, able to do it. Nowadays the same thing, the same skill, can be seen by some people as stuck in your own ways.

What you're doing at one age and what you're doing at another age is perceived differently; the motivation is seen as different, although I've been promoted because of these skills. At 40 it's 'Melanie questioning this because Melanie knows what's going on out there, the pitfalls', now can be perceived as 'Melanie's past it, is against change'. My questioning is seen as blocking rather than a director who's asking.

continued

BOX 2.1 Continued

It varies with the age of the colleague you're working with. Colleagues of the same age as me or older, there's no issue at all. It's some of the younger ones. It's an image. An image of the older woman and older worker wanting to be stuck in the past, not being innovative. It's been explicitly stated—'you're stuck in the past, you're a blocker; you're the old school, you're from the past, holding on to past ways of working'. And this was what a colleague recently said to me:'Your default position is to look back to the past.' I wasn't modern, I wasn't innovative.

This one's new to me. It came as a huge surprise; I've never come across it before and I've been working since 18. I've got potentially 10 years to go; it's something you've got to manage and handle.

First thing I did was to try and counteract it by appearing to be frightfully innovative right away! No. What I'll do is watch it and monitor it. I'll certainly watch it as a director, valuing staff and not discriminating against them because of race, gender, age or whatever. The danger is to deny yourself—and skew your judgment pretending to be young—saying 'cool' and 'guys'.

These accounts reveal the sudden realization that one's age appearance matters. As earlier noted, age visibility can come in spikes, often unexpected, sometimes startling. What was once taken for granted can no longer be so. Workplace competence and skills are filtered through others' 'age' eyes. To younger colleagues, Melanie appears out of tune, out of step, retrograde. Rachel feels short-changed because she is perceived as younger than she is. The narratives also show that age work can be reactive or proactive. Melanie experiments with impression management to 'pretend to be young', while Rachel hopes that dressing 'professionally' will do the trick.

Masks and masking

> QUESTION: I happen to be one of the youngest account executives at our investment firm. My boss still factors in my age when delegating tasks to my colleagues and me. He thinks that many of his long-term clients will have as much of a problem with my age as he does, even though he is the only person I know who has this issue. What can I do to appear older?
>
> ANSWER: The questioner should mirror whatever his boss wears; whenever his boss removes and replaces his jacket, so should the questioner; glasses will make him look older as will good shoes that are well-maintained.
>
> *Beyond Business Casual What to Wear to Work If You Want to Get Ahead.* (Sabath, 2004: 48–9)

Age masking is intrinsic to age work. It is fashioned (experimented with, mimicked, invented) from one's early years when 'acting your age' is seen to acquire social capital (Laz, 1998; Biggs, 2004). In childhood this often means creating the appearance of age that better matches others' (parents', friends', teachers') expectations of what 'someone your age should be'—often in terms of 'older' behaviours than the child would, otherwise, spontaneously produce. Later in the lifecourse, we witness the reverse: masking to look and behave younger, but again to acquire social status and capital.

Masking presumes skill at reading cues that particular age-performances matter, without which one is stigmatized in some way—not taken seriously, not heard, discredited. Age masking is a way of 'passing' for an age category that one might not feel or normally appear to others, and gaining kudos from 'pulling off a good performance'. Masking, therefore, is a synchronizing mechanism that goes to the heart of self and social-identity creation and its negotiations (Renfrow, 2004). Clothing plays a major part. Our everyday judgments about age are heavily mediated by clothing. Clothing transforms the naked body into a social product or object that reflects the garment fashions of the period and, importantly, how an individual signals their age, gender, status and sexuality.

Clothing's symbolic value is substantial. It is shaped by a vibrant, global fashion industry that subscribes to the notion that 'you are what you wear', a potent identity slogan (Fennis and Pruyn, 2007). Clothes are the first line of defence in masking bodily signs of a particular age or ageing. The tailor's and couturier's skills can smooth the appearance of bumps and bulges, accentuate others, disguise limb or skin imperfections and, through the judicious use of texture and colour, produce an image of youth or maturity, sexiness or conservatism, assertiveness or restraint.

The thrust of such endeavours has, traditionally, focused on women; however men, especially younger men, are now defined as major consumers of fashion clothing. The invention of 'metrosexual man' to characterize a new, narcissistic masculinity has contributed to loosening the gender divide. Metrosexual man is preoccupied with personal grooming, fashion, and self-image (Flocker, 2003; Twigg, 2007). For example, fashion magazine *Men's Flair* pitches its message directly to the 'worried young':

Tired of looking like a schoolboy? Tired of being considered immature? Want to be taken seriously? What you wear does make a difference in how you are treated by the rest of the world. If you don't believe that clothes really do make the man read this article.[9]

In work settings, 'dressing your age' is fertile ground for fashion writers' imaginations and tips. Opinion varies from a broad, 'While a lot of women try to look as young as they can, dressing in a non-age appropriate manner at work is not a good idea',[10] to age-banded advice of the sort:

Age 16–25—don't dress too old and enjoy being girly. Age 26-35 - learn how to take young fashion into the workplace. Age 36–45—girly no longer works, but don't go too far the other way. Start tidying up the look with clean lines. Age 46–55—go for good quality separates that really flatter your figure. Avoid 'amusing' hair colours.[11]

In the 1970s, 'power dressing' was seen as a way for the new influx of women in the workforce to assimilate, but on men's terms—suits and shoulder pads. It aimed to suggest assertiveness and competence and was commonplace in the UK and the USA. Today power dressing is presented more on age grounds, promising to make 'younger women appear older' and to provide older women with 'sophistication and youth'.[12]

MASKING MODES

Age masking can be light work or hard labour, depending on the consequences of inadequate or inappropriate masking. All forms, though, point to the dilemmas, ambiguities, and at times contradictions, in suppressing or denying the age one is in favour of the age that others expect. And it is here that chronology and culture intersect, and where marketing and consumerism are ever keen to get in on the act.

In 1901, Sylvanus Stall published a book boldly titled *What a Man of Forty-Five Needs to Know*. In it, he issued warnings of 'diminishment of sexual vigor' and other 'inevitable declines':

With the large and preponderating majority there is less pluck and push, less courage in understanding and pursuing new enterprises or large responsibilities. Cares and anxieties which were easily thrust aside now leave a sense of nervous anxiety.

(Stall, 1901: 64–65)

More than a century later, we find ourselves in a culture of compulsive self-improvement where, as Katz and Marshall (2003) observe, such assumptions have been completely reversed. It is a change due, in part, to people living longer, but also to the aggressive marketing of 'positive ageing', 'new ground for images of older people by providing role models for ageing well—active, healthy, attractive, romantic and sexy' (Williams et al., 2007: 19).

Marketers have revised their age-graded profiles of consumers' 'lifestyle preferences' to sell messages of 'vigour and youthfulness'. Their targets are not just the 45-year-olds of Sylvanus Stall's concern, but people in their late sixties and beyond. They aim to mollify people's fears about the prospect of ageing: greying, illness, loneliness, sexual inactivity, exclusion. There are fixes available, be they botox, hormone replacement, skin peels, Viagra, hair dyes, or exercise routines (Katz and Marshall, 2003; Taylor et al., 2009b). The seductive promise is to grow old without the appearance of ageing.

The popular media have played their part in this grand project. For example, a UK prime-time television programme, *10 Years Younger*, confronted participants, in clinical detail, with their decaying bodies. It then proceeded to reverse them through cosmetic surgery and corrective dentistry. The compliant subjects often appeared dazzled by their rapid new looks, stirred by effusive praise from the presenters. We learned nothing, however, about what happened after the studio lights were extinguished, or how they lived with their re-sculpted forms (Fineman, 2009).

Time magazine has added 'employability' to the rejuvenation menu. In a 2008 feature, '*How not to look old on the job*', readers are provided with a list of options, and prices, of cosmetic procedures, from tooth lengthening and neck tucks to hair restoration and earlobe repair. All enhance, claims the article, an individual's competitiveness in the workplace, reducing embarrassment for those 'who must grow old in full view of their colleagues' (Cullen and Sachs, 2008: 5). A similar message is to be found in Charla Krupp's advice to women in her 2009 book, *How Not to Look Old*, a volume that has received best-seller acclaim in America and plaudits from the fashion press. Her message is forthright: 'It's every woman's dream: looking hip, sexy, fresh, and pretty— whether you're in your 30's, 40's, 50's, or 60's. Now it's every woman's necessity: looking younger will help you hold onto your job and your partner—particularly when everyone around you seems half your age'.[13] Feminist critiques are noticeably absent from Krupp's raw pragmatism— such as Anne Kreamer's exposé of the myths that drive women to dye their hair to disguise their true age, or Germaine Greer's views on the male medicalization of women's age 'problems' (Greer, 1991; Kreamer, 2007).

DEEPER INCISIONS

The *real politick* of surviving organizational life tugs hard at the coat-tails of the age-sensitive, increasing their susceptibility to body masking and the messages of bodywork gurus. Being 'old and female' is a double jeopardy, usually more detrimental than 'old and male'. Visible ageing for women in a culture that fetishises youthfulness and the body beautiful is threatening to those whose acceptability and, maybe, livelihood are at stake (Gimlin, 2001; Hurd et al., 2007). The dilemmas are palpable for older women who struggle with the implications of ageing for their values and vanity—as two Canadian women confide to Clarke and Griffin (2008: 668):

The media has always impacted me. I've never been able to ignore it or distance myself from it. I've incorporated the values of our mainstream media. So it's been a continual struggle for me to counter those values. As I grow older, it's very difficult to see the wrinkles appearing and the skin losing its elasticity. My radical feminism, on the one hand, is saying, 'Don't be so absurd'. The other side of me struggles. When I look through magazines and see all of these advertisements for wrinkle creams and the amount of cosmetic surgeons there are out there now, I am just absolutely appalled at what's going on ... but I've considered getting rid of these wrinkles, and the facelifts and all that. Whether I'll ever do it or not, I don't know, but certainly I've considered it.

I'm as vain as the next person around the corner.... I'm concerned about how I look which to me is a bad thing. I've always been told it's bad to be concerned about spending lots of time on stuff like make-up. I'm very critical of the cosmetic industry, but I like to look so-called young. I like it when people come up to me and say, 'Oh, you don't look 58!' I'm conflicted though. I feel bad about being vain because of how I was raised and because I did a lot of feminist work around how advertising sexualises women. I've been fighting it from an intellectual perspective for so long. I shouldn't be vain because I'm preaching against it, and I question am I being true to myself?

Older men feature less often in the age-masking story, but there is growing evidence that moves towards greater gender equality in Western workplaces (and families) have begun to change this. Some writers have dubbed the shift 'a crisis in masculinity' (Horrocks, 1994; Hise, 2004; Gill et al., 2005). The nub of their argument is that younger, brighter, and attractive women are displacing older men in the organizational power-hierarchy. Such a 'sociogenenic' shift (Elias, 1994) has challenged the long-standing gender advantage of older men and threatens their sense of competence and worth.

One response is bodywork: 'Businessmen are increasingly having face-lifts in order to maintain their competitive edge and middle-aged men look to cosmetic surgery as a way to match their aging bodies to youthful outlooks and life styles' (Davis, 2002: 3). Consumer capitalism has provided the cultural and material resources for male 'body enhancement', now a sub-genre of plastic surgery (Gill et al., 2005). The Harley Medical Group epitomizes attempts to normalize such procedures (see Box 2.2).[14] It seeks to reassure potential customers that 'wanting to look good' is no gender shame, and that cosmetic surgery is a fine solution for both low confidence and ageing

---

BOX 2.2 CUTTING OUT AGE

Cosmetic Surgery For Men

Men can be just as concerned about their looks as women, and for far too long the expectation has been for men to accept what they have and suffer in silence, though now more than ever before, there is an increasing pressure on men to look good.

At The Harley Medical Group we understand that wanting to look good doesn't mean that you want to give up your masculinity. Our Cosmetic Surgery procedures will help you to feel good and to give you the look that you want so you can face life with confidence.

Instead of just thinking about Cosmetic Surgery and not doing it, more and more men are now actually enjoying the benefits in increasing numbers.

The effects of ageing can be reversed and features that have bothered you for years can be changed and a new physique can be attained, which could not be achieved even with exercise and a healthy diet.

Permission kindly granted by the Harley Medical group

Atkinson (2008) suggests that some men 'tactically reframe cosmetic sur-gery along established masculine lines of power' (83). In evidence, he provides illuminating accounts of men's justifications for plastic surgery and related cosmetic procedures. For example:

Our company hired three new managers last year, and two of them didn't look any older than 25. What makes it worse is that they are well-spoken, bright, charming women who are gorgeous. So there is me, an ageing guy in a changing business environment who appears as if he's missed more nights of sleep than he should have. The superficiality of that realisation kind of makes you sick . . . but these people won't want me around unless I adapt, unless I change. (Peter, 54, cosmetic bodywork) (79)

I looked at my neck droop for so long before I mustered up enough courage to have it fixed. . . . I look like I'm 20 again; well, at least around my neck. At least no one calls me 'turkey neck' anymore . . . you have no idea how many times I wore a turtleneck sweater to avoid derision. I can't buy enough low-collared shirts to show off my work. (Tom, 46, advertising executive, facelift) (75)

I can't wait another 20 years to take action. I need to be a man who walks into the room and no one says, 'Damn, he looks tired.' If that continues to happen, I'll be out the door. I could have experimented with herbal remedies, creams or lotions to erase the years from my face, but it might take years, if it even works. Why wait when I can have better results from a doctor in only one day? (Derek, 52, marketing expert, botox and microdermabrasion) (80)

We see that the body, as a symbol of one's identity and capability, can be managed in culturally approved ways, and age remedies are ever more available on the production of a chequebook or credit card. The link between bodily appearance and chronological age is disconnected to serve an illusion of youth, an impres-sion that is accorded much social value. There are, though, some recurring fault lines in the masking project. It is often not difficult for a perceptive colleague, job recruiter, or potential romantic partner to see beneath the mask, either because it has visible cracks, because it looks odd or discordant, or because age can always be inferred from a person's life history. Moreover, in time, the mask will crumble, to defeat the best efforts of the masking industry.

Summation and queries

In this chapter, age work has been shown to shadow much of our lifecourse. We do not simply 'get older', dispassionately ticking off the years as they pass. Our societies and cultures define—mark, celebrate, insist on—what different ages mean. Age work operates at the interface of what we privately *feel* about our age and what 'they' see our age appearance and behaviours to be. Age work may be relatively stress free, but it can also be tough or tortuous—such as for the young person wanting to appear older, the older person wanting to look more youthful, or for those who simply want to 'look their age', whatever that might be by local norms.

Social capital is a capricious commodity when it comes to age, perceived age often linked to perceived competence. The capital diminishes steadily from the mid years onwards when the notion of 'decline' is widely canvassed. In this period, age anxiety mixes with nostalgia to enhance our receptivity to a gamut of purported age-defying products and procedures. Most are aimed at women, but men are by no means spared. Here age work moves into high gear, a hoped-for buffer against rejection in love, work, or life in general. In societies where the appearance of youthfulness matters so much, age masking can thrive, to the point of obsessiveness.

Such is the prevalence of age work and its various manifestations, how might we distinguish age work that enhances social identity and cultural cohesion, from that which is self-defeating and narcissistic? Why, for example, should birthdays, or *some* birthdays, be so special? How is the anti-ageing industry essentially fomenting, as well as exploiting, our age anxieties, effectively underwriting the narrative of decline? And what role is there for feminism? Has it lost its way in resisting the pressure to engage in body work to 'look good'—for whom?

3 Generations

Of the many ways that age is popularly conceived, 'generation' is amongst the most enduring. In biblical Scripture, Matthew reports 'fourteen generations' separating Abraham and David, each of seventy to eighty years. We speak of 'the current generation', 'my parents' generation', 'future generations', 'an older generation', and 'a new generation'. Generational 'clashes' feature in everyday accounts of social and political issues.

The term 'generation' (from the Latin *generare*, 'bring forth') is often used as a shorthand for the lineage of offspring. Kinship relationships define the different generations over time, via parents, grandparents, great-grandparents, and so forth (Morgan and Kunkel, 2007). Historical continuity or discontinuity characterizes the generational contours, each generation located by its period of birth or period of early adulthood—e.g. the 1920s', 1930s', 1940s', or 1950s' 'generations'. It is argued that each era will imprint a 'generational consciousness', 'the influence of the remembered past over the construction and maintenance of age identity in the present' (Edmunds and Turner, 2002: 143). The recalled past is generational in that it is shared amongst one's age cohort, evoking common memories. These could be of daily customs and practices (e.g. food preferences and shortages, patterns of authority in school and the workplace, gender and age relations, sexual mores, race relations), or of major historical events (such as the First or Second World War, the fall of the Berlin Wall, the Vietnam conflict, 9/11, the invasion of Iraq, deaths of major public figures or celebrities, technological or medical achievements).

Generationality is marked in various ways, often in family gatherings and in reunions of class, college, or workmates. They reinforce 'usness', often through a haze of age-differentiated nostalgia. We identify with 'our' generation, while feeling different from 'other' generations. Generation both binds and separates. Generational consciousness is essentially experiential, but it can also be virtual, stimulated, and 'recovered' from official documentation and records. The now burgeoning 'ancestry industry' organizes the past for mass consumption. It taps into the urge to deepen generational identity through snippets of our ancestors' lives. Websites are a major portal (Crowe, 2008), like ancestry.co.uk that promises that it can 'help you discover the stories of your ancestors in more than 4 billion historical records' and that 'the history you discover can be preserved and shared for future generations'.

In the workplace, generational distinctions are often coded in terms such as 'the founding fathers', 'new blood', 'new guard', and 'old guard'. In popular management, putative differences between these generations are said to explain conflict in organizations. Hans Hanson, at the University of Wisconsin is one such voice:[1]

The generational conflict in the workplace is here to stay and will probably become even more intense in the future. Issues that have helped create increased generational conflict are the worldwide economy; rapid changes in the workplace; downsizing of companies/organizations; mergers, acquisitions and consolidations of companies; elimination of many middle management positions; seniority as only one element of promotion; and technology.

  These changes in the workplace have made companies and organizations very flat with limited upward mobility, which causes people from different generations to compete for the same jobs.... This causes managers and employees to identify more with their generation and blame other generations for workplace problems and issues.

Social impact of generations

How do generations shape societies? In addressing this broad question, scholars have tried to steer a path between competing perspectives and definitions of generation, to focus on strata 'composed of people of similar age or life stage, who tend to share capacities, abilities, and motivations related to age' (Foner, 1974: 188). Age group and generational cohort, although not equivalent terms, are often conflated in such theorizing, producing generations such as 'the old', 'the young', 'the rebels', 'the veterans', or 'the conservatives'. Members of each generational unit are regarded as the same or very similar.

  Such aggregations are regarded as key to macro changes in society. Strauss and Howe (1991), for instance, identify generational cycles in America's societal transformation, a recurring sequence of 'peer personalities' where an 'idealist' generation is followed by a 'reactive' one, then a 'civic' one, and finally an 'adaptive' generation. The whole process then repeats itself. Some generational influences are transnational in reach, such as the 1960s' spread of youth consciousness, consumerism, and feminism, and the influence of the '9/11 generation' following the 2001 attack on the US World Trade Center—a national trauma to pass on to future generations well beyond the USA (Edmunds and Turner, 2005). Indeed, as travel, the media, and the Internet become globalized, generational movements are harder to contain within particular geographical boundaries (Ferrero, 2005; O'Duffy, 2008). In 2010, the cataclysmic BP oil spill in the Gulf of Mexico was being heralded as a generational turning point for the future of the world's deep-sea oil exploration and our dependence on oil.

The transformatory influence of one generation over another is, though, much dependent on the grip of the existing or 'old' order and the nature of local infrastructures of social change: democratic, tribal, or totalitarian. Many democracies embrace new-generational difference as an intrinsic, if not complex, part of societal evolution and change. In contrast, there are closed, tribal communities that value and protect generational stability and non-change: it is a widely shared cultural virtue (Toppo, 2001; Chacko, 2005). They differ from authoritarian regimes that fearfully suppress any signs of new-generational discord or difference in their midst (Richmond, 1972).

GENERATION BLUR

These broad-brush insights into the patterning of generations do, however, beg questions about the detailed dynamics of generational influence. 'Generation' is a hugely encompassing, crude concept when applied to the specifics of social and organizational change. This was touched upon by Mannheim in the 1950s. He was uneasy about assumed similarities amongst generational cohorts: some people will share common experiences and meanings, but others will not. He viewed each new wave of adults as engaging with the prevailing culture, both assimilating and adapting what is inherited (Mannheim, 1952). Old, new, and intermediary generations will vie to renegotiate the social order. Moreover, the cohorts that feel particular political urgency are those most likely to spearhead any change (Kertzer, 1983; Pilcher, 1994).

Once a society's (or organization's) age strata becomes blurred—overlapping, more permeable—then the influence of generational cohorts or clusters is much reduced (Gilleard and Higgs, 2005). A postmodern reading would suggest that some cultures of ageing, especially in advanced Western societies, now represent a mosaic of identities. The effects of age cohorts are diluted and dispersed, and that 'generation' now has lost its edge. We witness this in the loss of deference towards older generations; the fading of the modernistic expectation that time served and loyalty in the workplace is automatically rewarded; the 'instant' success of youth in media, music and other enterprises; the fragmentation of the nuclear family (no one to define and defend traditional generational boundaries and mores); and the ability to postpone childbearing and rearing until late adulthood or middle age.

There have been attempts to refine 'generation' for analytic purposes (see Giddens, 1991; Gilleard and Higgs, 2005). For Giddens, a generation only has meaning within a particular, fairly narrow, sociohistorical period of time, normally a decade (e.g. the 1950s, 1960s, 1970s, and so forth)—some half of that given to the popular typologies. Likewise, Gilleard and Higgs regard the particular time period as an important generation field in its own right, populated by overlapping age cohorts and lifestyle practices, or 'habitus'. These conceptions differ from defining a generation by particular historical events. However, they fail to circumvent the essential arbitrariness of the 'generation' time slot—why not half-decades, six-yearly, etc.? Each could be constructed as meaningful periods, sociologically speaking. Neither do they address the problems of imposing generalities to specifics, gliding over intra-generational perceptions and variations.

Investing in 'generation'

'Generation' may be a slippery concept in sociological analysis, but it retains a potent position in popular management and in the manner we categorize one another. The effects are not necessarily benign. Gullette (2004), for example, regards generational typologies as 'rhetorically shaped for their moment' creating false, often unbridgeable differences and divisions between people. In these terms, they resemble age's propaganda, a fiction that, after a time, is taken as unquestionable truth. And the wider their circulation, the more they become taken as fact. It is a 'demeaning by homogenising' (Blaikie, 2004: 83) that, like all typologies masks individual variation and increases the propensity to stereotype.

As journalists, marketers, and writers on management promote and filter generational cohorts, they define the popular generational landscape and those in it. Generational discourses thus become significant colonizers of identity, as well as tools for organizing social policy and prescription. Accordingly, organizations have been challenged to 'wake up to the generations in their midst', and to gear their management practices to the 'distinct' preferences of the difference generational cohorts in their employ. Amy Glass, in *Understanding Generational Differences for Competitive Success,* asserts the managerial position: 'by focusing on research about the character traits of workers in each generation, and identifying the types of conflict that can result, managers can better understand these characteristics and work styles, and can leverage them to enhance both team and organizational success' (Glass, 2007: 98).

GENERATING GENERATIONS

The default position for popular, and quasi-academic analysis has been four a priori, mainly US-centric, demographic groups: *the Silents, the Baby Boomers, Generation X*, and *Generation Y.* The precise labelling, birth years and characterization of each group varies somewhat between different authors, adding a fair degree of arbitrariness to the endeavour.

The Silent (or Veteran or Traditionalist) generation, born in the1920s and 1930s

They are typically characterized as dedicated workers and risk adverse:

The Silent generation is one of caution, indifference, lack of adventure and imagination, and basically just 'silent.' The first half of the generation is one born during the Depression and, as a result, gives freely to charity, have a tender social conscience and believe in a fair process more than final results. The last half of the generation can remember World War II from their childhood, and many joined the Peace Corps to show their generational bond.   (Pennington-Gray and Lane, 2001: 76)

The 'silent' label was initially popularized by *Time* magazine in 1951 in response to the rhetorical question, 'Is it possible to paint a portrait of an entire generation [then aged 18–28]...a million faces and a million voices?'[2] The generation's silence was, according to *Time's* correspondent, evidenced in its reluctance to 'issue manifestoes, make speeches or carry posters...no militant beliefs...not speak out for anything...fear of being tagged "subversive"...ready to conform'. The generation was 'working fairly hard and saying almost nothing'.

Ironically, the 'silent' generation eventually produced some remarkable, not-so-silent, social critics, such as Martin Luther King and the 1950s' film icon James Dean, famous in *Rebel Without a Cause* for his portrayal of a disaffected teenager, deeply at odds with his parents and their generation. The Silent generation in America, and much of Europe, has benefited more than any other generation from pensions and payout in later life, and has 'entered retirement with hip lifestyle and unprecedented affluence' (Howe and Strauss 2007: 43).

Baby Boomer (or Boomers), born in 1940s and 1950s

The end of the Second World War brought a steep rise in birth rate, a boom, in the US, UK, parts of Europe, and Australia. The boom was unevenly spread. In the UK and France there were actually two birth booms, one between 1945 and 1950 and the other between 1960 and 1965. But Germany and Italy had no immediate post-war boom, while birth rates declined for several decades in many Eastern European states (Gilleard and Higgs, 2007).

The precise source of the 'boom' descriptor is obscure; however an evocative entry in a 1951 edition of the *New York Post* is a strong candidate:

Take the 3,548,000 babies born in 1950. Bundle them into a batch, bounce them all over the bountiful land that is America. What do you get? Boom. The biggest, baby boom ever known in history.   (Porter, 1951)

Civil rights, activism, and Vietnam are said to have shaped this cohort, the 'indulged products of postwar optimism' (Howe and Strauss 2007: 43). For Jenkins (2008) they are 'more optimistic and open to change than the prior generation [and] are responsible for the "me generation" culture and the pursuit of their own gratification, which often shows up as a sense of entitlement in today's workforce. Because the fall of the dot-com marketplace eroded their retirement savings, many of the baby boomers now find themselves having to work longer' (20).

The 'upbeatness' of Boomers was explored by James et al (2007). In a large study of retail outlets in America they found that baby boomers and traditionalists actually shared similar, positive, feelings about themselves and their company, but 'outgrouped' their younger colleagues, seeing them as less reliable. Yet the researchers were cautious about placing too much weight on this finding—there were other possible explanations: 'In our study there are men, women, professional workers, hourly workers, people of different races and ethnicity, and those who are more and less educated. These are but a few of the within-generation differences that matter in thinking about people's values, attitudes, and work styles' (7).

Generation X, born between 1960 and 1980

The designation's popularization attests to Douglas Copland's novel, *Generation X. Tales of an Accelerated Culture,* in which its young, post-baby-boom, characters struggle for meaning and purpose in California:

[They] have been handed a society priced beyond their means. Twentysomethings, brought up with divorce, Watergate and Three Mile Island, and scarred by the 80s fallout of yuppies, recession, crack and Ronald Regan, they represent the new generation— Generation X. . . . Unsure of their futures they immerse themselves in a regime of heavy drinking and working at no-future McJobs in the service industry. (Coupland, 1991: back cover)

Generation Xers are portrayed as ineffectual, resistant to institutionalization, and, in the eyes of Baby Boomers, distinctly lacking in the required work ethic (Williams et al., 1997). However, they have recently been subject to reconstruction, given the significant positions and celebrity that some of them have achieved. *Time* magazine headed-up the reinvention with its cover story in June 1997: 'You called us slackers. You dismissed us as Generation X. Well move over. We're not what you thought.'[3] In the same year the *Independent* newspaper in the UK took up the cry: 'Generation X: The slackers who changed the world.'[4] Now, far from being ineffectual pariahs, they 'are willing to develop their skills sets and take on challenges and are perceived as adaptive to job instability in the postdownsizing environment' (Jenkins, 2008: 20).

As a robust categorization, Generation X falls short under close scrutiny. For example, do Generation X physicians differ from their baby boomers counterparts? This question was posed by Jovic et al. (2006) in a study of 54 physicians in the USA. They found that they did hold some different perceptions of each other, especially the Xers' belief that baby-boom doctors centred more of their identity on their work:

I think the older generation, if I can say that, medicine was who they were ... So there was a very different mentality as far as work was concerned. They were going to work 8 to 8 every day, be on call as much as they had to. (5)

You don't have to be defined by the job you do. Being a parent is good; being able to balance is good. ... I'm not working 365 days a year. I don't need to do that to be a better doctor. (6)

However, the study found far more convergence than divergence between the generations, the core values of medicine often transcending generational differences:

We're no longer these egotistical, godlike, you know, revered people. Now we're human beings. (Male Boomer) (5)

It's the men that are equally as interested in having a life and knowing their family and participation in their family life, even if it means that their work has to take up less of their time. It's a delightful change. (Female Boomer) (5)

When Generations Xers themselves are confronted with their stereotype, how much of it do they own? Williams et al. (1997) explored this question. They exposed a mixed sample of young people in the USA to an NBC News television programme 'America Close Up—Generation X', supposedly 'about' them. In subsequent discussions, the group revealed that they felt misrepresented by the negative images and stereotypes, were uneasy about the generational boundaries presented, and rejected the homogeneity of generational identity.

Generation X said much about white upper-middle-class parents' fears about the impending downward mobility of their children; fears that tuned out to be not altogether warranted (Ortner 1998; Down and Reveley, 2004). A 1994 *Newsweek* article, tellingly entitled 'Generalization X', captured the racial slant. It quoted African-American filmmaker Allen Hughes: 'The phrase "Generation X" doesn't mean much to twentysomethings of colour ... Call it racist, or whatever, but we don't count when it comes to Generation X' (Giles, 1994: 66).

Generation Y (or Millennials or Net Generation), born between 1980 and 2005

Familiarly and ease with information technologies are seen as the distinguishing features of this generational group. They are 'digital natives' (Prensky, 2001), 'bathed in bits' (Tapscott, 2008), and 'the most technically literate' (Eisner, 2005). For these writers, Generation Ys are very much 'the future' and are often misunderstood by prior generations as intellectually vacuous, narcissistic, and dumbed-down by their technologies (e.g. Bauerlein, 2008). Nadira Hira, writing in *Fortune* magazine, aloofly describes 'the problem':

Nearly every businessperson over 30 has done it: sat in his office after a staff meeting and—reflecting upon the 25-year-old colleague with two tattoos, a piercing, no watch and a shameless propensity for chatting up the boss—wondered, What is with that guy?! (Hira, 2007: 38)

She goes on to argue that because 'there are whole lot of them' they need to be accommodated, 'even it means putting up with some outsized expectations'.

Fields et al. (2007) are more expansive—and awe-struck—in their appraisal:

In sheer numbers, Gen Y is a force to be reckoned with. In addition to the population size of this group, they bring to our culture a new set of behavioral standards that have led them to become vastly successful as entrepreneurs.... Coupled with their unflagging confidence, technological superiority, and indomitable self-esteem, Gen Y is a cultural phenomenon. (3)

Characteristics attributed to Generation Ys include collaborative working, the desire for fast and regular feedback, freedom of choice, and an urge for personal development. Some suggest that they have acquired a unique 'hard wiring', a neuroplasticity that lends itself to special information-processing skills (Prensky, 2001; Shaw and Fairhurst, 2008). They enter a labour market far more volatile than that of their parents'. It is claimed that they are particularly attuned to self-managing their futures, improving their employability and marketability by enhancing their skills (King, 2003; Holden and Harte, 2004). They are cast as citizens of a 'post-organizational' era where their own proactivity and flexibility counts more than old-fashioned loyalty, and where moving between companies is the norm (Westerman and Yamamura, 2007).

The rhetorical claims for Generation Y have been examined by a number of researchers and, like the other categorizations, they prove flimsy. For example, Bennett et al's (2008) review concludes that there is far more variability than homogeneity amongst this generation. They also observe that Generation Y's supposed threat to established societal norms has been engineered by intense media focus and sensationalist language; it is a chimera, not shared by any actual panic in the populous. They add: 'We may live in a highly technologised world, but it is conceivable that it has become so through evolution, rather than revolution. Young people may do things different but there are no grounds to consider them alien to us' (783).

Kennedy et al. (2008) studied a Generation Y cohort—over 2,000 first-year students entering Australian universities. They explored the extent to which these 'digital natives' were fundamentally different in their use of, and preferences for, technology to support teaching and learning. Their conclusion was, 'not very much'. Beyond the now everyday usage of computers, mobile phones and-emails, the patterns and preferences for new forms of technological support varied considerably within the cohort. The researchers could find no case for radically shifting learning materials, as advocated by some writers, such as Prensky (2001).

Sturges and Guest (2001) interviewed fifty male and female Generation Y graduates three years into their employment. The group could be expected to epitomize the enthusiastic 'self managers'. But no: the graduates wanted considerable help from their employers in managing their careers. Half of those interviewed were dissatisfied because they had received less help than they had expected. These findings chime with the results of a 2003 survey of UK graduates by King (2003). King concludes that assertions about the decline of the traditional career have been premature, and that career behaviour should not be based on the 'vagaries' of Generations X or Y.

The multi-generational workforce

In recent years, 'the multi-generational workforce' has featured in popular writings on management, especially in trade reports, business magazines, and practitioner books. In 1998 the influential Chartered Institute of Personnel Development in the UK reported, in *Gen Up*, on the 'strategic implication of the four generations working together',[5] taking Veterans, Baby Boomers, and Generations X and Y as their starting point. The report was featured in the magazine *Management Today*, together with comments from a McDonald's corporate executive. He was impressed by the 'fascinating stuff' raised in the report, concluding that 'we need to undertake a fundamental review of the varied needs of a generationally diverse workforce, and embed the way we meet these needs into the strategy of our organisations'.[6]

In the USA, the Society for Human Resource Management, an association with extensive international membership, has made a similar plea:

For the first time in history, four generations work side-by-side in many organizations. The working generations span more than 60 years, including so-called Traditionalists, Baby Boomers, Generation X and Millennials/Generation Y. All bring different experiences, perspectives, expectations, work styles and strengths to the workplace. Despite the perceived 'generation gap' from differing views and potential conflict, organizations—and especially HR—have the opportunity to capitalize on the assets of each generation for competitive advantage.

(Lockwood, 2009: 1)

They go on to summarize the workplace 'assets' of the different generations:

Traditionalists: Hard working, stable, loyal, thorough, detail-oriented, focused, emotional maturity. Baby Boomers: Team perspective, dedicated, experienced, knowledgeable, service-oriented. Generation X: Independent, adaptable, creative, techno-literate, willing to challenge the status quo; Millennials: Optimistic, able to multitask, tenacious, technologically savvy, driven to learn and grow, team-oriented, socially responsible. (2)

An upsurge of practitioner books has echoed the theme:

- *Y-Size Your Business: How Gen Y Employees Can Save You Money and Grow Your Business* (Dorsey, 2009)
- *Motivating the 'What's In It For Me?' Workforce: Manage Across the Generational Divide and Increase Profits* (Marston, 2007)
- *Managing the Multi-Generational Workforce: From the Gi Generation to the Millennials* (DelCampo et al., 2010)
- *Leading a Multigenerational Workforce* (Murphy, 2007)
- *Work With Me: A New Lens on Leading the Multigenerational Workforce* (Magnuson and Alexander, 2008)
- *Plugged In: The Generation Y Guide to Thriving at Work* (Erickson, 2008)
- *A Practical Guide to Managing the Multigenerational Workforce: Skills for Nurse Managers* (Lower, 2006)

How might we make sense of this outpouring? What are its common rhetorical elements? First, they inflate a sense of the times, when four age/generational cohorts are co-present and active in wider society (primarily because the oldest group are living longer and working longer). Second, they redefine elements that are marketable and can be represented as concerns for business: how to get the 'best' out of this new constellation in the workplace. And finally, there is an uncritical acceptance of the received wisdom on how the generational groups divide in type and preferences.

In these ways, the seeds of a new management fashion—multigenerational management—have been sown. It contains various prescriptions, according to practitioner partiality, such as tailored motivational and reward systems, communication technologies that appeal to a particular generation, coaching and mentoring across generational groups, reversed mentoring where technologically savvy Generation Ys tutor their less cognizant elders, flexible work/life balance policies, and training and career development geared to specific generational 'learning styles' (e.g. Feiertag and Berge, 2008; Baily, 2009). Much of the advice plays, like other management 'fixes', on defining a problem that the manager is assumed to have or, if not, is very likely to have. In many cases this boils down to the assertion that a multi-generational workforce will have 'clashes' and 'conflicts' that can have dire consequences for business. It creates a spectre of disorganization and loss such that those who have the ameliorative know-how (experts, consultants) gain credence and voice. In other words, their services are 'essential'. The precise rhetoric varies, but the alarmist tone is universal.

Box 3.1 reproduces a sample of claims (along with bids for work) from different management consultancies and training organizations. Their sharp copy is peppered with apprehension and, often, impending catastrophe. We get a stark picture of the multi-generational workforce, characterized by strife:

Box 3.1 SELLING THE FIX

Boomers vs. Millennials: Eliminating Multi-Generational Friction in Your Workplace[7]

Today's HR executive must contend with as many as four different generations of workers with unique—and often conflicting work styles. While Baby Boomers tend to burn the midnight oil, Millennials desire more free time to spend with their families. Seniors and Baby Boomers often find themselves reporting to someone who wasn't even born when they entered the workforce.

If employers aren't careful, this cross-generational conflict can escalate into an expensive age discrimination lawsuit

Mixing Four Generations in the Workplace[8]

Generation conflict costs billions of dollars in lost productivity to organizations like yours worldwide—not to mention the incalculable effects on motivation and morale. Now there's help with generational expert Cam Marston's new DVD course, Mixing Four Generations in the Workplace.

The program will dramatically reduce workplace conflict . . . using the generation differences in a positive way.

Bridging the Generation Gap at Work[9]

Finally! There is help on how to overcome the generation gap in the workplace and managing generational differences that are a natural part of the cross-generational workforce. In this seminar, participants learn interpersonal skills to overcome generational differences that can create miscommunication and conflict within the cross-generational team and the entire workplace. . . . Not managing generational differences can result in a clash of communication styles and work ethics that can create cultural chaos.

---

continued

Box 3.1 Continued

Managing Multiple Generations in the Workplace[10]

Conflict in the workplace? Losing talent because of a lack of promotional opportunities? Generational stereotypes obstructing communication and productivity? You're not alone. Today's workforce is more diverse than ever, combining four generations with distinctly different values, attitudes, and work expectations.

So if age doesn't pop into your head when you hear the phrase 'diversity in the workplace', then you better start thinking about how different generations in your workplace affect productivity.

Generation Clash![11]

As so-called Traditionalists, Boomers, Gen Xers, and Gen Yers intersect in the workplace, their attitudes, ethics, values, and behaviours can sometimes lead to misunderstandings and potential conflict.

Companies need to look beyond this clash of the generations for ways to leverage multi-generational perspectives to their benefit.

Managing Four Generations in the Workplace[12]

For the first time in history, there are four generations in the workplace at the same time. Each of these age groups has different expectations and different demands, and employers who cannot recognize these will lose their best employees and see their workplaces in turmoil.

This program will teach you how to 'Gen-Flex' or move into another generation's comfort zone. . . . This is the basis for what we call Gen-Flexing, operating in another generation's world. Treat them as they want to be treated. Gen-Flex out your comfort zone into theirs.

How Interpersonal Conflict Hurts Organizations[13]

Interpersonal conflicts can wreak havoc on an organization. Whether it's a silent war between departments, a hostile relationship between two co-workers, or a damaging relationship with a vendor, when two or more people are caught in an interpersonal tug-of-war, the organization pays the price.

Managing Different Generations in the Workplace[14]

Miscommunication and conflict across generations can cost your company thousands of dollars in lost time and employee turnover. In today's economy, the skills and talents of every single employee are valuable. Your people are a vital resource in making your company successful.

Bridge the Generation Gap[15]

Age differences can create an insurmountable challenge if they take a company by surprise. As with most Human Resources challenges, communication and preparation are the best weapons to avoid a workforce disaster.

By embracing and encouraging this workforce diversity, a manager can turn a challenging mix of age and philosophy into an organizational strength and an investment in the future.

lawsuits, miscommunication, obstructions, clashes, misunderstandings, turmoil, havoc, tugs-of-war, hostility, huge financial costs, employee turnover, potentially insurmountable challenges, and workforce disasters. The business case for action is woven into the scenarios ('people are a vital resource', 'productivity', 'investment in the future', 'lose best employees', 'leverage perspectives').

Advertising and marketing consultants have been keen to employ a similar generational template. The *Generational Imperative Inc* of Ohio, for instance, claims that its strategy 'is grounded in this well-documented truth: each generation, during its unique formative years, molds unique core values. And those core values exert significant influence upon that generation's consumer decisions'.[16] A similar position is taken by Ann Fishman, President of Louisiana-based *Generational Targeted Marketing*: 'These generations are quite different in what they like, what they don't like and what causes them to make up their minds about a product, service, donation or even a vote. Good communication and marketing include some common traits, but what touches the head and heart of a Baby Boomer will not satisfy the needs of someone from Generation X or Y. Even some generational traits of America's newest generation, Generation 9/11, can be predicted'.[17]

The appropriation and selling of generational divisions and distinctions becomes more complete as the discourse is institutionalized, embedded in enterprises that normalize its meaning and package it for others' consumption. It achieves its considerable rhetorical feat by trading on simplistic and easily digestible distinctions.

Generation bust

We are on reasonably fairly firm ground in calling the offspring of parents a new *generation* in a family's lineage, a new filial line. Beyond that, the popular claims for generations are suspect, held together by a combination of repeated assertions and marketing panache. Moreover, there is something of a self-fulfilling prophecy in dividing populations according to preconceived segments and then explaining any differences on the basis of those preconceptions. The segments themselves do not get questioned.

It is a masterful (if unintended) deception to put down a host of organization ills to gaps and conflicts between whole generational cohorts in the workplace, as if they are lined up in battle formation in mutual incomprehension. In reality, inevitable overlaps between generational cohorts, as well as shared projects, will ensure some common ground, while there is little reason to suppose that someone born at the start of a generational classification will necessarily be 'the same' as someone born in the middle or end (Wellner, 2000). It is also likely that many people will identify with more than one generation—they straddle the interests and preoccupation of their parents' and their children's generations, and possibly their children's children's generation too

Four-generations-in-the-workplace is the much repeated mantra of the conveyors of conflict. The assumption of four generations needs to be set against the move towards early retirement and delayed entry (from increased education and lack of new posts) in many downsized or otherwise hard-pressed sectors of the economy, so restricting the age and generation range of those still in employment (Giancola, 2006). In the UK and the USA the oldest, 'silent', generation have experienced some of the highest rises in unemployment[18] (Johnson and Mommaerts, 2009). And where the generations are mixed, there is evidence of considerable congruence in preferences between Baby Boomers and Ys (Hewlett et al., 2009) and between Xs and Ys (Mulvey et al., 2000). Nolan and Scott's (2009) detailed analysis of over 8,000 respondents to the British Household Survey reinforces this picture. Covering an age range from 16 to beyond 80 the survey found 'more affinities between the outlook of the young and old than those who emphasize generational gulfs may acknowledge' (153). All respondents spoke of their particular age in terms of both progress and decline. The claims for intergenerational difference and conflict are much exaggerated.

Speaking of the American scene, Giancola (2006: 36) concludes:

Recent trends in our society, such as the rapidly increasing numbers of Hispanic workers and nontraditional career choices for men and women, have created a workforce with such diversity that global concepts, such as generation, which tend to oversimplify the workforce, contribute little to understanding its complexity.

It is hard to disagree with this summation, applicable in principle to most developed economies. Generation risks reducing the significance of age and ageing in organizations to clichés, a continuing predilection as writers compete to type and label the next, post-Y, generation (e.g. as US 'Homelanders' or 'Generation Z'). Clichés have their occasional place in everyday shorthand, but they should play no part in the design and execution of workplace policies.

Summation and queries

The idea of generation has had a strong hold on how we grasp changes in family lineage, the shared impact of a lifetime's events, and the predilections of cohorts of people born in the same year or period. It is the largest unit to include the 'age map' discussed in chapter 1. It has considerable intuitive appeal, especially to writers of popular management seeking uncomplicated or catchy ways of differentiating people at work, as well as to political analysts seeking ready explanations for major shifts in society and voting behaviour. As part of everyday speech and communication, generation has sufficient tacit understanding to inform our identity: who we feel we are *not* like (e.g. our parents and grandparents) as much as whom we feel we *are* like (e.g. our school, college, or work friends). It is a convenient, if crude, hook on which to hang our desired, or actual, differences and similarities.

The problems occur when generation is taken as the precise unit that it is clearly not—at least not in many of its applications. How valid is it to attribute similar qualities or concerns to a vast band of people who happen to have been born in the same decade or other arbitrary period? How appropriate is it to assume that major societal events are perceived and felt similarly by a given generation? Is there not something of a self-fulfilling prophecy in assuming there will be 'crucial generational differences' in the workplace (such as in values, outlook, and skills) and then proffering advice and management on the 'inevitable' conflict that this brings? And once one reifies one dimension, such as generation, others of possible greater significance—such and race and gender—can be obscured.

4   Ageism

> It's exhausting to prove your professional worth simply because you are younger, but in some ways it comes with the territory.[1]

> Fran Harrison, [Manager], has repeatedly made derogatory and offensive comments in regards to my age. Comments such as 'I don't think women over 55 should be working.' [She has also] encouraged my co-workers to refer to me as an 'old woman' [and] 'old bitch'.[2]

Adding an 'ism' to age is a powerful signal. It implies three things. First, stereotyping a whole class or grouping of people; second, prejudice towards that grouping; and, third, organizational or institutional practices that culturally underpin the 'ism', resulting in discrimination against or in favour of the grouping. In these terms, ageism holds similar terrain to racism and sexism and, for those affected, can have far-reaching consequences for their lives—psychologically and materially. Yet there are some crucial differences. Those who hold racist or sexist beliefs are unlikely ever to join the ranks of the people they decry or despise: we do not normally 'grow' into a different skin colour or sex. But we are all of an age, and most of us grow old, often very old. An ageist young adult will, one day, become a member of the very group that he or she now derides.

Over forty years ago Robert Butler (1969) wrote a prophetic article titled 'Age-ism: another form of bigotry'. In it he introduced the term 'age-ism' (then tentatively hyphenated) and the notion of age-ism as 'the great sleeper' in American life, a prejudice that was, then, just beginning to stir. Commentators on Butler's work have tended to present a rather truncated version of his contribution, stressing the effects of ageism towards older members of society. This was indeed a significant part of his concern, and has rightly dominated much current discourse on ageism. But Butler was also keen to point out that ageism is a two-way street: 'a prejudice by one age group towards other age groups...the young may not trust anyone over 30; but those over 30 may not trust anyone younger' (Butler, 1969: 243–244). The voices that open this chapter make his point,

Age is one of those instant, or primitive, categories that is automatically engaged when we perceive and seek to 'place' another person (along with their race and gender) (Nelson, 2005). It is how we value, and what we do with, this placing that defines ageism, or otherwise. Ageism's source or target can be any age grouping, be it 'teenagers', 'the young', 'the middle aged', 'the old', or 'the very old'. Stereotyping, or 'othering', is ageism's psychological crutch: 'All teenagers are...'; 'The problem with middle aged people is...'. Stereotypes serve to make simple and manageable the complex and varied: they chunk the social world into ready and undemanding categories. The othered group is invariably homogeneous in the perceiver's eyes. For youngsters stereotyping, old people are pretty much alike in their 'incompetence' while, in the eyes of old people, teenagers are 'typically ill-disciplined and thoughtless' (Cuddy and Fiske, 2002). In contrast, each see their own group, their 'in group', as a mix of different characteristics. The basic structure for ageist attitudes is thus set.

Fearing the other

The shift from stereotyping to outright bigotry—suspicion, intolerance, animosity—has been well charted in accounts of racism and sexism. But where does ageism rank in this analysis? Why should age trigger discomfort or extreme feelings towards others?

Explanations have tended to focus on ageism 'upwards', from younger adults toward their elders, and how ageism 'deals with' their existential concerns. Ernest Becker's thesis has been influential in this respect. In *The Denial of Death* (1973) he argues that frightening thoughts about one's own mortality are endemic to much of human existence. We get by by suppressing or denying these feelings. Western cultures, especially, have buttressed this denial by evasions about death, by *not* talking about it directly in families, schools, or medical settings, and by sugar-coating it in homilies and euphemisms. Even in funeral settings, where death is rather difficult to deny, most of our religions and accompanying rituals offer a soothing picture to comfort mourners. It all maintains the perspective that death is not to be dwelled upon, a necessary feature of a 'death-denying cultural belief system' (Goldenberg et al, 2000: 201).

Yet the system is under strain as people live longer and are longer dying. The presence of the elderly is a reminder of our mortality and feared selves: in decline, unable to participate in the work and social routines that we now take for granted, being marginalized. To young eyes, the suffering and loss from bereavement that comes in later life can appear strange, even a weakness (Kastenbaum, 1974). Ageism helps—by physically and psychologically distancing the elderly. They are not 'us', they are 'another being', as Simone de Beauvoir writes in *The Coming of Age* (1972: 3).

Ageism's psychology, however, evolves within a cultural context. Max Lerner's stark observations of old age in urban, 'achieving' America circa 1950, are one such image:

It is natural for the culture to treat the old like the fag end of what was once good material.... The most flattering thing you can say to an older American is that he 'doesn't look his age' and 'doesn't act his age'—as if it were the most damning thing in the world to look old....

Since the American has been taught that success belongs to push and youth, it is hard to revere those who no longer possess either. One can be fond of them, tolerate them, take reluctant care of them, speak whimsically of the crotchetyness and frailties; but these are far from the genuine homage of heart and mind. To build a code of conduct toward the old requires not only personal kindliness but generations of the practice of values from which the old are not excluded—of which they are the summation....

The style of aging in America is not a graceful one. It is filled with constant efforts to fight off anxieties ... There come then ... the loss of physical attractiveness, the loss of life partners and friends through death, the loss of status, the loss of useful and respected roles in the family and culture, and the final insult of being imprisoned in a body which is the shell of its earlier self. (Lerner, 1957: 613–614)

Some half-century later, Lerner's picture remains relevant in many respects—for America and for other advanced economies. Even more accentuated is the stress on youth: they are the productive and aesthetic icons of capitalism's projects. Deep old age has become even deeper, carrying with it stigmas and social strains—such as how the working, 'productive', population can continue to care for and fund a growing bulge of older citizens while, at the same time, many of its younger folk are struggling to find work.

Lerner wisely observes that it will need the sincere endeavours of several generations to dilute the values and sentiments that deprecate and exclude the aged—so it is perhaps early days yet. Nevertheless, there have been some positive shifts since the 1950s. Legislative changes have outlawed age discrimination in most Western societies. 'Age positive' programmes have sprung up in the corporate sector alongside governmental initiatives. And 'grey power' has given some organized voice to older citizens, a potential influence on the wider political agenda (see chapter 7). These ventures are not unproblematic (more of which anon), but they have begun to loosen ageism's grip.

Ageism and the law

I have suggested that ageism comprises three strands: stereotyping, prejudice, and discriminatory practices. The precise links between the strands are arguable. For instance, while stereotyping and prejudice are often closely interconnected, not all age discrimination is driven by premeditated stereotyping and prejudice. There are occasions when the discriminator is unaware of their prejudices: they act without malice aforethought. Such niceties have fuelled debates on institutional racism, a systemic, invisible process in an organization that disadvantages certain racial groups. The discrimination cannot be put down to the calculated actions of a single manager, or a small number of bigoted individuals. The discrimination is deeply embedded in the organization's culture and it 'just happens' (Feagin and Feagin, 1978; Murji, 2007).

Enter age legislation. Age discrimination law prohibits discrimination based on age—such as during recruitment, promotion, or termination. Age legislation is widespread in Europe and the Americas. The USA's has the longest pedigree, dating back to the 1967 Age Discrimination in Employment Act. Canada introduced legislation in the early 1980s and Australia in 1988. The UK outlawed age discrimination in the workplace in 2006.[3] Prior to that it relied on a poorly-observed voluntary code of practice (Wood et al., 2008). The different regulatory regimes share a broadly similar philosophy, but their precise conditions and implementation vary. UK law, for example, proscribes age as reason, directly or indirectly to:

- decide not to employ someone
- dismiss them
- refuse to provide them with training
- deny them promotion
- give them adverse terms and conditions
- retire an employee before the employer's usual retirement age (if there is one)

The UK legislation also makes it unacceptable for an employer to ask the age of a job seeker or to refuse them life insurance. Discrimination is permissible for 'objectively justified' reasons—a weasel term that requires the employer to provide 'hard' evidence, on a case-by-case basis, that the discrimination serves a legitimate aim of the business—such as efficiency, health and welfare, or training requirements. Employee-employer disputes that cannot be resolved internally can be submitted to an employment tribunal for resolution. Three cases (Box 4.1) illustrate what can come before such tribunals, and the outcomes.

The prima facie existence of *age* discrimination was proven in each of these cases, but much hinges on how age discrimination law is drafted and interpreted. In this respect, there is more divergence internationally than convergence—as revealed in an investigation by *Ius Laboris*, an alliance of human resources law practitioners. They asked legal representatives in twenty EU states to give their expert opinion on the approach their courts would take in

---

BOX 4.1 FACES OF AGE DISCRIMINATION

A 19-Year-Old Administrative Assistant Sacked for Being 'Too Young'[4]

Leanne Wilkinson claimed she had been unfairly dismissed from her job at Springwell Engineering in Newcastle, having been told she was too young for the job and they needed an older person with more experience.

The employment tribunal ruled in her favour, finding that evidence relied on by the company did not show Wilkinson lacked in performance, and judged she had been discriminated against on the grounds of age. The tribunal said the company had relied on a 'stereotypical assumption that capability equals experience and experience equals older age . . . age was the predominant reason for the decision to dismiss'.

Wilkinson was awarded £16,081.12 (£5,000 of which is injury to feelings).

NHS Manager Wins £180,000 Payout Over Age Claim[5]

An NHS manager has been awarded £187,000 compensation after she lost her job for being 'too old' at the age of 56.

Her hospital trust employer was criticised by a tribunal judge for attempting to 'defend the indefensible' and the NHS is likely to be landed with a bill of more than £500,000 once legal fees are included.

Mrs Sturdy, now 60, was the preferred candidate for a key role running the breast screening service for 124,000 women until she let slip that she was just over three years from reaching retirement age. A trust boss told her 'I didn't realise you were so old' and she was rejected for the better paid job in favour of a 43-year-old colleague with 35 years less experience.

She said after the tribunal: 'It was a horrible, horrible experience that I went through, now it feels as if a burden has been lifted. I can't believe that I am free from it. I can't wait to burn all the files and folders from under the stairs with a ceremonial bonfire. It will be cleansing, freeing—I have had to live with this for three and a half years.'

Age Discrimination Claim Costs Bar Owner £15,000 in Compensation[6]

The Carlisle Employment Tribunal found that Ronald Davidson was unlawfully sacked three weeks after his 60th birthday.

Davidson worked for the Globe Tavern in the Cumbrian town of Longtown for more than six years, but was then humiliated, made to do menial tasks and not given free uniforms handed out to younger staff, before being dismissed in June 2007.

The tribunal awarded him £14,695, including £5,583 for loss of earnings and £5,000 for injury to feelings, according to local paper the News and Star.

---

certain hypothetical age-discrimination situations. One concerned whether it was unlawful age discrimination for a wine bar to specify that its waiting/bar staff should be under 30, as it believed this would attract the youthful clientele it desired. Lawyers in France were alone in the view that this would be lawful. All the representatives were then asked whether their answer would change if the wine bar could show objective proof that the level of business would decline if it was unable to maintain the youthful image that it wanted. This time those in France, Greece, Luxembourg, and Portugal considered the age limit would probably be lawful, but the other fifteen thought otherwise. The authors conclude, 'when one looks at the likely approach... to different situations it is difficult to believe that is the same measure being implemented in each country'.[7]

Such international variation is problematic for a globalized economy with a mobile labour force. On the other hand, age legislation evolves in response to local economic and cultural conditions (see von Steinau-Steinrück et al., 2009). For instance, Ireland is highly prescriptive in its obligations and rights, obviating recourse to courts for many of the judgments, unlike the flexibility permitted in the USA or UK. The USA is alone in exempting small organizations (with fewer than twenty employees) from mandatory retirement, and unlike Canada, Australia, Finland, and the Irish Republic, it has a separate act for age discrimination. When age is combined in a single legal instrument with other grounds for discrimination—such as race or sex—age tends to be back-staged in the adjudication process; it is less a 'status' discriminator (Hornstein, 2001; Filinson, 2008).

DOES AGE LEGISLATION HELP?

For an aggrieved worker alleging age discrimination, the legal route is an ultimate, if onerous, avenue of recourse. Is it is worth the trouble? Taking the USA as a touchstone, the statistics reveal a mixed picture. Grievances focus predominantly on unfair termination (Neumark, 2009). The number of charges filed in 2007 was a little over 19,000, jumping to nearly 25,000 in 2008, but dropping back to around 23,000 in 2009.[8] The spike in 2008 has been described as a 'perfect labour storm' for that year, the cumulative effects of a greying workforce and bad economic times pressing employers to reduce costs by laying off workers who cost them the most (Wolfe, 2009).

In 2009 some 60 per cent of the claims in the USA were judged to be unsubstantiated: 'no reasonable cause to believe that discrimination occurred based upon evidence obtained in investigation'. Of the remainder, over $72 million in total was awarded to the discriminated parties. So, while the majority of claimants failed to prove their case, a sizeable minority were successful and compensated. Given the recency of the UK's legislation, the evidence is less reliable—but is suggestive. In 2007 there were 972 claims. This rose to 2,949 in 2008, climbing to 3,801 in 2009—a possible sign of the UK's 'perfect storm'.[9] But only a very small proportion achieved success at tribunal, some 2 per cent. The compensation awarded ranged from £9,000 to £90,000.

One wing of age legislation is to provide justice for disputing parties. The other is to bring about a shift in workplace attitudes and practices at source. On this second score, the current situation can, at best, be described as equivocal. Some up-front practices have been tempered, such as removing direct references to age in advertisements (e.g. 'Salary relevant to age and

Table 4.1 Percentage of older people in population: 2000 to 2040

Region	Year	65 years or older	75 years or older	80 years and over
North America	2000	12.8	6.2	3.8
	2020	16.5	6.9	4.0
	2040	20.8	11.6	7.3
Western Europe	2000	17.8	8.5	4.9
	2020	10.1	10.1	6.2
	2040	24.3	15.0	9.3

Source: Kinsell and He (2009).

experience'; 'Young, funky and ambitious?'; 'Attractive to those under 30'), or indirect ones ('Mature person required', 'At least five years' experience', 'Newly qualified') (Hornstein, 2001).

But legislation is a blunt instrument. If an employer is bent on using age as a criterion in recruitment, then it can be inferred, and surreptitiously used, in many different ways. Our CVs and biographies are saturated with age sign-posts, embedded in our educational and work history. Even a candidate's first name can be age-indicative, given the generational fashions for particular names (Bennington and Wein, 2002). To remove age completely would effectively erase the person. In this light, it is unsurprising that, in breach of employment law, many employers continue to find ways of gathering age information from job applicants, a particular handicap for older workers (Wood et al., 2004). This occurs at a time when 'active elderly' job seekers are increasing exponentially in numbers (Adler and Hilber, 2009; Macnicol, 2009; Neumark, 2009). The potential pool of older workers in North America and Western Europe can be seen from the projected demographics in Table 4.1. In both regions, 65- to 74-year-olds are likely swell to over 20 per cent of the total population by the middle of this century.

Rationality and stereotypes

Age discrimination can be 'justified' or defended on the grounds of economic rationality and/or stereotypical beliefs.

ECONOMIC JUSTIFICATION

Rational-economic reasons to discriminate are based on the view that, in liberal market economies, organizations depend for their survival on low-cost, low-wage work, especially in the burgeoning service sector. Favouring younger over older workers reduces pension costs, as well as insurance and health-benefit payouts. In these ways, businesses are safeguarding their prime function—to survive and profit in the most cost-efficient manner. Any long-term human capital losses can be offset against short-term cost savings. It is therefore right and rational to shed (such as through downsizing) those workers who cost the most, many of whom just happen to be older members of the organization (Loretto et al., 2000).

This astringent logic de-emotionalizes and depersonalizes what, for those affected, is often an emotional and very personal event. They are being discriminated against because they 'happen' to be more costly, in effect penalized for their age and experience. The approach hinges on the question-able assumption that a workforce is a homogenous, interchangeable resource, and that the long-term human capital losses can be easily offset. Recent economic theory (e.g. O'Sullivan and Sheffrin, 2003) casts considerable doubt on this reasoning:

[E]mployers' motivations are often grounded, at least explicitly, in the financial future of the company, and this strategy involves promoting and retaining employees who meet this objectives.... Such patterns seem to fly in the face of human capital theorizing and its assumption that discrimination does not make economic sense, because employing those who are better qualified, regardless of status, is in the best interest of productivity and profit ... Our data are rich with examples of very qualified individuals, with vast experience, knowledge and credentials who were laid off or forced into early retirement, usually in the name of corporate restructuring or downsizing.   (Roscigno et al., 2007: 326–327)

STEREOTYPES

Stereotypes are nourished from wider societal assumptions about age and ageing (e.g. Shah and Kleiner, 2005; Keene, 2006; Swift, 2006). By their very nature, they are self-reinforcing. It needs only the odd encounter with a person who is perceived to match the stereotype for the generalized belief and prejudicial attitude to be affirmed. To ingrained stereotypers, evidence to the contrary is often irrelevant: as the adage goes, 'Don't confuse me with the facts, my mind is made up.' Some of their targets can eventually internalize the messages they hear and react as 'as expected for their age', so completing the unvirtuous circle.

'Older people are simply poorer performers'

Supervisors' reports on performance are often biased against older workers, even in relatively enlightened regimes of human resource management, and even though the costs of retaining older workers can often outstrip the costs of recruiting, training, and retaining new ones (Perrin, 2005). Age, however, is a poor proxy for performance. There is no consistent effect of age on work performance. Older workers typically perform as well as younger workers and outstrip them in many areas (Salthouse and Maurer, 1996; Wood et al., 2008; Griffiths, 2009). As Cuddy and Fiske (2002) remark, 'Older people's alleged incompetence lies solely in the eyes of the beholder' (12).

Older people may well experience decline in some sensory and motor areas, such as vision and reaction time, but they are often more safety conscious than younger workers and have higher levels of organizational commitment and loyalty (Brosi and Kleiner, 1999). They are also likely to adopt different or compensatory ways of problem solving, such as enhanced anticipation and more efficient search strategies (Griffiths, 2009). Many have superior leadership skills. Physically demanding jobs are on the decline, but where work is physically demanding, level fitness can be more important than chronological age for sustained performance. People now in their 50s and 60s are generally fitter than in previous generations and, when combined with their job experience, they can maintain their work effectiveness (Landy, 1996).

'Older workers don't want to change or get into new learning'

This is a widely held conception. It can be heard from business students, human resource managers, and line managers (Gibson et al., 1993; Lyon and Pollard, 1997; Loretto et al., 2000; Henkens, 2005). A common claim is that older people are resistant to new technology, unable or unwilling to take it on board or to update their skills. Accordingly, as Malul (2009) summarizes, 'older workers face hard times when dynamic technology changes are taking place' (812). When workers reach their late 40s or early 50s, training and advancement opportunities drop sharply, seen by employers as a poor return on investment (Glover and Branine, 2001; Snape and Redman, 2003; McNair, 2006; AARP, 2008). Information technology workers can be particularly vulnerable:

I work in information systems where older managers such as myself are restricted to work on old mainframe systems, and not trained so that we are excluded from work on new technology projects.[10]

In terms of general *ability* to learn as one grows older, some cognitive abilities decline (e.g. short-term memory, processing speed) while others, such as intelligence, remain stable well into one's 80s. The brain activity of a healthy 80-year-old is said to be little different from that of a healthy 20-year-old (McCann and Giles, 2002). The *pace* of learning can be slower for older than younger workers, especially where complex skills are involved (Kubeck et al., 1996). But this is far from unequivocal. Mowery and Kamlet (1993), for example, found that older workers matched their younger colleagues when learning new technological skills, and a survey of employers by Munnell et al. (2006) reached a similar conclusion.

If older workers can learn as well, if somewhat differently from, their younger counterparts, some of the ageist stereotype is undermined. But maybe older workers do, simply, prefer 'not to get into new stuff'. The 'resistant' stereotype evokes an image of effete, late career workers stuck in their ways, ticking over and seeing little added value for themselves in learning new processes or procedures. Anecdotes certainly support the 'seen it all before' response amongst older workers: 'You start to get healthily cynical about the future'; 'We find that things keep turning over again' (Fraser et al., 2009). But such reactions may be more a reflection of a poorly conceived change or training programme than of the ennui of ageing workers. For example, on surveying a representative segment of older workers, the American Association of Retired Persons discovered that workers in their fifties were highly receptive to training opportunities that would upgrade their technical and business skills and improve their performance and career prospects (AARP, 2008). The desire to learn job-relevant skills was alive and well in this group, a pattern found in other studies too (e.g. Loretto and White, 2006; Pillay et al., 2006; Coupland et al., 2008). Those 65 and over in the AARP sample were a little less keen than the rest, yet when offered computer skills training they were equally enthusiastic. Overall, in the report's words:

These findings clearly contradict the myth that mature workers are universally uncomfortable with technology. Furthermore, workers age 65+ are just as likely as most other 50+ workers to report that they do not have difficulty keeping up with the technology needed to perform their work. (9)

We can conclude that the stereotype of the change resistant, cognitively enfeebled, older worker is highly suspect. In times when many workers are confronting a longer lifespan and when mandatory retirement is being questioned or already abandoned (scrapped in the UK in 2011), conditions are more than ripe for relevant and sympathetic workplace training—for those who want it. The block, it appears, is with those employers who remain wedded to the typecast.

'Older workers get sicker and are off work more'

It has becomes something of a cliché to say that our bodies deteriorate as we get older. The inexorable march of time brings with it weakening eyesight and hearing, bone and joint stiffening, and increased risk of both minor and major illnesses. This widely circulated narrative of decline, or 'diseases of ageing', readily colonizes our expectations: 'to get old means to get ill'. Indeed, when asked what challenges they expected when they reached their mid- to late 60s, a large sample of American 18- to 64-year-olds put memory loss and serious illness at top of their concerns (Frankish et al., 1998).

It would be perverse to deny that old age, especially deep old age, does not bring its physical challenges and debilitations, but in *Facts and Misconceptions About Age, Health Status and Employability,* Benjamin and Wilson (2005) contest the stereotypical view of older workers as sicker workers. Other than some special cases, such as the vulnerability of older workers to injury from physical work in the construction and agricultural industries, increasing chronological age in the workplace does not necessarily bring physical decline. Older workers tend to take no less exercise than younger workers—but it is usually not so intensive. Longevity, 'active ageing', and improved dietary regimes have resulted in a much more robust, older workforce compared to earlier eras of industrialization (Frankish et al., 1998).

On absence, older workers are less likely than younger ones to take short-term absences for illness—typically the most disruptive for employers (Barham and Begum, 2007). And they also appear more honest, 'less likely to abuse their employer's trust by fabricating reasons for taking days off sick'.[11] Older workers do take slighter more days off for longer-term, certified illness. Even so, absence due to illness across all age groups tends to affect no more than 5 per cent of the workforce at any one time.[12]

IT'S EASIER TO SLAY A DRAGON THAN KILL A MYTH[13]

To relinquish a stereotype means surrendering some emotional investment and power. To believe that workers over 50 are slow or reluctant learners makes it easier for managers to preserve a younger and cheaper team. To assert that a 60-year-old female job applicant will be a poor performer because of her age rationalizes the discomfort of employing someone who 'could be their mother'. Myths about dysfunctional older age die hardest when they are entrenched in the organization's belief system and cultural norms. Dissolving a stereotype, therefore, requires persuasive informational pro-grammes and inspired leadership. This has been the aim of 'positive ageing' initiatives.

Positive ageing

Positive ageing counters the stereotypes with a message of 'positive' moral and economic obligation. Older people are not to be judged according to invalid and inappropriate stereotypes and be socially excluded: they are to be integrated as productive and economically valuable citizens (Biggs, 2004). Governmental, NGO, employees' and employers' organizations have all em-braced elements of positive ageing. For example, against the background of its age discrimination legislation, the UK Government's *Business Link* publication (and associated web resources) disabuses readers of ageing's 'mythologies' and exhorts employers to garner...

benefit from an age diverse workforce. These benefits could include a reduction in recruitment and training costs, and increased productivity. Older employees may have valuable experience and knowledge and may be able to train or mentor less experienced colleagues. They can also help you to create a balanced working environment and may welcome the opportunity to work flexibly to enable you to cover your business hours or respond to unexpected changes in your business.[14]

The *Employers Forum on Age,* likewise, promotes as 'common sense' the business case for age diversity: 'By abandoning their prejudices about what make a "younger" or "older" worker, smart employers are gaining competitive advantage.'[15] In 2010, the Forum listed 170 paid-up members. This was a tiny fraction of the 1.25 million pubic corporations in the UK, but many were 'blue chip' and potential opinion leaders. All were eligible to sport an *Age Aware* logo to advertise their anti-ageist stance. The Forum does not audit its members but acts in an advisory role, offering guidance on legislation and 'good practice'. Its exemplars include British Gas's removal of existing age-bands for its apprenticeship and trainee positions; Kent County Council's scheme to make themselves more attractive to under-represented younger applicants; ASDA's efforts to recruit over-50s; and B&Q's mixed workforce, for which the company claims 'a huge age range from 16–95'.[16]

Beyond the UK, some firms are 'age positive' in response to local political conditions. BMW, for instance, the largest employer in Lower Bavaria, became conscious of the local reputational damage that would ensue from firing or retiring its poorer-performing older workers. Befitting its technological reputation, it applied an ergonomic approach to the problem, reengineering workplace equipment in its assembly plant to reduce the physical strain on older workers (Loch et al., 2010). Despite some initial resistance to 'a pensioners' line', the move appeared to provide benefits for both employer, in terms of increased performance, and employees (who could be retained and exercise more of their potential).

But not all organizations have been total converts to the age positive message. My own interviews with human resources directors in 2009 reveal something of their thinking. For example, one spoke for a large, UK-based, financial services company:

Well, we haven't really had a big reaction to the age regulations yet. There's no area of my business that's coming to me saying 'Mark, we want to do stuff around age.' Yes, we've worked with the Employers Forum on Age, and we've discovered it was our younger people, more than ones over 60, who felt they were being passed over; their talents weren't recognised. The Forum's gone down the track of having award ceremonies for age which you find lots of big companies love, getting awards; it ticks all the boxes with the MD. But their biggest dilemma is how to get age on the wider agenda, as it is not quite the big thing yet. Certainly, we respond to legislation, fully and comprehensively... but that doesn't always get put into practice; things don't go right all the time. But, to be frank, we've had to change the way we look at early retirement and make the payouts less generous. We simply can't afford it. And I have to admit, particularly on retirement, other organizations are far ahead of us.

Another director worked for a worldwide telecommunications corporation:

Actually we firmly believe that all of that legislation is a bit of a red herring in that it's obviously very good practice but we're not into positive discrimination and therefore we believe that as long as you manage people effectively and you've got a proper performance culture then that's the only thing that matters. The key criterion is can people do the job to the standard that is required. I suspect that people only start thinking of themselves as 'old' when the physical demands of the job start making them feel tired and they can't so easily adjust their working regime to make sure that they look after themselves.

With the advent of Blackberry it's a 24 by 7 existence and when you're operating in 33 countries across 11 time zones, 6 languages and 5 continents, it never stops. It's highly rewarded and it demands its pound of flesh and so it is absolutely not a place for the fainthearted and it's absolutely not a place where anyone could hide. So there's a constant refresh going on and there is a constant review of structures, performance, people, management layers, reporting lines, spans of control, and if ever there is an opportunity to do it with less or to do more with less we always take that opportunity. It's not something you want to be doing at the age of 55.

In sum, age positive projects constitute a broad attack on ageism and related discriminatory practices in the workplace. The projects are, inevitably, filtered by organizational gatekeepers, so their impact varies—depending on organizational cultural values, on the persuasiveness of the business case and on the strength of sanctions for non-compliance. Positive ageing, though, does appear a welcome antidote to ageism in the workplace, so much so, that it is easy to overlook its own internal contradiction. Some variants insist that the old can be judged on a par with the young, on the same playing field, thus impressing the priorities of one period of the lifecourse, 'youth', on another, the 'old'. This is itself ageist, or a version of *youngism*. It can eclipse the unique contributions that older age can bring, such as experience, tacit knowledge, and cultural capital to pass on.

Gendered ageism

A person can belong to more than one discriminated or oppressed group; ageism rarely operates in isolation. It intersects with other prejudices, such as racial or social class. However, it is especially corrosive for women. Compared to men, women will experience age discrimination at a younger age and are seen (particularly by men) as older at an earlier age (Loretto et al., 2000; Granleese and Sayer, 2006).

There is a 'prime age' preferred by many employers—25–30 in the private sector, and a 'golden decade' of 35–45 in the public sector (Itzin and Phillipson, 1995; Loretto et al., 2000). Because of career breaks, such as maternity leave, women are more likely than men to fall outside these bands—and so miss the optimal time for promotion. Maternity leave, confusingly, frees women to care for their children while simultaneously excluding them from opportunities for advancement at work: they are out of the political flow. The handicap is less serious, or absent, for men, who often have less desire or opportunity to take paternity leave. Indeed, there are wide international differences in the proportion of pay reserved for the father, and whether he is permitted to share leave-allocation with the mother.[17] Ageism thus compounds women's long-standing difficulties in breaking through the 'glass ceiling' of workplace advancement. Corporate boardrooms remain predominantly male preserves. The global average for women reaching top management posts is 22 per cent (IBR, 2007). Japan ranks lowest at 7 per cent, and the Philippines highest at 50 per cent; the UK and USA hover in between at 19 and 23 per cent.

LOOKISM: THE BEAUTY BIAS

Ageing erodes the cultural capital attached to physical appearance, especially for women. Women's appearance compounds with their age and gender to constitute a triple jeopardy. The fears of women in their 50s and 60s are poignantly expressed in the following two testimonies reported by Clarke et al. (2008: 660–662):

I wish I could say that I feel at peace about ageing and that I will let things play out the way they do, but if I gave you an honest answer today, I think I'm scared because I know that essentially the world thinks old things and old people are kind of like garbage. I'm just holding my own and when I look like a piece of garbage, it's probably how I'll be treated.

I've felt for the last 10 years that I'm completely invisible to men [particularly if there is] a tall, long-legged blonde in the room. Nobody even sees me...that's why I don't like to go to very many events where people are in their thirties. I am invisible. I am not there. I get introduced to somebody but they're looking at somebody across the room. It's as though you're invisible. You're not there.

The workplace can concentrate such feelings:

The reason why they [co-workers] treat you differently—it's a visual thing. I'm not saying I was drop dead gorgeous when I was younger because I wasn't, but they're [co-workers] far more likely to spend time with someone who appeals to them.

(Walker et al., 2007: 43)

One senior team member sent an e-mail when I forgot to sign a form . . . 'Tell the dried up old maid to get her teeth in'. On another occasion a team leader called us a bunch of 'old fuckers'. . . a coach asked us which was greater, our team's combined ages or [the] bank balance . . . to name but a few incidents.

(Duncan and Loretto, 2004: 107)

The principal factor at play in all these accounts is appearance, or looks. *Lookism* favours those who look 'good', 'attractive', 'beautiful', 'handsome', over those who are 'ugly' or physically blemished in some way. The beauty bias is popularly seen to give the good looking a decided advantage in life— the best breaks, the best jobs, even the best pay. Daniel Hamermesh and his colleagues have attempted the challenging task of testing out this belief, focusing on the possible financial advantage of having good looks. They visited male and female Americans and Canadians in their homes to gather labour market and demographic information, while also quietly rating their physical appearance (a procedure of questionable ethics). The researchers then isolated the effects of 'beauty' by factoring out other likely contributors on earnings, such as education, race, region, tenure, firm size, and so forth. They concluded that there is indeed a financial payoff for good looks for both genders, those with 'below average' looks earning consistently less (Hamermesh and Biddle, 1994). Taking the proposition a step further, the researchers speculated that an organization's bottom-line performance could be influenced by the good looks, or otherwise, of its leaders. They gathered evidence to suggest that the beauty of Dutch executives in advertising firms raises the whole firms' sales, even proportionately more than the enhancement of the executives' own earnings (Pfann et al., 2000).

These, and related, findings prompt Warhurst et al. (2009) to conclude that lookism is 'the next frontier in the struggle against discrimination in employment':

The conclusion is stark: employee looks matter. Employers appear to discriminate in favour of people perceived to be better looking or who are perceived to have the 'right look' and penalize those perceived as less physically attractive or having the 'wrong look'. (132)

Lookism sits at the crossroads of social constructionist and evolutionary theories. The former, popularized by Naomi Wolf in *The Beauty Myth* (1990), argues that we are fed gendered images of ideal beauty through an onslaught of media images. We know what is beautiful because we are taught what is beautiful. The images permeate our views about what a beautiful (vigorous, healthy) woman ought to look like—such as slim, toned, youthful, and blemish free. In doing so, they exercise a considerable hold over women, in effect imprisoning them in their bodies. Less captively, male beauty is promoted via male 'style icons', such as an assemblage of media, film, sport, and other celebrities. Youth still tends to triumph for men, but less rigidly. A man can also be 'elderly and handsome', 'old and attractive'.

Evolutionary theory downplays cultural influences. Over millennia, claim evolutionists, our preference for symmetrical, strong bodies with clear skin and shiny hair, has evolved as a product of successful mating, producing a gene pool most conducive to survival and thriving (Fink et al., 2001; Rhodes, 2006). Particular aesthetic impulses are, as a result, 'hard wired' into us—which generally favour the young of our species. In evolutionary terms, some beauty standards may be learned, but the default position—to youth and symmetry—always predisposes our preferences.

LOOKISM'S GRIP

Lookism has a stronger hold over employees in some sectors than in others. Indeed, in certain occupations 'good' looks can be a positive disadvantage; one can be *too* attractive to 'fit in', such as for professional women in dominantly male organizations. For example, female lawyers seeking partner-ship status have found beauty to be a handicap (Biddle and Hamermesh, 1998), and similarly female academics in a male university environment. As one young, female university lecturer explains:

If you stand out...you seem like a threat to others, or others feel uncomfortable of your image and that makes you feel uncomfortable. So the more you blend in because it is a male dominated environment...with colour, with style, the more you are like others, the more others feel comfortable towards you.

(Granleese and Sayer, 2006: 509)

In frontline services, though, lookism has an ever tightening hold. Front staff in the catering, leisure, hospitality, and travel industries often have to assidu-ously act the 'youthful', or 'sexy' brand of their service or product, an exercise in aesthetic labour reinforced by corporate training (Fineman, 2003; War-hurst and Nickson, 2007). This may feel uncomfortable, even compromising, for some young workers, but for older female workers it can present a stiff, if not impenetrable, barrier. An employment consultant is blunt on the matter:

I think the physical presentation is probably the key thing. We place value on experience but some people have the perception that you're clapped out when you reach a certain mileage on the clock. It seems to be a beauty thing, as you become more mature some people might perceive that you're not so attractive.

(Handy and Davy, 2007: 93)

Lookism is deeply entrenched in the popular visual media—television, film. A youthful appearance may not be everything, but it has become a key consideration for survival in the trade. Prime-time television programmes typically under represent old people, particularly women in advanced old age. And when older characters are featured, they are often portrayed in traditional, stereotypical, gender roles (Harwood and Anderson, 2002; Healey and Ross, 2002; Kessler et al., 2004). The trajectory of the programme presenter encapsulates this trend.

OUT-CASTING THE BROADCASTER

In television, male programme presenters have the longest shelf-life, admired for the 'maturity', 'authority' and 'gravitas' that attends their greying hair and lined face. Lookism is gentler on the older male presenter than the older female presenter. The gendered bias came to a head in the UK in the late 1990s and 2000s. An ageist fuse was ignited when television executives of the male-led BBC announced the 'retirement' of some of their older, female, television presenters. One chose to sue for age discrimination, commenting ruefully, 'I felt sick to the pit of my stomach. . . . We have almost come to accept it as the norm that if you are a woman you have to be a size 8 and have unlined skin. I hoped to be judged on my work as a journalist and broadcaster, not the way I look'.[18] Another presenter, still clinging to her job after cosmetic surgery, added her voice, 'There are a lot of pretty young things with not much talent appearing on television. I'm quite pragmatic. If there was a lovely blonde with huge breasts and long legs who had my experience and wit, I'd be out of a job'.[19]

As protests mounted, television viewers aired their views through newspapers and blogs. One woman blogger captured the prevailing, female mood:

You know, it makes me so weary when I hear people saying 'no need for feminism' or 'feminism is dead' when the evidence to the contrary is out there, right in our faces. When oh when will men grow up and acknowledge the fact that women do not exist, first and foremost to look good for men? This tendency seems to be so ingrained in them—it's absolutely pathetic. Women also—shock! horror!—have education, egos and ambitions—just like men. As well as newsreaders, I'm utterly fed up with shows presented by grey-haired old men alongside attractive young women. As ever, we are surrounded by the sexual fantasies of men wherever we look.[20]

Such remonstrations underscore the dilemmas faced when lookism becomes institutionalized. It can be testing for the most ardent of feminists. The musings of feminist sociologist and gerontologist Toni Calasanti encapsulate some of the dilemmas. She struggles to align her own values with the 'consumer options' of her own ageing: 'Even though my theoretical background helps me understand why my multiple identities as a women, feminist, and scholar of aging conflict, it doesn't necessarily make me feel better about it' (Calasanti, 2008: 156).

Summation and queries

Ageism has long been the poor relative of other 'isms', especially racism and sexism. There are now signs of change as stereotypical beliefs about what particular ages bring have been challenged by researchers, by policy makers, and by employers' associations. It is illegal in many countries to discriminate on the basis of age. As more of the 'age positive' discourse permeates social consciousness through various channels—exemplars in industry, governmental projects, outspoken social scientists—there is the spectre of age becoming redefined, liberated from its old stereotypes.

But ageism does not disappear without a struggle. Ageing confronts us with some of our deepest fears about mortality, triggering the impulse to distance those—especially older people—who remind us of that fact. It makes prejudices towards older people particularly tough to dislodge. Age is such a primitive and emotive category that, other than in its most blatant forms, ageism may be impossible to entirely dislodge. It can be circumnavigated by employers offering apparently rational—though questionable—justifications for their decisions, and by inferring age from other personal or biographical characteristics. The law, moreover, presents a challenging burden of proof on litigants, more of them currently failing than winning their cases. Older job applicants and older employees can find it hard to avoid covert discrimination, a particular challenge when a longer working life becomes an essential rather than a luxury. Ageism interweaves with gender, and is at its most insidious when physical appearance—especially for women—is commodified, an appearance that can rapidly lose its value in a marketplace that reifies youthfulness. All such factors feed tendencies towards narcissism in a society.

Ageism cuts two ways, often overlooked by commentators in the field. There is insufficient attention to its effects on young people. How are younger people's struggles for social legitimacy and status impeded by ageism 'downwards'? Are their abilities and ambitions curtailed by an ageist urge to categorize them as 'simply too young'—and so protect existing age hierarchies, in and out of organizations? And where, and in what settings, are there exceptions to this 'rule'—and why?

5 Capturing Age Cohorts

Some organizations are expressly designed for a particular age group. There are youth orchestras and clubs, schools and hospitals for children, military camps for young men and women, 'third age' societies for the retired, residential centres for senior citizens. In all these cases, the organization's culture evolves around a relatively narrow age-band of members, people who are at an early, mid or late point in their lifecourse. How might such age-clusterings influence organizational processes and member experiences?

I have divided this chapter into three sections to explore contrasting age settings, organizational worlds invisible to most of us. Two are about young people. The first focuses on young offenders, youngsters who have fallen foul of the law in the UK and are held in institutions that deprive them of their liberty—but also aim to 'reform' them. The second penetrates the murky world of child labour, toil that can underpin the supply chains that bring us many of the products that we have come to desire and value. The last section highlights older people who are dementia sufferers. Dementia is growing exponentially as longevity increases, and many sufferers are institutionalized in care homes, often where the cared-for and carers can struggle to cope.

Young offenders

BOX 5.1 OFFICERS HURT IN YOUTH JAIL RIOT

Four prison officers were injured in a riot involving more than 30 inmates at a young offenders' institution.

A wing at Stoke Heath, near Market Drayton, Shropshire, was badly damaged during the disturbance, which went on for nine hours on Sunday evening. It began when 33 inmates on 'A' wing refused to return to their cells. The national control and restraint team later moved in with riot gear.

A dozen inmates had to be sent to other jails because of damage to the cells. One of the officers suffered a broken nose in the disturbance at the centre.

The wing houses 70 teenagers, aged 15 to 18, and the site has about 650 young offenders in total.

Occasionally organizations that, for the most part, are obscured from public gaze, are catapulted into public consciousness. The BBC's news report above, of a riot at a young offenders' institution, Stoke Heath, in 2006 was one such instance.[1] Coincidentally, around that time Her Majesty's Inspectorate of Prisons was undertaking its periodic survey of young people in custody. Amongst their findings, they compared fifteen different institutions on the 'respect' offenders experienced from staff. Stoke Heath had the worst rating. It also had one of the highest proportion of young men feeling unsafe and victimized by staff (Parke, 2008).

This is a peek at world where an age cohort is literally captured—and incarcerated. In birth and age range (15–21), the young offenders fit the parameters of so called Generation Ys or Millennials (see chapter 3). But in no way do they resemble the purported characteristics of that generation: highly technically literate, solid self-esteem, entrepreneurially agile. As 'convicted offenders' they are cast to the shadowy margins of society. And as *young* offenders, they are stereotypically stigmatized as 'hoodies', 'feral', 'thugs', 'predators', 'blade carriers', or 'troublemakers' (Stevenson et al., 2009).

THE INSTITUTIONAL CONTEXT

In 1985, the General Assembly of the United Nations adopted a resolution on *Minimum Rules for the Administration of Juvenile Justice*. It included the following two requirements:

- The placement of a juvenile in an institution shall always be a disposition of last resort and for the minimum necessary period.
- The objective of training and treatment of juveniles placed in institutions is to provide care, protection, education and vocational skills, with a view to assisting them to assume socially constructive and productive roles in society.

These provisions convey a clear message: young offenders' institutions are to care for, protect, and develop those in their charge. It is a picture that jars with that of rioting inmates and anti-riot officers. But the contrast encapsulates a core tension: an institution that, on the one hand, is psychologically debilitating in depriving young people of their liberty, but on the other hand, reforms them. The philosophy of sentencing enshrines the apparent contradiction: retribution and punishment to deter further offending; rehabilitation to reduce the risk of re-offending.

Young offenders are a potentially volatile group to contain, let alone to address the effects of the social deprivations to which most of them will eventually return. The majority of young offenders have experienced an insecure or chaotic family life and been excluded from school. Many have suffered sexual, physical, or emotional abuse and have routinely misused drugs or alcohol (Lyon et al., 2000). Contrary to media accounts, youth crime has not risen in recent years in the UK (Wilson et al., 2006), but the statistics belie a generational anxiety and more than a modicum of moral panic. There is a popular perception that many young people are simply out of control (and always will be)—so harsh punishment is the only answer. Respondents to Maruna and King's (2009) survey of public attitudes towards offenders echoed this view, exemplified by one 61-year-old:

These children—a good deal of them—are going to be criminals, aren't they, because they've got no respect now. So the penal system has got to reflect this. . . . And has got to be, not these softer prisons, but they've got to be harder. They've got to know that they've been in prison. They've got to know that, 'Oh dear I don't want to go to prison again.' But unfortunately they say, 'Oh dear, I'm in prison again. Never mind, I'll soon be out.' (102)

Voices such as these have spurred populist moves by the state to toughen their approach to juvenile crime by broadening its reach as well as pushing custodial sentences downwards in age. But the official aim of rehabilitation remains, the UK Prison Service claiming to offer young offenders education classes as well as practical training courses that will improve their skills and enhance their chances of finding a job once they have been released.[2] The interventions include vocational training, education for national qualifications, fitness facilities, and expert help to reduce dependency on drugs, alcohol, or tobacco.

The detention establishment

In 2009, 2.3 per cent of the UK's prison population were young people, 15–17-year-olds. In comparison, the USA's was 0.4 per cent, Australia's was 0.1 per cent, and Denmark's 0.5 per cent.[3] Numerically, the UK incarcerated over 2,600 juveniles, the vast majority male and a disproportionate number from black and ethnic-minority backgrounds.

The UK's position reflects a recent trend towards criminalizing many more young people as public attitudes towards them have hardened (Morgan, 2009). They are held in fifteen regionally dispersed establishments on dedicated wings or units (see Figure 5.1) Their crimes include serious assault, attempted murder, robbery, housebreaking, sexual offences, vehicle theft, shoplifting, arson, vandalism, and fraud. What they carry into prison, apart from the immediate impact of their court sentence, is a cocktail of emotional and structural handicaps, particularly the absence of core stabilizing influences in their lives—educational, housing, family, leisure. Where a family member has offended, the risks of a child offending are raised markedly.[4]

A young offender will also be influenced by their peers, especially in gangs. Street gangs have thrived in disadvantaged, residentially unstable

Figure 5.1 An inmate in his cell at Feltham Young Offenders Institution, UK. Permission kindly granted by Martin Godwin

neighbourhoods and they now feature strongly in the UK's crime reporting. The gangs tend to reflect ethnic, territorial, or gender (but predominately male) allegiances, and some include children as young as 10 (Shropshire and McFarquhar, 2002). Gangs provide social rewards, countering a sense of exclusion, purposeless, and powerlessness. They are also identity enhancing, where crimes such as robbery reinforce a particular brand of masculinity: physical prowess, and toughness (Bennett and Holloway, 2004; Dupere et al., 2007; Muncie, 2009). While not all gang members engage in criminal activity (and some will desist after testing the waters), those who do offend will frequently be involved in drug supply, robbery, and carry weapons (Murray, 2009).

Insider stories

The realities of individual offenders' backgrounds are brought to life in their own accounts. Lyon et al's (2000) discussions with eighty-four young inmates in ten prisons are revealing in this respect. Involvement with drugs was routine, 'It's just life, it's just normal.' The researchers found very few examples of the positive impact of professionals on their welfare. The narratives below (see Box 5.2) suggest something of their daily life outside of prison—their family, education, community, and time with peers.[5]

BOX 5.2 AN OFFENDER'S LIFE

The way I am, the way I'm violent and that, it's because of my family and the way I've been brought up and that. All me uncles and me dad, even me mum's been to jail for violence and all that, I've got brothers and cousins who've all been to jail for violence, and I didn't grow up all cushy with a silver spoon up me arse or anything like that, I grew up the hard way. (Young man)

My dad's been in jail, me eldest brother's been in jail, me second eldest brother's been in jail, I've been in jail, me youngest brother's going the same way. (Young man)

[W]here I grew up there was fucking nothing, just riots all the time, shootings all the time, just violence all the time. I'd seen it all when I was a kid you know what I'm saying? (Young man)

Because I always got picked on by teachers, I used to have spelling difficulties and because I were always behind, they were pushing me too far, and in the end I took an overdose. (Young woman)

I was on bail for 8 months and about 3 weeks before I get sentenced, they send me a tutor! And they say 'yeah have a tutor, do it at home' but there's no point, I thought 8 months and they never done nothing, never come and see me and then for 2, 3 weeks. (Under 18 young man)

Me, I've never been a criminal in me entire life, I've never done nothing stupid apart from, I only got one conviction. It was my friends that I hang round with, the group that I hang round with, I got influenced I went along with them and I got into trouble. (Under 18 young man)

[W]e all hang round the flats, and you'd have like your friends, the older boys, and every one'd be smoking puff and that, and you're thinking 'I want to be like them'—in their nice clothes, and then you find out how they're making the money, so you have a go, and you succeed, and you think 'that's easy'. (Young man)

The impact of incarceration

An HM Inspectorate survey, *Children and Young People in Custody* (Parke, 2008), reports the views of over 1,000 incarcerated young offenders in fifteen young offender institutions across the UK. Most of the respondents said that they had experienced problems when they first arrived: upset and alone, away from family, and without tobacco or drugs. Even though they were assigned a personal prison officer, social worker, or probation officer, few reported any direct contact. A quarter of the group said they had been physically restrained, but few felt it was easy to make a complaint, and even fewer amongst black and ethnic-minority respondents. Victimization from staff was a problem for nearly 20 per cent, and more so for black and ethnic-minority respondents. Many felt unsafe, especially in the public areas of the institution.

In nearly half the establishments, daily exercise outside was seen as unavailable. Those who reported from learning new skills ranged widely across institutions, 4 per cent to 85 per cent; black and ethnic-minority respondents were the least likely to report that they had been learning new skills.

Given where they were now, would they be any less likely to offend in the future? The previous HM Inspectorate survey (2004–2006) found a 75 per cent endorsement of this question. This time it had dropped to 71 per cent, a statistically significant decline. But any aspirations to stop offending were rarely realized—over 75 per cent of them re-offended after release.[6]

This broad-brush survey exposes a mixed, often bleak picture of life 'inside', with more than a hint of racial division. Further details of prison life can be found in Lyon et al.'s (2000) investigation. In it, young offenders expose their vulnerability, mixed in with fear and bluster. For a few, though, there is a significant breakthrough: the forging of a positive relationship or an insight into their offending behaviour. Below (Box 5.3), some have their say.[7]

Prisoner sub-culture for young offenders is pervasively macho and edgy. Personal bravado and showmanship, sometimes inherited from gang life, is accentuated in a 'survival of the fittest' world, only a few seeking others'

BOX 5.3 INSIDE STORIES

On entering

My first time in jail, when I first come in, I was like 'woooooaaaaah'. You look at everything and you think 'is this what it's like then?' All the stories that you've heard and now you've finally found out. You don't really think much of it 'til you're behind your door and you're like that—man—thinking 'Nah man', 8 o'clock at night, you're behind your door. And you're like 'No shit. I'm in jail—man' . . . It kicks you in the head when you first come in. (Young man)

When you come in, they take you off the van, they tell you to come into that little room and you've got to walk fast, here and there, get yourself dressed and everything. And then you go get your food, get banged up, and as you go in there, there's an atmosphere, all the boys asking for cigarettes and that. (Under 18 young man)

Child or adult?

They've got in my file that I'm childish. And I went to sentence planning and he says 'are you childish?' I said 'No' because I'm a loud person me, I like to have a laugh and that, I don't like sitting being morbid. So they put in my file that I'm childish and I'm only 17. But they're going to get that behaviour aren't they, because I am a child. They should understand that when they're sending us all to prison. (Under 18 young woman)

I don't like the way they speak to you. Like because you're a younger offender, you're a little kid. They've all worked out that I'm childish where they've been a nobody, they've kept their mouth shut . . . And then they come here and suddenly they're working with a load of kids that they can shout at and they talk down to you. (Young man)

Respect

As far as they're concerned they're just paid to open your door and let you out and then bang you back up. (Young man)

continued

BOX 5.3 Continued

I think they're more interested in punishing you rather than helping you, there's no rehabili-tation here . . . You're entitled to your meals, your association and that's about it. (Young man)

The ones I respect more are the ones that go by the book but have a laugh and a joke with . . . (Young man)

Personal officers

We're supposed to work closely with staff on the [name] Wing because we've got an individual officer for each inmate, but it doesn't work like that. I haven't seen my personal officer for about 7 months . . . I haven't seen mine since I come here. (Young woman)

Our personal officer is just, oh I won't say it, but I won't talk to him. If I had a problem I won't go and see him, so I just have to keep it to myself, you know what I mean, cos, cos of his attitude towards us, towards me, I won't go and speak to him. (Young man)

The only person that's helped me out since I've been in jail is my personal officer, and that's it. (Young man)

Education and skills

Well, you're going to need references and qualifications, so you might as well do something while you're in jail. (Young man)

What's the point of getting all those qualifications if you're going to come straight back in? (Young man)

I've done the thinking skills and it helps, seeing things from people's points of views. I know it's helped me. (Young man)

Yeah, I've been on an offending behaviour course . . . and I think that it done one of the best things for me, to be honest. One of the best things I've ever done in prison . . . (Young man)

I'll do a drugs and an alcohol course because I drunk a lot on the out, but they're the only courses I want to do . . . I was a heavy drinker on the out yeah, and they showed us this video, that's what made me think. And the drugs ones, you just see people fucked up off drugs, losing arms and legs from fucking injecting—none of that for me, mate. (Young man)

On re-offending

I'm getting out in 12 weeks, and I'm getting so scared, because it's easy to say 'I'm not going to get into trouble', but it really creeps on me, like trouble just finds me. (Young woman)

They just think you can come to jail, stop your drugs, go out and you're alright, but it doesn't work like that. It's temptation, not withdrawal, it's temptation nowt else. (Young woman) support (Woodall, 2007). Trust does not come easily in the prison environment. Where help is wanted, offenders gravitate towards those who come from their own neighbourhoods, so reinforcing a familiar identity (Phillips, 2008). Aggression and pent-up frustration are exacerbated by limited contacts with family and friends, and by 'provocative' remarks from officers:

You could wake up in a good mood and an officer could say one thing and it puts you on a downer for the rest of the day... he's disrespectful and has no respect. He talks to you like shit. (Young offender)

Officers should leave their problems at the gate and not bring them into the prison or take them out on us. Some of them can be right miserable bastards. (Young offender)

(Woodall, 2007: 136–137)

Overall, there is a strong impression, from the young offenders, that it is containment that makes the running in institutional attempts to balance incarceration with rehabilitation.

THE PRISONER OFFICER'S PERSPECTIVE

Prison officers shoulder a weighty burden, cast by the House of Commons Justice Committee as 'a key figure in reducing re-offending'. The Prison Service outlines the officer's main responsibilities:[8]

- carrying out security checks and searching procedures
- supervising prisoners, keeping account of prisoners in your charge and maintaining order
- employing authorized physical control and restraint procedures where appropriate
- taking care of prisoners and their property, taking account of their rights and dignity
- providing appropriate care and support for prisoners at risk of self-harm
- promoting anti-bullying and suicide prevention policies
- taking an active part in rehabilitation programmes for prisoners
- assessing and advising prisoners, using your own experiences and integrity
- writing fair and perceptive reports on prisoners.

Control and security predominate in this listing (corresponding to young offenders' experiences), a reflection of prison officer training since its inception in 1935. In the words of one long-standing prison officer:

I have 25 years experience as a prison officer. I have lived and survived, through fresh start, 'de-militarisation' of staff attitudes, austere regimes, decency agenda, the emergence of a 'blame and claim' culture, too many reports and inquiries to list and at the end of all that, the bottom line is that we still lock up people that the courts deem fit to send to prison, only now there are more of them. (HC, 2009: 13)

BOX 5.4 PAPERWORK AND TARGETS

Real prison work, achieved interpersonally on the landings and in the prison yards, has given way to paper work, making sure the right box is ticked at the right time, and number crunching.

The idea that prison officers still have any role to play in rehabilitation is a myth. Staff spend half of their time filling out pointless checklists just to tick boxes in order to make it look as though we are doing something.

[P]risons are drowning under a growing raft of targets . . . . audits, with too little time spent on engaging with, and challenging offenders.

Source: HC (2009: 38)

Not included in the officer's job description is the recent infusion of manage-rialism, and some private-sector competition. Prison officers are now subject to closer, centralized scrutiny, and are more visible on a range of performance indicators and targets (see Box 5.4) And, like many other public sector employ-ees, they have found imposed targets and performance measurement often ritualistic and time consuming, a 'diversion' from their direct work with inmates.

Currently there are no minimum educational requirements to be a prison officer. Someone can join at 18, similar in age to some of the young offenders they will meet, and without the life experience that would probably help them appreciate their charges. Training for all prison officers is a modest eight weeks, with an extra week for those working with young people. It includes a half-day each on mental health, substance abuse, vulnerability assessment, and managing difficult behaviour—arguably a thin-skim of knowledge with which to confront some of the most challenging and vulnerable of young people. It is substantially less than other professionals working with adoles-cents, prompting the Howard League for Penal Reform to ask: 'Do we want turnkeys or professionals?'[9] Prisoner officers who, nevertheless, take their caring duties seriously can find themselves working against a sub-culture of prisoner officer 'heavies' who taunt the 'welfare screw' (HC, 2009: 44).

This background ill-equips officers faced with psychologically disturbed or handicapped young offenders. Their behaviours can be readily misunder-stood, treated trivially, or seriously neglected. The Howard League for Penal Reform, long-time advocate of humane and rehabilitive prison conditions, has compiled case files on such instances (see Box 5.5).

'Procedural' actions such as these can be seen, also, as officers' ways of coping with the pressures of prison overcrowding, a frequent 'churn' of governors, and high sickness levels amongst their own colleagues. They are

---

BOX 5.5 CASES FOR CONCERN

Our case files tell countless stories of staff inability to cope with these young people, with disastrous results. For example, the case of 'P', a young man who was hospitalised 84 times over an 8 month period, shows staff responding by the use of disciplinary sanctions such as segregation and punishment through external adjudications. Distraught and confused staff were clearly unable to deal with the bloodletting and other serious self-injury in any meaningful way. They set up a 'traffic light' system so that 'P' was told he would be on a basic regime with no activity, no reading material or television if he harmed himself but could progress to more activities if he desisted from self-injury. His self mutilation worsened because of the spartan conditions. The punishments inflicted on him by staff exacerbated his mental distress.

Another client, a profoundly deaf teenager, was promised a vibrating alarm clock to enable him to wake in time for education classes as prison staff simply shouted at prisoners to wake them. It was not provided, and when he was late getting up, prison staff in the private prison initiated disciplinary proceedings to punish him. With prison officers unable to provide health, mental health or specialist support, the problems of the many prisoners with complex mental and other health needs are simply exacerbated in the custodial setting.

Source: (Howard, *2009*: 9).

---

conditions that compel officers, at times, to leave prisoners locked up for days, all adding to officers' sense of malaise and disaffection (Howard, 2009). Very few speak well of the system (Duffy et al., 2008). Tensions are exacerbated by the biographical profile of prisoner officers. They are predominately white men and unrepresentative of the ethnic or religious background of the prison population.

IN SUM

Organizing for age in the UK's prison service is replete with conflicts and contradictions, a pattern to be found in many other countries, such the USA and Australia. Accepting that custodial sentences for some young offenders are unavoidable, their deprivation of liberty amounts to *the* punishment. Further punishment, by intent or default, through oppressive, overburdened, or inadequately skilled officers, or a insufficiently resourced system, is akin to a double sentence.

How well a society treats its young offenders, individuals with still most of their life before them, is a mark of its maturity, as are its efforts to eliminate the social conditions that contribute to their criminal behaviour. Prisons, surely, can do little about the latter, so the challenge is to do the best they can with individual offenders to help them improve their chances in life—a seemingly uphill struggle for a prison system dogged by overcrowding and caught between competing ideologies of containment and reform.

For some offenders, loss of liberty can be a sufficient deterrent to re-offending—it is just too unpleasant. But the statistics reveal that such an outcome is a rarity. The experience of incarceration does not produce a 'new' person, better able to resist the attractions of criminality. Precisely the opposite tends to occur, fuelling a cycle of recidivism. The trick appears to be the integration of imaginative, carefully targeted, supportive services—inside the young offender institution; outside it through linked, supervised projects; and in post-release follow-up to mitigate the stigma of having been in prison. At present, there are patchy elements of such practices, subject to unpredictable funding and shifting government priorities.

The prisoner officer and prison governor are key players in in-house initiatives. Despite the 'containment' ethos and institutional stress, some have managed creatively to forge their own path, indicating that the local leadership can make a difference. There are, for example, Governor Austin Treacy's endeavours in Northern Ireland (Figure 5.2). He turned dogs and a mobile home to his young offenders' advantage:

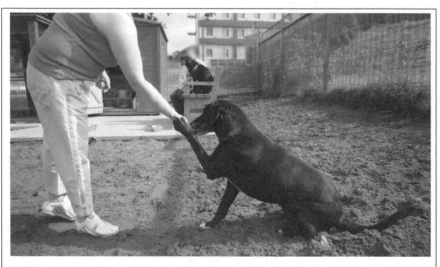

Figure 5.2 Winning hearts and minds. Photo: Paul McErlane

For the past two years the governor has been busy introducing a series of reforms including a 'pet therapy' project for prisoners struggling to adapt to life inside. These have prompted both sceptical media coverage accusing the prison of being soft on offenders, and public outrage.

Treacy strides around the complex like a man on a mission, enthusing about why a 'more progressive' prison regime in Northern Ireland's only young offender institution is 'absolutely' essential for prisoner rehabilitation. 'Look around you,' he instructs. 'This looks more like a school, I think you'll agree, than a prison.'

Amanda, who also has three years left to serve . . . 'The best thing is that it might help me when I get out. I'd like to get a job working with animals. I'm willing to volunteer first . . . but at least I might stand a chance now.'

Controversially, the prison purchased a six-berth mobile home that Treacy intends to use as an 'extended visiting facility' where parents can interact and even stay the night occasionally with their children; an improvement on the public, impersonal conventional visitors' centre.

Asked if what is happening here will rehabilitate prisoners in a lasting way, Treacy admits 'it is just too soon [to tell]'.

Source: O'Hara (2009).

The note of optimism in this account throws the spotlight on the organizational culture of the particular young offender institution—and the wider professionalism and leadership of its staff. Once liberated from an overwhelming pressure to control, staff can reach out to their charges in small, but very significant, ways.

Child labourers

There is powerful argument that much child labour is simply wrong. It is unethical when it (a) exploits children as cheap and easy labour; (b) robs children of their education, dignity in childhood; and (c) perpetuates an impoverished underclass (Figures 5.3a and b). The social reformers of the nineteenth century struggled to get this message across in times when child labour was regarded as a main source of family income—and a fine return for an owner-manager's capital outlay. Children were regarded as inexpensive labour; they (together with women) comprised some 40 per cent of the textile labour force in 1830s' America (Goldin and Sokoloff, 1982). Their particular importance was also apparent in the very design of some of the machinery that spearheaded the Industrial Revolution in Britain, such as the spinning jenny to produce yarn. It was engineered to accommodate the build of childworkers of 9 to 12 years of age (Berg and Hudson, 1992).

Today, on the face of it, things are very different. Many industrialized countries have child labour laws—but with wide variations in enforcement. By 2010, 155 states had subscribed to the International Labour Organization's (ILO) convention on minimum age for employment, most opting for 15 years, but some permitting temporary 'light work' for children as young as 12. No-one under 18 should be involved in dangerous work.[10] The most severe forms of child labour—such as child trafficking, slavery, and debt bondage—had been formally proscribed by 171 states.[11] Along with other non-governmental organizations—such as trade unions, UNICEF, the UN,

Figure 5.3a Nineteenth-century child labour, Georgia, USA. Lewis Hine, Library of Congress, Washington

Figure 5.3b Twenty-first century child labour, cocoa plantation, Ivory Coast. Permission kindly granted by Jessica Dimmock/VII Network

and Save the Children—the combined pressure on governments and employers to outlaw child labour has been considerable.

June 12th 2010 marked the ILO's eighth *World Day Against Child Labour*, a rallying point for action, coupled with strategies for poverty reduction, social protection, and education. The ILO's prohibition excludes work that can be a 'positive experience' for children; that is, within the legal limits and not detrimental to their health or schooling. The paper round, Saturday morning shop work or temporary holiday employment is acceptable. The child labour that is of most concern flaunts legal provisions and ignores international codes. At worst, it enrols children in bonded or forced labour, in prostitution, in the drugs trade, or in armed conflict. Much of this occurs in the unregulated, informal economy—small workshops, street work—often for long hours and disciplined through violence.[12] It is a conduit for sub-contractors in international supply chains, some for major high-street brands. Textiles, footwear, clothing and toys produced in Turkey, Bangladesh, India, China, and Egypt have relied on sweatshop child labour, in big and small manufacturing units, and in household operations, estimated to be 14 per cent of all child labour (ILO, 2004).

CHEAP AND COMPLIANT

Low-paid children help to reduce production costs and increase profitably and competitiveness. They are easier to control than adult workers, either through intimidation or inexpensive bribes (e.g. hair ribbons, chocolates). Girls are often preferred in the clothing industry because of their familiarly and dexterity with sewing. They perform their manual work in the macho, often oppressive, culture of male owners, supervisors, and machine operators (ILO, 2004). Girls have also been preferred for cross-pollination work in the cotton fields of India. Cross-pollination involves manually placing pollen grains from one genotype onto the stigma of flowers of the other genotype, an intensive and daily job. A seed farmer explains:

Cross-pollination work is very labor intensive and a large number of labourers is required to do this work. It is also delicate work and needs to be handled carefully. We prefer young girl children for this task because with their delicate fingers (nimble fingers) they can handle this work better than adults. They also work more intensively than adults. We can control them easily. They listen to us and do what ever we ask them to do. The most important thing is labor costs. Nearly half of our investment goes towards payment of labor charges. The wage rates for children are far lower than adult wages. We can reduce our labor costs considerably if we hire girl children. If we want to hire adult labor we have to pay higher wages. With the current procurement price we get from the seed companies we can not afford to pay higher wages to the laborers. (Venkateswarlu, 2007: 7–8)

BOX 5.6 THE CHILD WORKER'S PLIGHT

Shanthilal (12 years)

I lived in Gudapida village, and grazed the family cattle. We used to go together, as a group of friends—Pravin, Ishu, Shankar and I, with the cattle on the village outskirts. During this time, we met one Kanubhai Gautambhai Kharadi, who told us about probable employment at the BT Cotton seed farms in Gujarat, and having convinced us, he took all three of us with him on the bus. We were brought by Kanubhai—a mate himself, to a farm in village Jasaali, Taluka Deodar, District Banaskaantha.

Our parents were unaware about this, and the mate did not care to inform them. No advance money was given to any of us. However, we were at the farm for about a month, where we worked to cross-pollinate cotton flowers. We were harassed by the farm owner, beaten and confined so that neither could we purchase rations nor were we provided with enough food-stuff. Further, no payment was made during the whole month. Frustrated and tired, all three of us abandoned work one day, and fled on foot, from Deodar to Himmatnagar town (a distance of 200 kms), from where we retuned home, traveling on trucks. The journey back took us three days. We went without food for most of this period.

Shyamala (12 years) and Yoshoda 14 (years)

The lethargy of the government in preventing the smuggling of children violating all the laws resulted in the death of two innocent children. Doodekula Subbarayudu, a cottonseed farmer producing seed for 'Raasi,' one of the leading seed companies in India, in R. Pampally village, Uyyalawada Mandal, Kurnool district, brought young children from Gudur Mandal to do cross pollination in his farms against an advance of Rs. 1000 given to their parents during summer. Of these children, 12 year old Shyamala and her 14 year old sister, Yoshoda, were found missing on 7th October 2006 late in the night and found dead on the morning of 8th October. These girls were among the other 500 children who have descended in the Uyyalavada mandal. Until the post mortem report is given the cause of death would remain unestablished. Chinnashalu, one of the workers in the cotton seed farm along with his gang raped Shyamala on October 7th, in the late hours. After gang raping her, all of them together killed Syamala and Yasoda.

Source: Venkateswarlu (2007: 22, 3).

The taken-for-granted exploitation in this account hides an even darker side, where the risks of abuse, physical harm, and psychological trauma are ever present. It is revealed in reports from, or of, child cotton workers (see Box 5.6).

Attempts to curb child labour have not been without their successes, with a recorded fall in the number of illegal child workers over recent years, especially in hazardous occupations. Yet the raw statistics still make a sobering read. In 2004 it was estimated that, overall, there were 281 million child labourers, 126 million of whom undertook dangerous work (Hagemann et al., 2006). Moreover, as economic crisis squeeze suppliers' margins, they feel impelled to outsource work to ever cheaper sources—that is, to more children.

Table 5.1 The Products of Child Labour

Product	Countries
Bamboo	Burma
Beans (green, soy, yellow)	Burma
Brazil Nuts/Chestnuts	Bolivia
Bricks	Burma, China, India, Nepal, Pakistan
Carpets	India, Nepal, Pakistan
Charcoal	Brazil
Coal	Pakistan
Coca (stimulant plant)	Colombia
Cocoa	Cote d'Ivoire, Nigeria
Coffee	Cote d'Ivoire
Cotton	Benin, Burkina Faso, China, Tajikistan, Uzbekistan
Cottonseed (hybrid)	India
Diamonds	Sierra Leone
Electronics	China
Embroidered Textiles	India, Nepal
Garments	Argentina, India,Thailand
Gold	Burkina Faso
Granite	Nigeria
Gravel (crushed stones)	Nigeria
Pornography	Russia
Rice	Burma, India, Mali
Rubber	Burma
Shrimp	Thailand
Stones	India, Nepal
Sugarcane	Bolivia, Burma
Teak	Burma
Tilapia (fish)	Ghana
Tobacco	Malawi
Toys	China

The bulk of the child labour is to be found in the rural economy of developing countries—agriculture, fishing, hunting, or forestry—a proportion of which is devoted to cheap exports for the industrialized world. In 2009, the US Department of Labor issued an extensive list (Table 5.1) of such products and their sources, with this carefully worded caveat:

Based on recent, credible, and appropriately corroborated information the Departments of Labor, State, and Homeland Security have preliminarily concluded that there is a reasonable basis to believe that the following products, identified by their country of origin, might have been mined, produced, or manufactured by forced or indentured child labor.   (DOL, 2009: 46795)

The list in Table 5.1 implicates twenty-three counties exporting a total of twenty-nine different commodities, from beans to bricks, carpets to cotton, diamonds to gold, rice to sugarcane, teak to toys. It paints a picture of widespread child labour in developing countries. But child labour is not confined to the 'third world'; it can be found in the hidden economy of many capital cities in the developed world. Kruse and Mahony (2000) report the employment of children (especially immigrants) in New York sweatshops, all having slipped through the inspectorial net. They work in hazardous meat processing, in restaurants and in apparel firms. The authors estimate some 455,000 children and youths have worked in violation of federal and state laws since the 1970s. In the UK, UNICEF have found confusion amongst young people, parents, teachers, and employers about the age that children can be legally employed (it is 13 years, but highly restricted and regulated), and how many hours they can work (it is twelve hours during the school week) (Dottridge and Stuart, 2005). All working children of school age should be licensed by their local authority but, in practice, few are.

UNWRAPPING CHOCOLATE: A BITTER-SWEET CASE

The world has an insatiable appetite for chocolate, keenly and exotically marketed by the confectionery industry. Chocolate's staple ingredient is cocoa, sourced mainly from the Ivory Coast in West Africa (and rather less so from Ghana). Child labour is banned in the Ivory Coast, but the presence of children in the cocoa fields is a common sight. Children, many under 10, are engaged in hazardous activities as defined by the Ivory Coast's own regulatory standards. They clear land, carry heavy loads, harvest and break-open cocoa pods, weed, and apply pesticides (PCIDT, 2009). Some bear the marks of machete cuts, injuries of their 'trade': ripe pods are cut from the cocoa tree with a machete or knife and are opened with a machete or club to extract the beans (see Figure 5.3b). The US Department of State defines these conditions as amongst the 'worst forms for child labor', implicating more than 109,000 children who labour for long, gruelling hours, some suffering frequent beatings.[13] Parenti (2008: 1) offers a first-hand account of the terrain:

Outside the village of Sinikosson in southwestern Ivory Coast, along a trail tracing the edge of a muddy fishpond, Madi Ouedraogo sits on the ground picking up cocoa pods in one hand, hacking them open with a machete in the other and scooping the filmy white beans into plastic buckets. It is the middle of the school day, but Madi, who looks to be about 10, says his family can't afford the fees to send him to the nearest school, five miles away. 'I don't like this work,' he says. 'I would rather do something else. But I have to do this.' Working and living conditions are brutal. Most villages lack electricity, running water, health clinics or schools.

The physical and psychological distance from the child labourer gets progressively greater along the supply chain. The major cocoa exporters neither own the plantation nor directly employ the children: there are others in the chain, starting with the small, independent, farmers who grow the cocoa. They sell to local middle men who collect and warehouse the cocoa beans. These then sell on to the cocoa exporters, names such as Cargill, Archer Daniels Midland, Barry Callebaut, and Saf-Cacao. The manufacturers of chocolate buy from them. The made-up chocolate finally passes through wholesalers, distributors, and retailers, eventually to reach the consumer. The child labourer's imprint is by now well-obscured.

The wider cultural context

The child worker in the Ivory Coast is part of a complex social-cultural web. In 2009, the United Nations Development Programme Human Development Index ranked the Ivory Coast as amongst the lowest in overall development— 163rd out of 182 countries. Adult literacy was 50 per cent and average income $1,690 (compared to $45,592 in the USA and $35,130 in the UK).

High levels of poverty and low-growth economy combine to force families to depend on their children's income to survive and to place trust in an employer or agent (Raghavan and Chatterjee, 2001). Income from taxes on cocoa exports rarely finds its way into education and social services. In a depressed economy, education is not seen as an automatic route to employment, and children who quit school at 12 or 13 can readily melt into the informal economy, rarely pursued by the state.[14]

The Western abhorrence of child labour is not shared by communities that have lived it for generations—much as was the custom in pre- and early-industrial Europe. The sight of children working is familiar and normalized in many African families, especially where men have multiple wives and children. Polygamy is illegal in the Ivory Coast, but nevertheless persists (French, 1996). Many children start working at an early age, regarded as a family investment, often of more immediate value than schooling (Zeitzen, 2008). Some of this work is kept within family and kinship relations. It would be natural, for example, for the children of a cocoa farmer to assist their father in the production process. But the potential for harm increases markedly when the child is involved in migrant work for remote outsiders (IITA, 2002).

These local practices exist within a volatile world market for cocoa exports. The price that cocoa farmers receive for their effort depends on much beyond their control. It includes varied crop yields, seasonal weather patterns, and plant disease ('swollen shoot' virus infected much of West African's orchards in 2010, the only cure being to uproot and burn the plants). The farmer's dependence on a single crop adds to their vulnerability, especially if civil instability persuades international purchasers to seek supplies elsewhere.

As the price offered to farmers drops, their profit falls, and they look for ways of trimming their overheads. Cutting labour costs is one of the few available options. They are less likely, therefore, to send their children to school when times are hard, enrolling whatever 'free' support they can. If needs must, this can include the smallest children who would normally be exempt from the toughest work. Bøås and Huser (2006: 48) explain the economic reasoning:

> During the harvest, the cocoa pods are removed from the trees with a machete tied to a long stick. This work is both difficult and heavy. If the cut is not made at the right spot the tree will be damaged, and since this work is also physically hard it simply cannot be conducted by too small children. They will become tired and too often place the cut at the wrong spot and thereby accidentally hurt the tree. Too many cuts like this will reduce the ability of the tree to produce pods the next year and thereby also diminish the future profit of the farmer. Thus, using very young children in this type of work does not make sense, and there is little reason to believe that farmers do not know what they are doing. However, there may be exceptions to this type of long-term economic rationality, and they are most likely to occur in times of crisis.

Rough regulation

Chocolate's labyrinthine journey, from the hand of the child labourer to the mouth of the consumer, presents a considerable challenge for regulation that will ensure the protection of children, especially when child labour is so embedded in a culture of poverty. But a voluntary agreement between the World Cocoa Foundation and the Chocolate Manufacturers Association was designed to achieve exactly this, and to end forced and trafficked child labour in cocoa supply.[15] The protocol was facilitated by the US Department of Labor and human rights activists in 2001, based on the premise that manufacturers had considerable control over the cocoa market and its price at the farm gate: they were key players in the ultimate employment of children. The long-term aim was the complete removal of child labour from the cocoa fields, to dovetail with educational and material support for the children and help for farmers to improve their yields.

In the early days of the protocol things got worse, primarily because of the civil war that absorbed the Ivory Coast from 2002 to 2004; 'blood chocolate' provided ready income for armed groups. Since then there have been moves by key stakeholders, including the Ivory Coast Government, to put into place child labour monitoring and certification systems, and remediation programmes for the children. But despite their good intentions, many of the initiatives have become ensnared in the politics of vested interests in the industry. Certification of improvement and remediation for child workers are easily evaded or ignored, further weakened by a lack of measurable and binding targets, by few independent audits, and by the absence of a trustworthy seal or logo. Some alternatives, such as 'Fair Trade' cooperatives, look promising, but they cover just a tiny proportion of smallholder cocoa farms— 1,400 of 500,000 in the Ivory Coast.[16] As a detailed report from Tulane University concludes, 'all actors agree that more remains to be accomplished' (PCIDT, 2009: 12).

ON REPRESENTING CHILDREN

Press headlines (see Box 5.7) about child labour are typically terse and alarmist.

Behind these headlines are exposés of questionable corporate practices, some at odds with an employer's proclaimed ethical standards. A critical mass of media interest, combined with NGO and governmental pressure, can inflict reputational damage on a company, sufficient to stir it to reparative action.

BOX 5.7 ALARM AND SCANDAL

Child labour scandal hits Adidas

Brutality, poor wages and 15-hour days in the Asian sweatshops
Observer, 19 November 2000

Scandal of silk industry where child 'slaves' work seven days a week

Independent, 24 January 2003

US blueberry farms accused of using children as pickers

Independent, 2 November 2009

Child labor cases uncovered in China

New York Times, 30 April 2008

Gap in child labour scandal

TheStar.com, 29 October 2007

Ghana: slave boys go home

New York Times, 12 September 2003

BOX 5.8 H&M'S MANIFESTO

- H&M does not accept the use of child labour.
- Efforts to prevent child labour in the supply chain H&M has around 60 auditors around the world whose job it is to check that H&M's Code of Conduct is being observed, including the ban on child labour. In addition, there are quality controllers, who can look out for suspected child labour on their visits to suppliers' factories. The auditors also fulfil a preventive role by monitoring the employment procedures of the suppliers and advising them on how to avoid employing underage children. Together with the supplier H&M tries to find the optimum solution, taking into account the child's age, education and social situation.
- In most cases the solution involves the child being given the opportunity for schooling, which is paid for by the supplier. The supplier also compensates the family for loss of income.
- If we are to get to grips with this problem in the long term, the social conditions of children in poor countries must be improved. This isn't something that we can achieve alone, and so H&M works with a variety of organisations and authorities to address this issue.[17]

Some of those accused choose to disengage from all work that implicates child labour and source their supplies elsewhere. Others seek to remove children through progressive involvement. They engage with parties in the supply chain and with local issues on child labour while committing to a longer term programme of support (Winstanley et al., 2002). The international fashion retailer Hennes and Mauritz (H&M) declares such an approach in its statement of corporate responsibility (see Box 5.8).

Company codes on child labour are proclamations of intent with public image in mind. They can be easily dismissed as cosmetic, but they are symbolically important and, as public declarations, can be used to hold a company to account. Currently, though, substantive codes like H&M's are a rarity. Sampling fifty-five multinational companies, Kolk and van Tulder (2002) found less than 20 per cent had specific provisions on child labour in their ethical codes, and those that did were vague on verification. Some organizations in their study argued defensively against the need for code. They claimed that it could be counterproductive to create standards that differed from those of the host country. It could make it difficult for a company to operate in that country and to benefit children in a more gradual, but no less sympathetic, way.

Different voices, different ideologies

In the clamour of revelations about child labour we witness a mix of motives and voices—but most are infused with a Westernized notion of enlightened progressiveness. The obliteration of child labour is presented as an incontestable goal, a moral must. It is a viewpoint matured through many years of economic development and carried by Western corporations with more or less conviction, but as a pragmatic necessity when their business and reputation depends on it. When, then, a shopper is guaranteed 'no child labour' on purchasing their toy, chocolate, or shirt, is the now ex child labourer better off?

Perhaps. It depends on the style of engagement by the company with the cultural, gender, and poverty issues that produce child labour in the first place. This, of necessity, means working in partnership with different stakeholders, such as the children themselves, local employers, NGOs, and local and national government (a process that has been estimated to amount to just a tiny fraction of the savings made from international sourcing (Winstanley et al., 2002)). But even the best intended efforts can misfire, cogently illustrated by the 'Sialkot soccer ball scandal'.

In April 1995, a CBS documentary featured images of children stitching together the panels of soccer balls in grim, one-room workshops in Sialkot, Pakistan (see accounts in Khan et al., 2007; Khan, 2007). Nike and Adidas were key players. It triggered a vigorous media campaign to persuade the soccer-ball industry to change its ways and stop using child labour. They did.

The companies, together with UNICEF and the ILO, shifted the stitching to centres that could be regularly monitored. The children were provided with regular local schooling and their families offered systems of credit and skills training to increase their independence. It appeared a textbook intervention. Amongst its effusive endorsers was President Bill Clinton:

Let me cite just one example of the success being achieved, the work being done to eliminate child labor from the soccer ball industry in Pakistan. Two years ago, thousands of children under the age of 14 worked for 50 companies stitching soccer balls full-time. The industry, the ILO and UNICEF joined together to remove children from the production of soccer balls and give them a chance to go to school, and to monitor the results.[18]

But a detailed review of the case (see Husselbee, 2000; Khan, 2007) reaches a very different conclusion. It transpired that few panels were originally sewn in remote workshops: most were distributed to the villages around Sialkot to be worked on in homes by some 15,000 children with their families. Children were traditionally part of the household economy and worked with their parents, but now the household economy had been disrupted. The local schooling provided was punitive and lacked food; children much preferred to be working and, by 2004, the project's education schemes had wound up. Of fifty women stitchers (interviewed by Kahn) only two preferred the centres: they could produce more at home because they could fit the work into any hours of the day or night. They saw soccer-ball stitching as essentially low status, but now made more visible to others in their daily trip to the stitching centres. Gibes and harassment accompanied their journey:

If we go to factories, people say nasty things about us. [They say] putting [on] red lipstick, going out, what do you have in mind. [We] do it [stitching] out of necessity. Common feeling [in villages] is that if one cannot do anything [else, i.e. if one is useless], then stitch. [There is] no respect in [the] village. (85)

Kahn's conclusion is forceful: 'It is quite instructive that in all the media discourse that articulated this crisis, this research could not unearth a single article in which women were given space, such was the overwhelming prominence of the child labor question, which blinded the self-appointed and self-righteous media representers to all other critical and relevant matters' (86). One could add that neither were children's voices heard, on whose behalf the elaborate programme was conceived and executed. Paraphrasing Grier's (2004) critique of child labour in African scholarship, children are often represented as passive and voiceless, rarely as meaning-makers in their own right, and at least part-agents of their own preferences and destiny.

IN SUM

Using and abusing children in the world's economies has a long and chequered history. When children are deemed as cheap units of production, rather than age-vulnerable individuals, the seedier side of capitalism's mega projects is exposed. Economies of scale and ever cheaper goods take on a sinister meaning when they rest on the shoulders of the youngest and most defenceless members of society. But much of this is obscured to the bargain-hunting consumer and profit-hungry investor. Regulatory regimes, pressure group actions and genuine corporate social responsibly, are necessary, if imperfect, counterforces.

But there is a danger in that well-meaning attempts to improve the lot of children can appear as a postcolonial residue, patronizing those who know their own lives and cultural niche far better than anyone else. The challenge for those who engage with child labour is to appreciate that it is deeply embedded in poverty, and in a mesh of economic, political, and cultural practices. The risk in 'taking out' the most obvious—to the outsider—manifestation of child labour is that it can unintentionally impact on local cultural ways that are co-dependent—which can, ironically, end up leaving the child and their family worse off.

Dementia Care

Dementia care sharply accentuates what can happen when two societal stigmas combine: ageism and a 'disease of the mind'.

Dementia is a term that describes different, currently irreversible, forms of cognitive impairment that are caused by diseases of the brain. Symptoms include decline in memory, reasoning, ability to carry out many routine tasks, communication skills, and a loss of control of bodily functions. The most common cause is Alzheimer's disease (named after its discoverer in 1909, Alois Alzheimer), where the chemistry and structure of the brain progressively deteriorate. But there are some 100 different types of dementia, including vascular dementia where mini-strokes starve the brain of oxygen.[19]

The age link is crucial. While some forms of dementia can be early-onset and affect the young, the dominant picture is of an affliction of the old. The World Health Organization's *World Health Report 2003*[20] puts Alzheimer's and other dementias amongst the top four diseases that burden people over-60, accentuated in developed counties where there are longer life expectancies. Statistically, one in fifty people between ages 65 and 70 are likely to suffer dementia, but the risks increase to one in five amongst the over-80s. Ferri et al (2005) estimate that there are twenty-four million people with dementia globally, a number expected to double every twenty years. It has been described as a 'time bomb' for policy makers as dementia diagnoses become more commonplace and include ever greater numbers. In the UK, there are currently around 700,000 people with dementia.[21]

WHERE ARE DEMENTIA SUFFERERS?

In the UK one-third of dementia sufferers live in care homes, housing approximately 240,000 people. There are some 18,500 care homes, a mix of state (local authority) run and private establishments. The remaining sufferers live privately in their own homes, reliant on support from family, friends, and/or professional carers.

Living with dementia can be demanding for all parties, especially as the condition becomes more debilitating and as available support become strained. Ideally, the state steps in when a individual and/or their family can no longer cope, but state's position on dementia in the UK has, until very recently, been guarded and limited—not least for reasons of cost. That began to change—in principle—in 2009 with the publication of the Department of Health's *National Dementia Strategy*,[22] so joining England with the few other countries (currently France, Australia, and Korea) that have such strategies. It is an impressive five-year plan that promises improved health and social care services in England for everyone with dementia and their carers. However, in 2010, the National Audit Office, an independent watchdog on government initiatives and programmes, concluded that the strategy was far stronger on rhetoric than realism. It was, in their view, considerably underfunded and without the necessary backup of leadership and training: 'At the moment this strategy lacks the mechanisms needed to bring about large scale improvements and without these mechanisms it is unlikely that the intended and much needed transformation of services will be delivered within the strategy's five year timeframe'.[23]

STIGMA

Stigma overshadows much of the public discourse on dementia. The lack of prioritization of dementia in many nations' policies on health and social welfare can be seen to reflect the low value placed on 'old' citizens who are no longer amongst the economic productive members of society, combined with an unease about engaging with 'psychiatric symptoms' that have no simple fix and are often only likely to get worse. Dementia thus shares the stigma long experienced by the mentally ill; it produces a systemic, negative, discrimination: 'dementiaism'. Those who eventually get a definitive diagnosis are left with little support, information, or advice (McCormack, 2004). More generally, the fear of dementia adds to the stigmatization of sufferers, a self-protective distancing, despite ample evidence that those afflicted often cope with their condition and are active agents up to the advanced stages of their disease (Hertogh et al., 2007). As novelist Terry Pratchett, observed on being diagnosed with a rare form of Alzheimers at 59: 'It's a strange life when you "come out"—people get embarrassed, lower their voices and get lost for words'.[24]

'Coming out' is a courageous counterforce to stigmatization, but is relatively rare—despite the good offices of organizations such as Age UK and the Alzheimers Society. Hiding dementia behind closed doors, either at home or in an institution, is more typical (see Box 5.9 below). The nature of concealment is in part culturally shaped; how the stigma is perceived by dementia sufferers and by those in their local community. Mackenzie (2006) points to the nuances of stigma management amongst home-based South Asian carers in the UK. The carers were well attuned to caring for older relatives, but dementia was seen through the lens of superstition. The illness was regarded as a curse from God, a punishment that, if revealed to other people, would compromise the family's reputation and honour. It was therefore hidden from view—and in doing so, further isolated both carer and dementia sufferer.

BOX 5.9 CARE IN CRISIS?

Sixty-two per cent of care home residents [in England] are currently estimated to have dementia but less than 28% of care home places are registered to provide specialist dementia care. Few care home staff have specialist nursing qualifications or have been trained in dementia care. There is a high turnover in staff and high vacancy levels and some staff do not have English as a first language. Poor standards of care have resulted in instances of inappropriate medicines management and complaints that people are not afforded sufficient dignity and respect.

Source: House of Commons, 2008.

Around half [in Scotland] of all people never went out of the care home and there was very little planned activity outside the care home.... No care homes had a system for recording medicines.... We found care homes where staff did not understand the legal safeguards...Doors were locked in the majority of care homes we visited. Only a very small minority of people had the freedom to come and go as they pleased.... Only a third of care home managers had undergone a recognised training course about caring for people with dementia...The law on medical treatment for people who lack capacity is not being obeyed.

Source: CareCommission, 2009: 10–12.

THE CARE HOME

The bleak image portrayed in Box 5.9 contrasts radically with the 'quality care' promises in advertisements by care homes, often embellished with photographs of relaxed, smiling, residents.

Dementia care is gradually being prised from the shadows to expose its personal, social, and economic ramifications. Stories from media celebrities who have cared for a family member with dementia, or have dementia themselves, have contributed to public awareness. Sir Gerry Robinson, 'business guru', is one such example. In December 2009, he headed-up two prime-time BBC television programmes titled, provocatively, *Can Gerry Robinson Fix Dementia Care Homes?*[25] The venture was prompted by his own experiences in caring for his late father. The programme was billed as follows (Box 5.10):

BOX 5.10 CAN GERRY ROBINSON FIX DEMENTIA CARE HOMES?

In the next twenty years over a million Britons will have dementia, and sufferers are likely to end up in one of the country's privately run care homes. It's a huge business worth six billion pounds, largely paid for by taxation, yet a great deal of the care is woefully inadequate.

Can Gerry, whose father had the disease when he died, change a culture of stagnant lounges, a lack of specialist training among staff, and a focus on keeping people alive rather than helping them to live a happy life?

The programme featured care homes that displayed many of the short-comings highlighted by the commissions of inquiry (above). There were distressed residents, docile residents, and harassed staff unable to provide little more than basic bodily attention for those in their care. In contrast, Robinson featured an exemplar of 'good practice': a residential home that provided 'person-centred' care. Staff were trained to understand the best ways of appreciating the realties and experiences of residents and were encouraged to spend much one-to-one time with them. Robinson's key message was: the dignity and happiness of residents is paramount, and that is also the bedrock of a profitable business.

The programme touched a raw nerve amongst some viewers:[26]

- I visit my father every day and stay for several hours. This program put into film and words just the things which distress me all the time, but are so difficult to convey to anyone else, because they're often not things which you can 'put your finger on'. Gerry got to the nub of the problem: the care that is given is a matter of getting tasks done, boxes ticked. The care that is really needed is people CARING ABOUT other people. Every time I go to the home, I see scenes of heartbreaking and desperate neglect.

- I have just watched the first programme regarding dementia care. My father is 80 and currently living in a care home as a result of vascular dementia. Since his admission several years ago I have and still do, constantly fight on his behalf to get even the basic care he deserves. They are happy to take all his pension to pay for 'care' that is at best adequate in terms of watering, feeding and cleaning and little else. Just thinking about his treatment makes my heart break. As a younger man he was intelligent, articulate, funny and above all always kind and gentle—he does not deserve this. I cared for him myself in the community until I could no longer manage.

- Gerry Robinson's findings in the less well performing homes coincided exactly with my own. In particular, I too have heard distressed residents calling out for help over prolonged periods, their cries ignored. These residents are trying to cope with a world they no longer fully understand. They are confused, anxious and often very frightened because they do not know where they are. I cannot imagine how dreadful their mental turmoil must be. Many residents are left sitting on their own and even if seated in the communal lounge, they receive minimal stimulation. . . . A kind of supervised neglect prevails, fuelled partly by ageist attitudes towards the residents. . . . Care of vulnerable older people in general makes me both sad and angry. So often they seem to be treated insensi-tively, like carcases of meat. We will all grow old—all you have to do is live long enough. It's time we started 'doing as we would be done by' when caring for older people.

ON THE POLITICS AND ETHICS OF CARE

'Care' can mean many things. I can care about my car, care for my plants, care to have my breakfast at 8.30 a.m. In organizations, care has been turned and twisted in many different directions. There is, for example, the salesperson or waiter who 'cares, above all, about your satisfaction'; there are the scripted flight attendants trained to look and sound caring for their passengers; there are the immaculately attired hotel receptionists who 'care so much that you have a comfortable stay'. Care has become corporatized and sloganized such that it is often void of moral import; its role is essentially commercial, transactional, and ephemeral, a fleeting pleasantry that aims to reinforce a future sale. The care home has, ironically, been infected with this kind of discourse.

Care as an ethic, though, has a special connotation. It underpins the essence of being in a 'caring profession' or being a 'carer'. Virginia Held explains:

Persons in caring relations are acting for self-and-other together. Their characteristic stance is neither egotistic nor altruistic; these are the options in conflictual situations, but the wellbeing of the caring relation involves the cooperative well-being of those in the relations and the well-being of the relation itself. (Held, 2006: 12)

The ethic of care is at the centre of the positive ties that we construct with one another, a 'key dimension of identity, interpersonal relations and social institutions... especially in societies like ours that must care for large numbers of old, young, sick and weak' (Gabriel, 2009: 383). In other words, without caring of this sort, much is lost, especially trust and the emotional bonds that help carer and cared-for meaningfully connect.

For older people, entering a care home can be a confusing, even frightening experience, adding to the disorientation of their dementia. Thereon, organizational features can conspire to create an ethos of care that is little more than a thin shell or carapace. The actualities are low-paid, poorly trained staff under pressure to get through the day by 'containing' their clients, people who can appear odd, demanding, and sometimes erratic. The carer's preoccupation is the daily round of physical management: feeding and cleaning tasks. Care is reduced to control and client compliance. The care ideal of mutuality and empathy is rarely discernible. As Innes astutely observes, there is an inward entrenchment of low status, stigma, and power that sustains the care home culture:

Low-status workers (predominately female) are caring for a client group that is undervalued and objectified rather than as individuals of value to society. However, the low-status workers are in a position to exert power and control over a similarly low-status client group. (Innes, 2009: 63)

Dementia clients' complaints and distress can fall on deaf ears in these circumstances, disrupted only by persistent protests from 'outside' others, such as family members or social workers.

PERSON-CENTRED CARE—THE ANSWER?

> It is very painful to go into crowds. When I sit in the middle of a large audience, I find myself becoming more and more panic-stricken and I will leave the church service, confused and drenched with sweat.... I do know that in times of emotional stress I have tremendous headaches that produce confusion and finally produce physical exhaustion. At the end, my mind blanks out, and I become unresponsive and uncommunicative.
>
> Robert Davis clergyman, *My Journey into Alzheimer's Disease* (1989: 104)

Rarely evident in policy debates about dementia are the voices of dementia sufferers themselves. This remarkable omission is partly a legacy of the dominant disease-model, the medicalization of dementia. Here, dementia is defined as a neurobiological phenomenon that requires physical and pharmacological intervention (Cotrell and Schulz, 1993). Consequently, the 'patient' is objectified. Memory loss associated with dementia is assessed in terms of pre-formed questions on standard protocols, such as *The Mini Mental State Examination*, where the score achieved determines the drug prescribed. The clinical expert is in charge, a stance that encourages a 'hygienic' approach to dementia care.

What this misses, crucially, is the experiential world of the dementia sufferer, a fundamental cornerstone to the care ethic. It treats the sufferer as a bundle of individual symptoms to 'manage', somehow divorced from the politics of the care context (Innes, 2009). It also raises the intriguing possibility that what is observed as 'demented behaviour' speaks as much, at times more, about the kind of care received than the 'nature' of the condition. In other words, the 'odd', 'unruly', or 'challenging' behaviour of residents is their attempt to resist unwanted restrictions in the only way that they can, constrained as they are by the culture of control and stigma (Gubrium, 1991).

Clues as to how dementia-diagnosed people feel about their predicament can be located in a few sources. Bowers et al. (2009) report care-home residents' voices in *Older People's Vision of Long-Term Care*, and de Boer et al (2007) locate the dementia patient's perspective in a review of the dementia literature. A selection of these findings is presented in Box 5.11.

These narratives convey three themes. The first is of care home residents feeling trapped and isolated; there is sense of resignation and despair.

BOX 5.11 VOICING DEMENTIA

Inside the care home[27]

- 'There was a meeting the other night. Some people talked but nothing special. Would be able to talk better on a one-to-one basis.'

- 'I wouldn't tell anyone if I was depressed—just get on with it—which happens quite a lot.'

- 'I've lost the ability to communicate as there's no one with the same interests here as me.'

- 'It would be great if we could use some of the fee we pay for our own leisure, maybe have someone for two hours each week to do what we want with us—take me out on the bus, sort out my wardrobe.'

- 'I would like the care assistants to talk to me when they come to care for me.'

Inside dementia

- 'Lose my mind, ability to know what is going on—I want to observe and feel part of life.' 'There is nothing left when you lose your mind.' 'Not be able do anything . . . I don't want to lose everything.'[28]

- 'Can it be that the term "Alzheimer's" has a connotation similar to the "Scarlet Letter" or "Back Plague"? Is it even more embarrassing than a sexual disease?'[29]

- 'I must be one of the victims, I've got a change to be one of the contributors. I feel good about that.'[30]

- 'I haven't thought so much about the memory lark, because it hasn't really affected me . . . When I read about that, it doesn't worry me. I don't think a lot about it because I don't' want to seem to walk around the wrong way or anything like that, you know, that's what I think . . .'[31]

- 'I think I am very fortunate. I have really managed to accept it to say that I'm a lot luckier than a lot of other people. I could be a lot worse.'[32]

- 'As long as I can do something safely and do it properly, then I don't want to have to depend on somebody else. Because you feel useless then and I don't want to be useless.'[33]

As others have noted, it is the social, not the physical, aspects of care that is often of greatest importance to dementia sufferers (Goldsmith, 1996). The second is that the lived experience of dementia is highly individualistic. Some people are gripped by fear and confusion; some are wrestling with the social stigma; some are revaluating their identity and competencies; and some are almost at ease with their predicament. Time with the disease, personality, and the quality of support will all be at play, but the variations reinforce the final point: any meaningful caring relationship needs to begin with what the dementia sufferer says and feels.

This conclusion is germane to the backlash to over-medicalizing dementia—compressing dementia into a cluster of cognitive and physical deficits or damages which turn the person into an object. Kitwood (1990), for example, advances the notion of 'personhood', to be celebrated and nurtured in dementia caregiving. Personhood effectively polarizes the state of dementia care, rejecting 'ignoring', 'disempowerment', 'stigmatization', 'intimidation', and 'withholding', in favour of 'recognition', 'giving', 'validation', and 'collaboration'. It asserts that, however advanced the dementia, there is a 'person within' who can be reached with sufficient patience and skill.

Personhood challenges our 'cognitively dominant' culture that reifies cognitive skills such as quick thinking, coherence, problem solving, rapid and accurate recall. It posits that all is far from lost when such facilities atrophy or disappear: the 'person' is not totally destroyed. Sabat, for example, studied dementia case histories to conclude that, while the outward manifestations of self do become fragile and fragmented, other features remain intact, such as personal preferences and a sense of what one can or cannot do well, (Sabat, 2002, 2006). Others observers reach a similar conclusion:

I have seen deeply demented patients weep or shiver as they listen to music they have never heard before, and I think they can experience the entire range of feelings the rest of us can, and that dementia, at least at these times, is no bar to emotional depth. Once one has seen such responses, one knows that there is still a self to be called upon, even if music, and only music, can do the calling.   (Sacks, 2007: 346)

A man does not consist of memory alone. He has feeling, will, sensibilities, moral being—matters of which neuropsychology cannot speak. And it is here, beyond the realm of an impersonal psychology, that you may find ways to touch him, and change him.   (Luria, 1985: 32)

RECONFIGURING THE CARE SETTING

Person-centred care attempts to understand the world from the perspective of the person with dementia, to recognize the unique expression of their feelings despite their cognitive impairments, and to tailor care accordingly (Brooker, 2008). The potential for reward and social connection, therefore, should always be possible if carer and care institution frame dementia in this manner. If the deeper, emotional centres of the brain remain intact, music, art, and reminiscence can be more appropriate forms of communication than ones that press cerebral tests on the person (Zeisel, 2010). Tools such as 'life history' can be used to help the carer appreciate the individual's place in time and build a relationship that appreciates the resident's lifespace and interests, past and present.

Attracted to its essential humanism and optimism, person-centred care has been embraced enthusiastically by critics of traditional approaches.[34] Controlled studies are beginning to emerge which appear to support its efficacy compared to traditional care models (Chenoweth et al., 2009). Meanwhile, devices such as 'dementia-care mapping' have exposed the care process to constructive scrutiny. It evaluates, through third-party observations, how much, and how well, person-centred care is practised (Brooker, 2005). Person-centred care, however, is not without its critics. Some scholars are uneasy about the assumption that aspects of self are 'always there', possibly 'until the end'. As (over?) committed carers and family members, are we too anxious to see personhood in our charges or loved ones, regardless? Is it then more to do with the carer's attributions and desires than the realities of the individual with dementia? As Davis (2004) asks, can it lead to a false sense that death is not, inevitably a desolate event, the disease having eventually robbed the person of all vestiges of personhood?

IN SUM

In an ageing population, it is increasingly likely that we will know someone near or dear to us who experiences dementia. Organizing for dementia care confronts our cultural prejudices towards ageing as well as the 'afflictions' of older age. It adds a sharp twist to our fears about getting old. If the latter years are an unwelcome reminder of our mortality, the prospect of dementia adds a further note of gloom. The cultural tendency to hide away and subdue its oldest, sickest members in institutions or 'homes' is mirrored in dementia care, where care is much medicalized, despite the evidence that social and emotional attention should be paramount.

Public dementia policies expose a struggle to reconcile the ballooning statistics on the incidence of dementia with other economic priorities—in which the older and infirmed play little part. The tension is apparent in the way person-centred dementia care now appears in various policy documents issued by the UK Government and its advisory bodies. While person-centred care is favoured, there remains a wide gap between wanting a major change from 'bed and body' attention in the residential care sector, and the political will, financial resources, and skills to help make it happen.

Person-centred care cannot be grafted onto the current system as yet a further task 'to do', leaving current carers bewildered and overwhelmed. It requires a cultural and organizational infrastructure comprising committed, experienced, managers; well-trained and well-remunerated care staff; staffing levels that permit significant quality time with residents (currently a care-home resident spends just two minutes with staff or other residents over a six-hour period),[35] and the cultivation of an open, 'person' culture that seamlessly mixes staff with residents and visiting family members. There is considerable scope here for an exciting and challenging new professionalism in dementia care, providing a worthy societal service—and not just for those who can pay.

6 Retirement

> Retirement brings a radical break into a man's life; he is entirely cut off from his past and he has to adapt himself to a new status. This status does bring certain advantages such as rest and leisure, but also serious disadvantages—it makes him poorer and disqualifies him.
>
> Simon de Beauvoir, 1972

> This short book will help you work through the very personal process of discovering what's likely to be consequential to your happiness in retirement... the discovery of eternal Saturdays.
>
> Richard E. Grace, 2010

Ageing has long been associated with retirement. In the 'normal' lifecourse people will eventually retire from their work when they are old. They will withdraw, pull back, ease into to a life of non-employment, popularly portrayed as a period of well-earned rest and leisure.

Before industrialization retirement was almost non-existent: work ended in illness or death. The recipe for comfortable old age was amassed personal assets, the advantage of the merchant and professional classes. A regularly funded retirement was available to but an elite few, often state bureaucrats and the military (Marshall and Taylor, 2005). The rest relied on family support, begging or any menial job that they could come by. The advent of the Industrial Revolution was no kinder to older workers, most of whom were rendered obsolescent. In the words of a 1906 economist: 'The old man today... slow, hesitating, frequently half-blind and deaf, is sadly misplaced amid the death dealing machinery of a modern factory' (Achenbaum, 2006: 52; see also chapter 1).

Wider retirement is a relatively recent, twentieth-century invention, institutionalized post Second World War with the availability of surplus capital and state pensions (Quadagno, 1982; Phillipson, 1990). Those who reach 60 or 65 years of age and have made sufficient financial contribution are typically regarded as eligible for a state pension—a financial lifeline for many. State pensions, though, have been dispensed differentially and discriminately, often failing, for instance, older women, as Pat Thane observes:

The obstacles to women building an adequate pension have been known ever since state pensions were first proposed in Britain over a century ago. The challenges were the same then as now: women did, and do, outlive men; women were/are likely to be poorer than men in old age because they had/have, less opportunities to save due to more restricted job opportunities, lower pay and interrupted careers due to caring responsibilities. They were/are, more likely than men, to experience poverty due to the ending of a partnership. A hundred years ago this was caused by widowhood, now the chief cause is separation or divorce, but the proportion affected and the material effects were/are similar.[1]

Age eligibility for retirement and state pension has varied somewhat by occupation. For example, in the USA official retirement for commercial airline pilots is 60, for federal firefighters 57, and for police officers 55–60. Physicians, though, can retire in their 70s, while Supreme Court judges can dispense their wisdoms up until their 80s. In Greece there are currently 580 jobs deemed sufficiently hazardous to merit early retirement—at 55 for men and 50 for women (Thomas, 2010). Some of these are clearly dangerous, such as coal mining and bomb disposal. Others appear odd or arguable, such as hairdressers (chemical hair preparations), radio and TV presenters (risk of bacterial infection from microphones), and musicians playing wind instruments (risk of gastric reflux).[2]

Saving for retirement

Saving for your retirement is one of the most important financial plans you can make. You can choose to save in a pension scheme and/or a savings plan, but whatever you decide, you'll want your funds to grow and be worth as much as possible in the long term.

Figure 6.1 UK Government advice on retirement planning[3]

All such variations point to the social construction of retirement and its age-links, rooted in localized practices. With increasing life expectancy, retirement can constitute up to a third of a person's lifespan, straining available income-tax revenues for pension support (Glover and Branine, 2001). One response has been to increase the age of pension entitlement. For example, in the USA those born after 1959 will be unable to receive their full state pension before they are 67. Germany's pension age will be 67 from 2012 and the UK's is planned to increase progressively to 66 and then by steps to 68—for both men and women.

The onus of responsibility for care in retirement and old age has shifted gradually away from the state to the individual, described by Rose (1996) as the 'death of the social'. The UK government's official line in 2010 illustrates this (see Figure 6.1). It promotes the virtues of 'a savings plan' (idealized through an image of smiling, grey-haired, white, heterosexual couple).

In this new era, goes the counsel, young people will need to save more and work longer than their parents' generation to fund their retirement. The paradox of this advice is that it occurs at a period when, structurally, many young people are disadvantaged in the labour market, facing low or no earnings. For some, there is a sense of disengagement or remoteness from the realities of later-life pensions, a 'what's the point' (Furnham and Goletto-Tankel, 2002).

THE COMPANY

Private, company pension schemes can considerably augment, if not replace, state pensions. Historically, they were a rarity in the USA until the late nineteenth century when the American Express Company broke rank and paid its over 60s workers a small amount—if they agreed to quit (Achenbaum, 2006). On the other side of the Atlantic, the UK's venture into company pensions was inspired by a Quaker, George Cadbury who, in 1906, donated the then not inconsiderable sum of £60,000 into a pension fund for his employees. Today, some pension schemes are voluntary (an employee can elect whether or not to join); others are mandatory. In Australia, Switzerland, France, Chile, Argentina, Hungary, and Poland, and, from 2012, the UK, for instance, it is required that employers provide a private pension for all their employees. Given that the company pension is tied to earnings, its potential for divisiveness is considerable (Hills et al., 2009), especially when it is calculated as a multiple of a final salary. The substantial pensions that have been awarded to some executive retirees belie the description 'fringe benefit'.

Company pensions are now particularly attractive to governments keen to hive-off retirement/old age support to the private sector. But they are far from risk free. They are exposed to economic downturns, insufficient equity to provide for the increase in eligible retirees, and the longevity of retirees. In recent times we have witnessed insolvencies and early closures of some superannuation schemes, the poor returns of others, and the radical adjustment of employer and employee contributions of still others (Bräuninger et al., 2010). In the UK, the worst effects of total foreclosure have been mitigated by a Government pension protection fund, outlawing the plundering of corporate pension funds to buttress a fading business. It followed a succession of corporate failures that left employees with little pension benefit. One event was particularly noteworthy: the premature death in 1991 of Robert Maxwell, owner of the Mirror group of newspapers. It transpired that he had siphoned off some £400 million of his company's pension fund in an attempt to rescue his ailing corporate empire.

As social reforms are contemplated (new social care taxes, individualized self-help schemes, raising the pension age, longer working life), the stark contrast with poorer countries becomes even starker. In North and Sub-Saharan Africa, Asia, and parts of the Middle East, older workers have thin protection, or, more often, none at all. Agricultural workers in rural areas have to work well into their old age or up until the point when they are unable to continue. The burden of their care then falls to their family, or to no one.[4]

Retirement's fragmentation

The ageing population and economic instability of the late twentieth and the early twenty-first century have created a mosaic of 'retirement' scenarios. Some people choose to work past their state pension age out of financial necessity, or simply because they prefer to: it provides a structure and meaning to their 'still active' lives. Others, if they can afford it, voluntarily retire before the state pension age, a pattern observed across many European countries, especially amongst relatively well-off baby boomers (Romans, 2007). There are individuals who prematurely retire because of poor health or inability to cope with the physical demands of their job—a particular risk for workers in manual trades. Still others are victims of organizational downsizing and recessionary retrenchment, forcibly 'retired early' in their 50s or early 60s. Here retirement euphemistically blurs with redundancy, a fate that befalls older workers disproportionately in declining industries (Marshall and Taylor, 2005). Historically it has hit hardest the less skilled, but the recessions of the 1980s and 2000s have been less discriminating, leaving managers and professionals in their wake. Some see this as a painful end to their career (Fineman, 1983). Others resist the 'retired' label, as a 59-year-old IT expert explains to Gabriel et al. (2010):

Retired! [*Laughs heartily*] No. I'll, hopefully, I might do some more lecturing and I hope to—I hope to—I might do some other things, like maybe set up a business as well, but I just like keeping active, I mean my philosophy basically is if you're in good health and you want to do something then you should do it. So that's my main thing, work's not a driving force these days as much as it was.... Unemployment used to be almost a taboo, but these days it's become almost like it's acceptable and you're not a weak employee or anything like that. (15)

The *way*, not just the reason why, people retire adds further complexity to the picture. There are older workers who are able to part with their employer gradually, working part time on 'bridge jobs' between work and retirement. It softens the shock of a sudden stop or 'falling off the cliff' (Beehr and Bennett, 2007; Feldman, 2007). Such opportunities are, however, more the exception than the rule. The sharp break is more typical—well captured by a male transport manager:

It's a very big step to go from working full-time to stepping over into what looks like the abyss of retiring and it's a psychological thing that you've got to come to terms with. One minute you've got the security of a wage coming in, which is a good wage.... The next you're just a dog's body.   (Vickerstaff and Cox, 2005: 85)

'Semi-retirement' and 'part-retirement' have become common additions to the lexicon of retirement. They can apply to people who have retired from a career post—voluntarily or otherwise—but are now self-employed, 'the seeming oxymoron of working while retired' (Beehr and Bennett, 2007: 278). 'Retired = old' begins to dissolve in these circumstances. There are self-employed professionals—consultants, writers, artists, financial advisors—who may adjust their workloads as they age but never consider themselves retired. Academics can formally retire from their university, yet still continue to write, publish, and occasionally attend conferences—even though they are now out of the mainstream of their profession. Sociologist Robert Weiss, one such person, wistfully relates the tale of his encounter with a young person at a conference who had read something he had written some four decades earlier: 'She felt honoured to meet me as she had thought I was dead' (Weiss, 2005: 3).

Young—and retired

As different ways and times of stopping, pausing and re-starting work emerge, it is becoming plain that not all retirees are old, nor are all the elderly retired

(Luborsky and LeBlanc, 2003). The ultimate flip in the age/retirement expectation is when very young workers retire—effectively finish with their chosen career. This is particularly apparent with elite athletes, people groomed for success since they were children to be footballers, gymnasts, tennis players, swimmers, or the like. Some may have achieved considerable public acclaim, bathed for a time in the glow of celebrity status. Others will be less high-profile. Most, though, will retire young—as young as 18 for gymnasts, often in training since they were 6.

Their retirement occurs because they can no longer compete or score as they once did. In the fiercely competitive, close surveillance, world of top sport there is little room for stragglers or for those who can longer 'make it'. Unsurprisingly, the process is traumatic for some, triggering depression, eating disorders and emotional difficulties (Brewer et al., 1999; Kerr and Dacyshyn, 2000):

I definitely identify more with the athlete role. That is an issue I'm trying to deal with in terms of retiring. I have been swimming for 13 years and swimming is a big part of me, a big part of my identity.[5]

There was nothing else to me but gymnastics, so you take away the gym and there is nothing.'[6]

When you're a gymnast you're so enclosed and watched over every day, 24 hours a day. As an 18-year old you're treated like a 12 year old. . . . you're told what to do.[7]

When attachment to one's sport is total, and identity is narrowly defined as an embodied sense of self, retirement can be devastating. At worst it prefigures a life where nothing ever quite matches up to one's early passion. At best it can eventually lead to self-acceptance as an 'ex-athlete' and onwards to negotiating a new sense of self (Perna et al., 1999; Lally, 2007). Time, after all, is on their side, even if adequate preparation is not.

The older retiree—saying goodbye

There are those faced with reconstructing their later lives following retirement. The pace and reasons for retirement—expected or unexpected, mandatory or voluntary—will play a part in any adjustment. Also, how wedded the person is to the meanings and routines of previous work and what they imagine their 'third age' will be like. It is a process that can shift in subjective meaning over time, such as from initial euphoria (the promise of unfettered freedom), to disenchantment (an emotional let-down as a meaningful life role becomes illusive), to an accommodation to one's new lifestyle, including a transition into old age (Atchley, 1976; Hanson and Wapner, 1994; Reitzes and Mutran, 2006; Beehr and Bennett, 2007).

For some, looking back on a long working lifetime, retirement can be an abrupt reminder of their mortality. They are entering a period when the hour-glass is well past half-empty. Three senior managers ponder this:[8]

Let's face it, when one retires, one is saying one has entered the final phase of life. This is it. There is no more after this... you are walking down the last corridor... And it may be wonderful, but it is still the last one.

When you're sixty, you think: Well. I'm probably not going to live to be a hundred, so that means I have maybe twenty more years to live. Maybe I have only fifteen. You get to a certain age and you know that there is no possibility that you're going to live fifty more years.

I have disbelief in my age, I just can't believe it. You know it's not possible that it can end. After all, thirty-eight years.

Reflexivity of this sort is mediated by how parting from work is organized for, or by, employees. Some companies hire pre-retirement consultants to do the job, to help retirees manage the transition. Practical issues concerning health, pensions, and financial planning are typically central to the agenda; rarely addressed though, are the emotions of adjustment.[9]

Exit rituals can leave their mark, for good or ill. They range from the curt and impersonal ('I just got a just a brown envelope containing my P45 form—I was out, finished'), to the elaborate and ceremonial. As a rite of passage, the retirement ceremony commonly features a boss's carefully crafted speech celebrating the incumbent's past, and a gift funded by a collection from colleagues (some more willing contributors than others), all lightened by food and alcohol. The transition ahead is seldom mentioned, other than in the broadest, clichéd, terms: 'lots of time now to do the gardening'; 'you can get on to that golf course every day'; 'no more tedious meetings!' (Atchley, 1997). A familiar parting refrain is 'It would be great to see you here, any time'. A human resource manager tells a cautionary tale for those who take this sentiment too literally:

Brian was a production executive. He loved his work with us; I guess he was a workaholic. He's been retired about a year now. We gave him a lavish send off; a huge party. He was a popular man, you see. About a month after he left he popped in to see us. Of course it was great to see him and to exchange stories. I got the feeling then that he wasn't adjusting too well to retirement. He said he'd keep in touch with us, and that he did! It seemed like every week he'd be in—trying, really, to be where he thought he belonged. Eventually one of his old colleagues came to see me, in despair. 'He's driving us mad' he said. 'He's a nice guy, but we don't want him any more. He wants to do our job for us; he can't let go.'   (Fineman et al., 2010: 22)

The interpersonal bonds of working, even when honed over many years, can turn out to be fragile and instrumental. Retirement ceremonies, for the most part, signal that the strands are now broken and a new age/stage transition has formally begun (Savishinsky, 1995). If meaningful to the retiree, they can, like other rites of passage, ease the shift into a new age and place. But for some, the event is too formulaic and sanitized: it rings hollow:

I know people will plan a party and that sort of thing, I just don't want anything like it. I've attended retirement parties and its embarrassing, all the lies that get told, all the conflicts that get washed over and whitewashed. And I just didn't want that.

(Weiss, 2005: 49)

Still others hover between these positions, rather like not wanting another birthday acknowledged but disappointed if no card arrives to mark the occasion:

I was with the company thirty-seven years. And I'm sure that I'm the only person—and I was a senior officer of the company—I'm sure that I'm the only one in the company's history that left at retirement age that wasn't offered some kind of retirement party. I didn't want a party actually. I've been to enough company parties . . . but . . . . it would have been nice to have an offer . . . . I got the feeling that there was really a kind of void in the end that should have been filled in.   (Weiss, 2005: 53)

For those long disenchanted with their work, eager to leave 'the daily grind', a drink with a few self-selected colleagues can be a preferred way of parting. It is an occasion where both past feelings and future hopes and worries can, perhaps, be shared.

In retirement—confronting oneself

Recently, I was enjoying a meal out with friends—Alan and his wife, Arlene. Alan, aged 65, had retired earlier that year after a long and distinguished career as marketing director of a multinational firm that manufactured top-of-the-range lighting. He had enjoyed all the accoutrements of executive status, including first-class international travel and a team of supporting staff. I asked him how things were going. He broke into a brief grin: 'Fantastic! I can take so many holidays now and really enjoy my hobbies. It's good, really good!' I sensed he was a little over-effusive but I politely—and somewhat enviously—congratulated him on his new lifestyle. In the middle of the meal he left to go to the bathroom; Arlene grabbed my arm. 'Don't believe a word he says!' she said. 'He's been like a bear with a sore head. He's lost without all his props, his secretary, his expense account and being "boss". I'm really very worried about him'.

(a)   (b)

Figure 6.2 Retirement—how it should be? Permission kindly granted for Figure 6.2(a) by www.carttoStock.com and for Figure 6.2(b) by Max Gathings

These differing descriptions touch on some of the conflicting tensions of retirement: having to live up to a public representation of what retirement *should* be like, and the lingering, private, imprint of a previous work identity.

The images in Figure 6.2—a sample from many greeting card lookalikes—stereotypically portray retirement as a state to be eagerly anticipated, when happiness is on the cards (literally in this case) and leisure and pleasure abound. Its positive gloss is total. Disappointment, illness, incapacity, or poverty is efficiently airbrushed from such presentations. Retirement is a release from work's obligation and is unquestionably a good thing for one's spirit and well-being. Some such experiences may indeed occur for certain retirees, especially when leaving a job that has long become stale and void of purpose (Van Solinge and Henkens, 2008).

But what if the experience is very different: a sense of displacement and loss? How can you face retirement's promise of fun and freedom when feeling displaced and marginalized (Weiss, 2005)? Alan's response is not untypical: deception and emotion work. Pretend, especially in public, that all is going well. Alan wanted me—and presumably others—to believe that his retirement was unalloyed pleasure—because that is what retirement is 'supposed' to be. Declaring otherwise would be a self and public admission that he was failing to manage, to cope with or adjust to his new life, an uncomfortable position for a man who has long held the position of successful top manager.

THE IDENTITY LINGERS ON

The move to total retirement effectively ends a person's work role, but not necessarily their job identity. For a time—sometimes several years—the ex-role can live on, providing an identity cushion during adjustment to retirement (Reitzes and Mutran, 2006). The job has disappeared but the memory lingers on, occupying the liminal space between pre- and post-retirement identities. Given the premium in industrialized societies on having, and describing oneself through, a job, it can be a shock to relinquish that identity in favour of an amorphous, roleless role—'retired'. It is not uncommon to hear people not long retired describe themselves in terms of their past occupation or job title, valorizing their past achievements. As continuity theorists suggest, we are constantly working at our narratives and feelings to create meaningful bridges between past and present (Atchley, 1999). Inflating one's prior identity can provide an important anchor, especially when retirement is felt as a stigma or loss of purpose.

Living off old identities is helpful, perhaps essential, to offset the unease of status loss. But it is inherently unsustainable. A retired manager in a study by Jones et al. (2010: 112) captures the dilemma:

I'm still living off the camel's hump of my previous jobs, but I could see that could happen, depending on whether I turn into a vegetable or not...they will suddenly work out that actually, this chap's a no-good waster and not in fact important any more! [T]hen you really will know that you are sort of yesterday's man.

The sense of impending uselessness that pervades this man's account hints at emasculation, the gendered nature of his loss of standing. For women retirees, a gendered retirement can mean defaulting to a traditional role of housewife and domestic carer—an uncomfortable position for those who hold feminist ideals. As Caroll (2004: 6) dryly notes, 'domestic spaces are not necessarily places of endless leisure/pleasure for "retired" women'. A retiree in Jones et al.'s study confronts that very prospect:

I guess as a woman, I don't want to just be 'the housewife' and I never have been, so I certainly don't intend to be now...I don't want to, you know, go to the local Oxfam shop or something!... So I don't want to be doing mundane things, I want to be doing something that really will make a difference.   (112)

Professional women are no less immune to loss of purpose on retirement than professional men. However, some can find the initial transition rather less destabilizing than men because of their familiarity with previous discontinuities in their life (e.g. multiple relocations, marital disruption, child rearing, parental care) (Bateson, 1990). Thereafter, though, the move can be a painful one because of loss of social contacts, a diminished professional identity, and ageist stereotypes (Price, 2000).

Manufacturing the third age

The notion of a *third* age harks back to the early, and arguable, theorizing that the lifespan can be divided into discrete 'ages' (see chapter 1). It presumes a *first* age—a period to complete one's formal education; a *second* age of parenting and paid work; leading to a *third* age of *active* retirement, free from work, financial and social obligations, and the enjoyment of good health. It is a time for personal exploration, development, and growth, the 'bonus' of an extended lifespans (Laslett, 1996; Hunt, 2005). Frailty and dependency are not (yet) vanquished: they come much later in life—in the *fourth* and final age.

'Third age' as a descriptive term is now to be found in education ('The University of The Third Age') and the marketing of goods and services of all sorts. Counsellors and market researchers have staked their claim (see Box 6.1).

Marketing to third-agers has been facilitated by virtual and hard-copy magazines, such as *Retired and Living, Retired Magazine, AARP Magazine* ('World's largest circulation'), *Saga Magazine, Best Retirement Spots, Grand Times,* and *Living Well.* Their formula is to mix promotional material and advertisements with upbeat 'lifestyle' advice, often embellished by accounts

---

Box 6.1 MARKETING THE THIRD AGE

The Third Age designates the 'bonus years' of extended middle age and active elderhood, roughly from age 50 to frail old age. Sometimes called Second Adulthood, this 'grace period' presents both challenges and magnificent opportunities.

Why is LifeCrafting for the Third Age important? The structured process enables you to create the life you want through your choices and actions, rather than drifting and hoping for the best while settling for less. Flexible planning allows for changing course in response to unexpected opportunities.

Meg Newhouse, *Third-Age LifeCrafting*[10]

We have explored the dream fulfilment made possible by a lump sum at retirement and the various opportunities this can present: a new car, exciting holidays, new home appliances, furnishings and fittings.

The 3rd age is often a time of major change. For some, it's a time to take up new challenges or to indulge latent hobbies and interests; whilst for others, it is characterised by 'settling and sorting' and putting affairs in order.

In the later stages of the 3rd age, individuals may become less confident, more risk averse, more cautious and nervous. Our experience in this market has included projects relating to healthcare/personal care and home/leisure products assignments relating to grocery shopping, branding and individual product line development.

Hirst Research & Marketing[11]

from 'retired' celebrities and 'real retirees' ('*Retired and loving it! Six satisfied Americans share why they love their postwork lives*').[12]

Market targeting is sometimes broad-brushed, other times variegated—where third-agers have been deconstructed to produce an array of different groupings or types. Baby boomers, according to Green (2003) can be 'leading edge' or 'trailing edge', while Moschis et al. (1997), on the other hand, see them as 'healthy indulgers' (they like travel, home care services, and town houses), 'frail reclusers' (need overdraft protection, exercise equipment, and home health care), or 'ailing outgoers' (require investment products, health club membership, and special clothing). The American Association of Retired Persons has divided near-retirees into five attitudinal types: 'the strugglers', 'the anxious', 'the enthusiasts', the 'self-reliants' and 'today's traditionalists'.[13] Yet other taxonomies trade on catchy acronyms, such as 'woopies' (well-off older persons), 'glams' (grey, leisured, and moneyed) and 'grumpies' (growing number of mature professionals) (Blaikie, 1999).

These labels are quirky and certainly contentious, they nevertheless provide ways of manoeuvring consumption patterns by defining—for a time—the heterogeneous texture of a field that marketers consider profitable. Moreover, professionals' vocabularies are often translated and incorporated into personal narratives (Gubrium and Holstein, 1998), thus some the third-age categories (including 'third age' itself) are ready hooks onto which elderly consumers can hang their identities should they desire, while simultaneously attending to products and services created 'for them'. In these ways retirement's experiences become inexorably, and often powerfully, entwined with pressures to consume.

TIGHTENING THE SELL

Many writers take baby boomers as prototypical third-agers, a generation born in the 1940s, now facing retirement in relative affluence and security (Blaikie, 2002). Putting a specific age to who does or does not belong to the third age is a somewhat arbitrary exercise, given the variations in retirement age and the third-agers who unretire to seek further work or education. There is, therefore, some dissatisfaction about the analytic robustness of 'third age', some writers prudently preferring to construe it more as a generational cultural phenomenon (see Gilleard and Higgs, 2009). In other words, third-ageness is akin to a zeitgeist, a spirit of the generational times, marked by older people's patterns of consumption and use of leisure.

The consumption/leisure ethos is aptly illustrated by intensive marketing events aimed at older retirees. *The Retirement Show* in the UK is one such manifestation. Its fourth annual event took place in London in 2010 in the substantial Olympia Exhibition Centre (and also in Manchester and

Glasgow). The show's organizers boasted some '60,000 mature visitors'. It enticed exhibitors with the promise that they would face 'a captive audience who are ready to spend—with you!' Moreover, it was...

a unique opportunity to interact with the UK's fastest growing and most asset-rich population group. The over-50s control 80% of the UK's wealth, have little or no debt and huge spending power. The pot of assets and cash held by people over 50 is valued at over UK£175 billion. By 2031, the number of people aged 80 and over will rise from 2.2 million to 4.9 million. Net worth of visitors to The Retirement Shows in 2009 was estimated at over £2bn. With fixed or index-linked incomes, the over-50s sector is largely recession-proof.[14]

Retirement's 'fun' was built into the show's design. It included 'exciting sessions' on cookery demonstrations, gardening questions and answers, tango dancing, Pilates and yoga. In the gaps between entertainments, the 'affluent visitor' could peruse a wide range of product and services, many focusing on holidays, tourisms, property abroad, financial planning, and aids to health and mobility. The powerfully orchestrated message was clear: (a) the new-retiree market is there for the picking, and (b) its 'unique selling points' are tailored activity, fitness, fun, leisure, and financial investments.

Where to retire

Where to retire has, traditionally, been an uncomplicated matter. You retire where you live, close to or with family members, augmented when necessary by community support and services. You retire and age 'in place', in your mixed-age neighbourhood. As 'naturally occurring retirement communities' (Hunt and Gunter-Hunt, 1986) they are, in their 'pure' form, neither planned nor designed for older people, but evolve appropriately when more than 50 per cent of residents are aged 60 or older (Callahan and Lansperry, 1997).

Most retirees prefer to remain in their own home and community as they age (AARP, 2005). It offers them a sense of continuity, belonging, and the potential for cross-generational support. But there are drawbacks. One's home can eventually become ill-suited to changing health and security needs (see chapter 5). As the nuclear family has atomized it has become progressively less likely that one's kith and kin will be nearby. Often considerable distances separate family members, communication and support dependent more on virtual links than face-to-face ones. So, left to themselves, there is nothing inherently 'natural' about naturally occurring retirement communities that guarantees a comfortable, inclusive lifestyle for the retired. Those that do are likely to be a product of an unusual confluence of family and friends, of social policies targeted at the elderly, and of supportive services (Cohen-Mansfield et al., 2010).

GETTING AWAY

There are retirees who have a vision of retirement as renewal that requires breaking old geographical ties. In the UK, 'seaside bungalow retirement' has had an iconic place in this vision. The lure of the British coastal resort with its image of clear air, calming sea view, easy climate, and ready-made leisure facilities has attracted urban visitors since Victorian times. And since the 1950s, permanent retirees have added to this population. Those who consider themselves as 'permanently on holiday' have shifted the age-demographics of resorts such as Bournemouth, Eastbourne, Worthing, Paignton, Colwyn Bay, and Blackpool. These places host urban retirees who have uprooted and re-settled in a new home, often a bungalow or a purpose-built apartment.

Yet, for a growing corpus of wealthier pensioners, such seaside retirement has now lost much of its lustre. Historic market towns and attractive, upmarket, country settings beckon (Doward, 2009). Coastal 'bungalow quietude' remains—but now more the preserve of the less well-off.[15] And for them it has brought both joys and disappointments. As Mellow recorded nearly half-a-century ago: 'Some people have seen the place of their choice only in the summer, and have not considered what it offers, or looks like, in winter when entertainments are reduced and the coast can be cold and un-inviting, and the resident is thrown back on the quality of indigenous community life, which may or may not suit the newcomer' (Mellor, 1962: 43).

The retirement village

As retirees have become more willing to shift their financial assets into a retirement property, the retirement industry has geared up to the challenge. Town planners, speculative builders, financiers, and estate agents have taken up the opportunity. Many were present in *The Retirement Show*. Developers and their agents offered 'luxury', 'ideal', retirement properties—some yet to be built. Kei-Homes' development in Spain (*'Quality not Quantity'*) is not untypical, advertised in ebullient prose with an image of a smiling elderly couple bathing in crystal-clear water.[16] It promises a 'truly unique and remarkable retirement haven for those who prefer to be right on the sea front', with the added attraction of 'a huge outdoor swimming pool, indoor swimming pool and sauna, as well as a fully equipped 700 square metre gym, a massage room and a beauty salon'. The 'payment options' are crafted to make purchase look easy and risk free. The unwary purchaser could be forgiven for believing that property slump of the 2000s was little more than an unfortunate blip in the world economy. The hyperbolic 'haven', tone of this promotion plays, like others, on an idealized view of retirement; a time of leisure and luxury. Retirees can purposively co-locate to enjoy an active, leisured existence—free from worries, inconveniencies, and threats to their safety. They are with many others of like age and mind yet, at the same time, preserve their individuality—a curious mix of our postmodern times (Blaikie, 1999).

Manufactured retirement communities—'villages' and 'cities'—epitomize the trend towards designer living for the retired. They have long been option for retirees in Australia, New Zealand, and North America; more recently, they have come to the UK. Some have been specifically designed for gay and lesbian retirees, a response to their experiences of institutionalized homophobia.[17] As a major European report concludes:

At retirement homes, awareness of LGBT [lesbian, gay, bisexual, transsexual and transgendered] persons' needs is rare. Under these circumstances, 'invisibility' becomes a survival strategy.   (EUAFR, 2009: 4)

All retirement villages share a number of characteristics. First, they are age segregated, exploiting loopholes or exceptions in anti-discriminatory age legislation. So they can exclude anyone under, say, 55 or 60. Second, they are activity centred, a cornerstone of 'positive ageing' (Lucas, 2004). Retirement as a period of inactivity and decline is replaced by a different narrative: managed leisure and active fun. The fit retiree buys into a serious playground for the elderly that aims to reproduce positive-aged identities (Laws, 1995). The enterprise co-ops the residue of the work ethic amongst retirees and re-forms it into a 'keeping busy' ethic; in effect, working *at* leisure. As Ekerdt (1986) astutely observes, it 'justifies the leisure of retirement, defends retired people against judgments of senescence, and gives definition to the retirement role. In all, it helps individuals adapt to retirement, and it in turn adapts retirement to prevailing societal values' (239).

A third feature is that they are closed institutions. Many are constructed behind solid, high walls with electronic security doors, tapping into latent fears amongst the elderly about crime in society 'out there' (Lucas, 2004). They are often assiduously policed by the residents themselves and by security personnel—to ensure that only eligible people are present. Security measures are typically high-profiled in a community's marketing literature and in accounts of what residents say that they appreciate (Graham and Tuffin, 2004). Finally, the places are actively managed. In part, this is down to the residents themselves as they create a 'community of identity' tied to the place and location (Gilleard and Higgs, 2005).

As with all organizations, a village's culture and sub-cultures evolve over time, a product of the varied participation, leadership, values, and informal practices of its members. But none of this takes place in a structural vacuum. There are formal covenants and house rules, there are professional managers and administrators with job descriptions, there are site owners, and there are wider civic and regulatory authorities that periodically interface with the community. Retirement communities are not frozen in the cheery, idyllic images of promotion material but are politicized settings where differences and tensions can arise; where aged people age; where partners die; and where, beneath the jolly, 'active' surface, feelings of loss and loneliness can linger.

The physical separation by a stratum of society in this manner raises questions about the nature of lifecourse social provision in a market economy. In many ways it appears a retrogressive move, fostering a fortress, 'golden ghetto' mentality that can add to societal fragmentation and stigmatization of the elderly. Moving into a gated geritopia may have advantages for the individual retiree, but it weakens the possibilities of a mixed, age-tolerant society. Arguably, retirement villages are a mark of societal failure to provide meaningful and attractive ways of integrating some of its ageing population into their home communities. So, those who can will 'buy out', but simultaneously remove themselves from opportunities to contribute to their local neighbourhood, reducing its variety and stock of knowledge (see Hunt et al., 1983; Grant, 2006). Set against this, in emphasizing *active* ageing in retirement—albeit for a minority of the elderly—the communities offer a contrast to entrenched stereotypes about the debilities that accompany ageing and retirement. They stand for another, more positive, way of being (Croucher, 2006). But in principle, it should be possible to achieve this in a more age-inclusive way.

Inside retirement 'havens'

Del Webb Corporation's *Sun City Hilton Head* (Box 6.2) in California is representative of the current state of the art. It is one of fifty-two age-restricted, 'active adult' communities in the USA, built and run by the company. There is no whisper of 'old' or of decline in its publicity. In a marketing seminar to Del Webb sales staff, a Del Webb executive explains why:

Don't mention aging in place! Tell them it'll make life easier when their parents visit. Nobody wants to be reminded that his or her body is deteriorating. Call them 'lifestyle features' for 'easy living'... Don't call your development 'age restricted', 'senior', or even 'retirement' housing. That's a no-no in our business. These folks

---

Box 6.2 SUN CITY HILTON HEAD

Lowcountry setting gives active adults the power to imagine

Make the best decision ever. Why wait? Stop dreaming and start living today at Sun City Hilton Head, the Southeast's signature destination for active adults age 55 and better.

Offering endless opportunities for residents to explore, Sun City Hilton Head has activities sure to please fitness enthusiasts, arts and craft gurus, seasoned golfers and jetsetters alike. Home to three impressive amenity centers, an entire sports complex, state-of-the-art fitness centers, two social halls and over 100 clubs and resident community groups, Sun City Hilton Head is not only a place you can call home but a luxurious and fun retreat as well!

Play like a pro on one of our two championship golf courses, or test your skills out on our new executive golf course before heading off for a drink at one of the three clubhouses. If you're not in the mood for a nine iron, you can always pump some iron at the Hidden Cypress Fitness Center or the Purrysburg Fitness Center, complete with such luxuries as a cushioned floor aerobics studio, outdoor pool, state-of-the art fitness equipment and an on-site therapy spa.

Our full-time Lifestyle Director will help coordinate special events, gatherings and activities to ensure that you experience all of our world-class amenities; the true essence of the active adult lifestyle found here at Del Webb Sun City Hilton Head.[18]

Permission kindly granted by the Del Webb Corporation

---

aren't seniors, and they're not retired both . . . We're selling an ageless lifestyle, and the lifestyle should be the tagline.   (Blechman, 2008: 194–195)

'Ageless' activity is writ large. Residents can canoe, kayak, swim, fish, dance, dine, bike, garden, play pool or tennis or cards, go to in-house movies or theatre, work out in the gym, or do crafts. Golf courses are standard fare in such developments, and each community is coordinated by a full-time manager, aka 'lifestyle director'. The 'Sun City' tag is given to nine of Del Webb's developments indicating something of the early history of the marque, when the communities were located mainly in the Sun Belt region of the USA. Their size befits 'city'—often large, sprawling and self-governing. Sun City Hilton Head covers some 5,000 acres with more than 4,000 homes and about 8,000 residents.[19] In 2008, the original Sun City in Arizona contained 41,565 residents, the vast majority white. Seventy per cent were 65 or older.[20]

Del(bert) Webb himself—who died in 1974—was a well-heeled and well-connected property developer, who keenly explored the potential of age-segregated retirement communities in the 1960s. His Arizona venture was a leap of faith which proved a shrewd move. Reputedly, its opening on New Year's Day 1960 drew a crowd of 100,000 potential purchasers, forming a mile-long traffic queue. Many bought a property on the spot (Blechman, 2008). Webb's success was the feature story of *Time Magazine* in August 1962, bannered 'The Retirement City. A New Way of Life for the Old'. The report is a chatty interview-cum-eulogy to the man's achievements—especially Sun City, on which Webb reflects:

When I see what we've built...it's the most satisfying thing that's ever happened to me. An old fellow came up to me once with tears in his eyes and thanked me for building Sun City. He said he was planning to spend the happiest 40 years of his life there.[21]

The Villages in Florida parallels Sun Cities in many respects in philosophy, demographic composition, and design. Under the munificent gaze of a full-size statue of its late founder, businessman Harold Schwartz, The Villages offers its heavily Republican residents a Disneyesque vision: *'a retirement community where people's dreams can come true'.*[22] Founded in the 1960s, it has none of the higgledy piggledy, time-honed, character of European villages, but is a meticulously planned, age-restricted, mini-metropolis of over 75,000 people and rising.[23] It promotes a cosy, 'mom and pop' image of a 'home-town' steeped in leisure: *'Our hometown offers the finest recreational opportunities and facilities to provide our residents with endless ways to have fun and enjoy life'.*[24] These include thirty-seven golf courses. Indeed, the golf cart plays a major role in personal transportation throughout the whole community, facilitated by special roadways and tunnels. Ease and leisure are residents' lingua franca, filling the void created by a lack of shared history, but where an impression of a past is manufactured in 'quaint town squares'.

The neighbourhoods of The Villages are managed by committees of residents, but overseen by the developer's employees who, under Florida law, are able to take a controlling interest over the governance of the 5.6 square miles of the development.[25] This extends to minutia of landscaping and carefully ordered living, enshrined in formal covenants and restrictions which include...

the removal or weeds and the edging of lawns, which must be at least fifty-one percent sod. Hedges over four feet high are prohibited, as are clotheslines, individual mail-boxes (mail is collected at central kiosks), the keeping of more than two pets, window air-condoning units (all homes must have central air-conditioning), door-to-door solicitation, and Halloween trick-or-treaters....In newer neighbourhoods, lawn ornaments are forbidden except for seasonal displays 'not exceeding thirty-day duration. (Blechman, 2008: 56)

Age limitations are specifically laid down: no one under the age of 19 can live in The Villages, but they can visit—as long as it for no more than thirty days a year.

Such an inward-looking social order has triggered stiff criticism from some scholars. Panitt (1993:12) mocks the illusionary liberty of the 'we're free to follow the rules' ethos of the community, while Houseman (1992: 36) regards it as a dreary world 'devoid of youth and spontaneity'. 'Emplacing' old age in this contrived manner, argues Laws (1995), exacerbates a young/old, ageist, split. It is where 'beleaguered' seniors become more entrenched in their antipathy towards the young, a view to be found amongst residents of The Villages, as one elucidates:

Children don't fit the lifestyle we've got in The Villages.... You can't mix the two. It's either one or the other, but not both. If this place was mutigenerational, there'd be a lot more crime. We'd have drug busts, wild parties, loud stereos, auto accidents. It wouldn't be the same. We'd be shoved to the side. And afraid.

(Blechman, 2008: 171)

Like a walled medieval city, occupants can resist invasion from the foe, which, for the many conservative minded, includes youngsters and other distur-bances to a traditional American way of life. Residents feel justified in seeking a safe, self-enhancing retreat from what they see as a crumbling wider society that often demeans its senior citizens (Kastenbaum, 1993). They aim to make their retirement as comfortable and self-contained as possible, free from hassle and family burdens. An ex Sun City resident observes:

[T]those white walls around the community mean a great deal to them. It keeps out crime and it keeps out people they don't want. It keeps out young people and it keeps out children and it keeps out all the things that were attendant on their lives when they lived in other places. And so there is a concerted feeling of splendid isolation.

(McHugh and Larson-Keaghy, 2005: 251)

Box 6.3 JOY IN PARADISE[26]

It's a great community . . . In most cities, the elderly are not accepted as full card-carrying citizens. They're looked down upon or they're shuffled aside. They have gifts you know.

An awful lot of people are here . . . because they got turned off in their former communities. . . . I mean, it was as though people were being pushed away because now they were retired, and the assumption was they had nothing to contribute. . . . We really need communities like this to prove to the average communities what older adults, retired—whatever you want to call them—can do for a community which they're not being permitted now.

And, you know, there are many people who criticize Sun City. . . . I think it's part envy and part is the fact they can't envision living without children and schools and all of those things. But when you get old enough to retire, then you begin to see how good that kind of life will be. You're among your kind. Everybody is old. Everybody is not young, let's say.

I love it here. . . . The neighbourhoods are neat and clean. We've got covenants here and they're enforced, which is good because it keeps out the riffraff.

Residents of Sun City and The Villages comfortably embrace these ambitions, as they reveal in Box 6.3.

Village communities are structured to ensure that off-the-shelf, 'rejuvenating' identities are readily available, and that illness narratives are rarely heard (Biggs et al., 2001; Grant, 2007). They are newer to the UK, in part due to the shortage of available development land. Until recently, the main choice for

Lark Hill
Village
🦌 An ExtraCare Village

With over 85 different activities, there's something to suit everyone. The Village is built around a host of superb facilities that include arts and crafts, ceramics, gardening, woodwork, IT, and health and well-being therapies.

Lark Hill Village offers a huge range of activities for its residents within a safe and busy environment. There's tailored support for people who need it and an active well-being programme which is driven by the residents themselves. . . . Commenting on his future Village life [71 year old Bill Hodder] said: 'Barbara and I will be living in a safe community with full and active lives and it's a relief to know that we will have support and care if we need it and a joy to have made so many new friends even before we have moved in. The concept is inspired'.

Figure 6.3   Lark Hill Village

UK retirees has been a somewhat dated stock of sheltered housing (Croucher, 2006). Now, alert to the baby-boom market, retirement villages appear in many developers' portfolios, some linked to charitable trusts that specialize in providing the infrastructure for 'active lifestyle' retirees.[27] Lark Hill Village is one example, with 327 age-restricted homes and 'traditional village' amenities[28] (see Figure 6.3).

In 2009 there were approximately eighty retirement villages in the UK, each designed with 100 or more properties.[29] None resemble Florida's mega development in scale (it has some 5,000 properties), but most, like Lark Hill, enthusiastically embrace the 'active' agenda.

Trouble in paradise

The utopian picture painted by developers and residents is clearly at odds with the unease of social critics who reside outside their walls. Are the communities, as Blechman (2008: 220) opines, 'based on a selfish and fraudulent premise—the exclusion of children and families' and, whatever their benefits, they fail to 'compensate for the high societal price for this exclusionary lifestyle'? Certainly, developers' interests are shaped by the profits to be gained from a pool of financially secure elders, with an eye on their turnover and on generations to come. But societal costs are relative, in that many naturally occurring retirement communities are not, as previously mentioned, socially inclusive in the way that Blechman implies or hopes for (Reed et al., 2004). In this light, we can see the emergence of privatized retirement villages as the market stepping in to plug the gap. It capitalizes on a climate of frustration and fear amongst a proportion of its elderly citizens, and the fantasy of rejuvenation.

There is, nevertheless, a side to retirement village life that is less spoken about. It is not all Shangri-La. What can appear so attractive on the brochures and start well for residents can turn sour; the activity package, especially, can wear thin. Carol, a resident of a Florida retirement village, confesses her disenchantment:

Everything is the same here. There's nowhere to go. We're in the middle of nowhere. Where's the art museum? Where's the library in Copley Square? Where's the Boston Pops? I miss the mix. I miss not seeing any children around.

And Dotty, another resident, regularly plays bingo because, she explains, 'I'm too old to be doing anything thing else fun'.[30] There is, of course, considerable pressure to take part once one has committed to an 'active lifestyle'. Non-participants risk being marginalized. For some retirees this is a major reason *not* to join such a community. Dorothy, observing a nearby retirement village in Florida, balks at the recreational director's micro-managed, tightly packed events programme: 'You have no idea—exercise—it's just like you were back at school, as if you're such imbeciles you couldn't think of a thing to do yourself'. And Harriet adds: 'You have to decide what a "senior citizen" is. Do you want to be told what to do, when you should go and play golf, when to join a group, or do you want to do things because you enjoy them?' (Katz, 2000: 146).

A central premise of positive ageing is that keeping busy and being with others is a recipe for positive mental health (Griffin, 2010). The advice, though, fails to acknowledge that there is no guarantee that life will feel of value or significance when the activity is persistently purchased 'ready made', in McDonaldized portions. A thin line separates retirement villages as places of liberation and self-expression, from enclaves where personal agency and choice is trammeled, and where compulsive activity is a substitute for age anxiety and emptiness of meaning. If retirement and longevity are to be times to savour, then the ephemeral, narcissistic distractions of consumer choice can turn into existential dead-ends. Meaningfulness is rarely obtainable off the shelf.

LONELY IN THE CROWD

As we age, we tend to narrow our choice of social partners, minimizing the social and emotional risks of new friendships and investing in fewer, but familiar and reliable relationships (Carstensen, 1992). Residents of a retirement village can, therefore, find themselves facing a paradoxical situation. Having escaped the loneliness of their traditional neighbourhood, they now feel even lonelier in the socially active crowd—especially if they are without partners or have been recently bereaved. As pre-existing friendships melt away, a succession of acquaintances, rather than deeper friendships, characterize the social scene (Adams et al., 2004). A community premised on intense social capital can end up one dimensional. The veneer of play and jollity requires a high degree of emotion work to sustain, which can become burdensome, especially for the frailer—physically and/or psychologically—members of the community (Bernard et al., 2007).

One thing that retirement villages solidly represent is a refuge from an ageist, stigmatizing, society and its everyday worries. Broadly, that is what they seem to deliver, with residents keen to avoid conflict (Streib and Metsch, 2002; Evans, 2009). Yet this is not the whole story. There is a dearth of research on long-term experiences inside retirement villages, complicated by national differences in how the villages are managed and where they are in their own lifecycle. Nevertheless, there are discernible cracks in the much vaunted carefree image. Particularly revealing is Kestin and Hoonaard's (2002) ethnography of a 10-year-old Florida retirement village, 'Eldorado'. The village appeared, on the surface, like others of its type—a well-ordered, homogeneous community. But several groups sat at its fringes: newcomers, 'snowbirds' (seeking a warmer climate for part of a year) and the widowed.

Newcomers found it hard to integrate with established residents, 'the older generation', whom they found cliquey. As one newcomer observed: 'They may have been friendly when they all moved in at the same time, but if you came in later, they have their own cliques, their own group. There's no question about that' (57). Allusions were made by newcomers to the 'quietness' and inactivity of the older generation betraying, ironically, an ageist strand in a community intended to be anything but. In their turn, older residents saw newcomers as victims of their own reticence to join in. Snowbirds were regarded by year-round residents as marginal because of their lack of commitment to important issues—such as the everyday management of the village and the continuity of gaming and leisure activities.

Most poignant of the out-groups was the widows. In a ten-year period the proportion of widowed residents had climbed from a modest 9 per cent to nearly 30 per cent. They found themselves, in Erving Goffman's terms, with stained identities (Goffman, 1963). Their prior married-coupledom granted them access to friendships with other couples who were (as they perceived it) now reluctant to include them in the social rounds. But married couples saw things differently. They put the problem down to the widows' reluctance to socialize and their desire to maintain their own privacy. And so the fissure was fixed.

This case reveals that retirement villages can develop informal divisions and sub-cultures—as do most complex enterprises. As the community ages and shifts over time, vested interests harden and tensions surface. Age-band similarity does not magically inoculate an organization from the effects of age differences; they simply become more refined or subtle. Along with structural demarcations, some can be hard to negotiate or resolve. Evans (2009), for example, found that a gated retirement village in the UK was socially divided by the tenure of its residents: rented, privately owned, or shared ownership. The different tenures were a well-meaning managerial attempt to improve access to different social groups, but instead they reinforced social divisions and class prejudices. A resident clarifies:

I think that there's obviously an automatic, not barrier, but wall between the council people and the people who bought theirs, it's different. I mean, it wasn't cheap to buy here and obviously you're in a different, well, not social position, but financial position to them, and that is always a bit of a barrier to communication. (209)

The most serious disputes in villages tend to occur when residents' lifestyles or economic interests are threatened in some way. Streib and Metsch (2002) reveal how key stakeholders (residents, management, owners, developers, outside agencies), in various combinations, become implicated. The disputes expose power differences, prejudices, and different perceptions on issues—such as change in nearby land usage. The thought of having a nursing home on the edge of a community was, according to the researchers, 'repulsive to the residents who viewed their community as a place for "youthful" newly retired' (75). Another matter concerned the renewal of ageing sewage and water utilities. It sparked a triangular conflict between residents, local county government, and the developer. A rather different concern involved a resident's challenge to the village rule that prohibited children as permanent residents. It was contested unsuccessfully when a pair of residents took in, and assumed care of, their developmentally disabled grandchild. Rules are rules.

At times, though, the very existence of a dispute can add spice to residents' lives. Streib and Metsch note that being engaged in, or heading up, a conflict was purposeful and pleasurable to some retirees, especially those who had once held significant management or leadership roles. The conflict provided them with an opportunity to exercise well-practised skills and prior identities, but now more for leisure than 'work'. It rekindled part of their old selves, enhancing their feelings of importance and control in the community. Some 'fun' is especially satisfying when it is not on the lifestyle director's list of activities.

Summation and queries

Retirement, once a seemingly straightforward contract between the individual, the employer and the state, has now become fragmented and contentious—a touchtone of our postmodern times. Age cut-offs for retirement are fast disappearing or being renegotiated, splintering generations. There are young people who face a future and old age with little financial provision; there are over-60s who cannot afford to retire but simultaneously have no guarantee of continued employment; and there are those of the 'old order' who are able to retire comfortably, if not in some luxury.

The niceties of pension pots and life savings, as important as they are, obscure the complexity of retirement's meanings to individuals. Popular images about retirement's joys, choices, and entitlements can create dilemmas, and much emotion work, for those who find their actual experiences very different. The routines of retirement life can prove a pale substitute for deeply ingrained work identities, bringing fears of mortality out of the closet.

We live in cultures preoccupied with, often obsessed by, preparations for work. Little attention is given to preparation for, and emotional survival, for non-work, post-work or post-career. How might such considerations best be integrated into our education and socialization systems, especially when many people have little, or a short, experience of work to retire from, while others continue working well into their latter years? Is it time to shift our thinking about the relationship between work and retirement and, indeed, the very validity of retirement as a construct?

7 A New Age?

There are eras in history that shake our taken-for-granted assumptions and beliefs. The 1930s Great Depression was one, and the period in which I write this book is another: the Great Recession. It is prudent to excavate beneath such social-economic upheavals to locate some enduring truths about our aged-shaped cultures, and indeed many appear in the preceding chapters. But the recession and its aftermath have also reconstructed age in some important, possibly enduring, forms.

In various ways, a major recession exposes and amplifies hidden, or taken for granted, age demarcations and oppressions. A financially strapped economy is more likely to default to its common prejudices and to pockets of self-interest. We see, for example, a jump in legal filings for age-discrimination.[1] Some of the vulnerable groups highlighted in chapter 5—young offenders, and the elderly who need dementia care—find themselves further marginalized as the hope of new state funding fades. Child labourers in the cocoa fields of Africa, in a curious twist of fate, may not be even worse-off because of the recession, as pitiable as their circumstances are. Chocolate is one luxury that has bucked the recessionary trend, increasing in sales—a consumer comfort, perhaps, in hard times.[2] However, not all is quite so straightforward in the labyrinthine world of cocoa trading. There are commodity speculators who regard cocoa as a means to quick profit. Some have hoarded vast quantities to create an artificial shortage and price rise. The knock-on effect is that chocolate manufacturers use less cocoa, destabilizing the livelihood of the cocoa producer and their child employees.[3]

As governments rein in public expenditure and institute sharp austerity measures to lessen huge public debt, the 'recovery' shockwaves are felt by the oldest and youngest in the workplace: first in line to be 'restructured' out of their jobs. They are cast onto an over-burdened social security system and a job-placement apparatus that has few, if any jobs, to offer. Ageism bites at both ends of the age spectrum, the youngest perceived to be 'too inexperienced' or 'inadequately skilled' to be attractive to remaining employers, while older workers are regarded as 'too/wrongly experienced' or 'too expensive'. The job outlook for those under 25, or those just out of university seeking their first job, is particularly bleak, while those 45 and older face employer bias against hiring older workers, illegal though it may be (Morin and Taylor, 2009).

Children choosing schools have felt the effects of the recession too, or to be more precise, their parents have. In the UK, many parents who regularly elect to opt out of state education for their children and purchase places in private schools have found it hard or impossible to meet the large fees. The knock-on effect has been the closure or merging of private schools unable to survive, and staff redundancies.[4] It has also meant pressure on state schools to absorb the children, schools previously shunned for ideological, pedagogical, or status reasons: an ironical turn around.

The much-discussed baby boomers have received something of a generational shock. The assets of those nearing retirement have shrunk or collapsed following the stock market plunge in 2009 and the bursting of the housing bubble in the USA—estimated to have destroyed more than $10 trillion in household wealth (Rosnick and Baker, 2010). Weller (2010) notes that, compared to other recessions, it was the first time in the USA that older families had the largest increases in bankruptcies and it was the first recession where social security cuts had been phased in. Weller also observes that older workers and retirees have struggled to get sufficient health insurance, exacerbated by employers saving money by cutting back on their contributions.

A depleted state pension and social security system is no match for the economic needs of the elderly and the retired, nor is it up to repairing shattered retirement dreams. The ubiquitous retirement industry, likewise, takes a hit, be it Sun City type developments or the more-modest accoutrements of a leisured retirement lifestyle. But pre-boomers, and those with recession-resistant wealth, will ensure that the industry does not disappear. Many of them have escaped the full impact of the recession with enough income in spendable form, or with well-insulated annuities.

Grey politics

In democracy's pluralism, pressure groups and special-interest organizations have long played a lively role in shaping national political agendas. Given the demographic prominence of an ageing society and its impact on public services, health care, pension rights and retirement, who speaks for the needs and desires of the older citizen?

There are US lobby groups such as the American Association of Retired Persons (AARP), Gray Panthers and the National Council for Senior Citizens. There is Grey Power in New Zealand, Green Seniors in Europe (dedicated to putting over older people's perspectives on environmental issues), Histadrut HaGimlaim in Israel, lobbying for older person's rights. And in the UK, there is the trade-union affiliated National Pensioner Organization and Age UK. Canada's Raging Grannies is one of the quirkier groups where, amongst other things, women of 'grandmother age' dress up in ways that mock older women's stereotypes. In all there are some seventy-eight organizations representing seniors within Europe, the most to be found in France, Germany, and Spain (Gilleard and Higgs, 2010). In short, 'senior' has proved a significant rallying point for a potpourri of advocacy groups representing older people's concerns.

But to what extent have these concerns coalesced into a politically defined identity? In the Netherlands, Poland, Romania, Russia, and Serbia-Montenegro there are seniors' political parties, but there are none in the USA—a symptom of a 'first past the post' election system that disadvantages minority parties (unlike the proportional representation in many European countries). Indeed, the fledgling *Pensioners Party* in the UK points to the handicap of the big-party system in the UK:

Every society is judged by how it treats the less fortunate. It does not matter how old you are, unless you die you will eventually become a pensioner and left to the mercy of an uncaring society. Just think about it!! Let us hope for electoral reform—it may give us a better chance to obtain some representation in Parliament.[5]

Some seniors' parties have won parliamentary seats, but few have managed to consolidate their gains (Kohli, 2000). And typically, most fail to cross the threshold of eligibility. There is, then, an apparent oddity. Older people are a growing majority in Western societies; they are more likely than younger people to express an interest in politics; they are more likely to turn out to vote; many share concerns over pensions, employment, health care, and a raft of ageist societal attitudes. Yet... older citizens resist political identification when it is offered, thus adding to their own cultural invisibility (Naegele and Walker, 1999).

The explanation why transcends the particular voting system (although that undoubtedly makes some difference). Old age fails to galvanize in the same way as, say, race or gender, because it has yet to be *felt* sufficiently in terms of a common identification or shared oppression (Gilleard and Higgs, 2010). People are 'old' in many different ways and at different points on an increasing lifespan, so their specific concerns, their means and their coping, are more individualized, despite the broader worries and injustices. This factionalizes the 'older voice' in favour of traditional party-political allegiances, parties that may or may not address the systemic issues that older citizens face.

Ostensibly, a government with a fair proportion of elders should be better attuned to 'grey matters'. As yet, there is no strong evidence that this is the case: older politicians do not necessarily fly the flag for older citizens, nor do they themselves share the social and economic disadvantage faced by many older citizens. The outcome of the 2010 national election in the UK is instructive in this respect, returning dominantly professional, business, and often mon-eyed, candidates. Many were privately/Oxbridge educated (Hackett and

Hunter, 2010), and over three-quarters were male, thus unrepresentative of over 50 per cent of the population—women—who face some of the most pernicious effects of ageism in their middle and later years.

Where age matters

Our journey through age reveals the deep and sometimes insidious reach of age in the way we make our interpersonal judgements, in how we construct our identities, in how organizations dispense their favours, in how societies arrange their priorities and resources, and in how consumer capitalism carves profit from age gradations and stereotypes.

Age carries with it a weighty baggage of status or stigma. It is unsurprising, then, that we have evolved an array of devices to disguise the most burdensome elements and enhance the more desirable features—for young and old alike. But it is a curious feature of the modern state that its major institutions depend, on the one hand, on chronological age to order and regulate their affairs while, on the other hand, they create the conditions where age denial, disguise, and prejudice can flourish.

Postmodern living has mixed matters somewhat—the young do not all have to progress through the age/status hierarchy to reach 'the top', and the old can continue working, learning, or playing well into their late years should they so desire. But for both groups there is institutional drag. Adolescence, especially in the UK, is fettered by an educational system (and cultural identity) that places dominant emphasis on 'the academic' and 'the cerebral', marginalizing craft, technical, and aesthetic skills. Coupled with grade inflation—each higher level of academic attainment is worth progressively less in a competitive market place with fewer jobs to go around—swathes of 'insufficiently' or 'inappropriately' qualified youth have nowhere to go. At root here is how a society defines and positions itself in relation to its new cultural capital—its children and youth—against the vagaries of market determinism.

For older people, ageism shadows many of their opportunities, in and out of work. A by-product is a robust anti-ageing industry which taps an inexhaustible demand for its services while also stoking endemic age-anxiety. The visible marks of ageing are, of course, not intrinsically 'bad', but are defined so in a society preoccupied with the aesthetics of youthfulness. And when powerful commercial players enter the fray—cosmetics, surgery diet, fashion, media—narcissism is firmly fixed and normalized. Yet, as a project of the 'self', it is ultimately bound to fail: biological ageing will win out in the end.

The spillover into age-grading particular jobs varies according to sector. As we have seen, television, the performing arts, fashion, and many customer service settings literally trade on images of youthfulness and/or blemish-free bodies, reinforced by audiences enchanted by the spectacle. But in jobs out of the public eye, age appearance also matters. Given the prevalence of stereotypes attached to age, the age that one *looks* is frequently taken as a proxy for chronological age, and that in turn influences others' judgements of one's work competence, status, and reliability. We can see this in micro-encounters between colleagues. We can see it also in management practices where perceived or actual age 'infect' staff recruitment, selection, appraisal, promotion, or termination. The law is able to restrain the grosser manifestations of ageism in the workplace, but it competes, often unsuccessfully, with entrenched rationalizations about the economic and 'investment' value of people of a particular age. Very junior appointments and older women, as earlier shown, can fall particularly foul of the discriminatory undertow.

THE RETIREE

The first blasts of the demographic time bomb have shaken the nature of support for retirees, exposing an outmoded model of 'working lifespan' and of social protection. The near retiree, keen to continue working, will find only some employers able or eager to oblige, most falling back on a default retirement age, where there is one. The retiree who depends on a state pension faces a tougher future, their modest means under constant threat from inflationary pressures and shifts in government policy.

Class and wealth have long divided the retired population, but now a combination of longevity and income has exaggerated the distinction. Retirees in the West are living longer, but the wealthiest and socially privileged do the best. They are particularly welcome in active ageing's supermarket. Living longer also means postponing—or a longer wait until—the failings and decrepitude of advanced old age. Once again, the market offers alternatives and choices to ease the pathway, such as special care at home or in dedicated institutions. Those without sufficient capital are dependent on a second-tier system and on the devotion of a family member or friend willing to undertake the carer role. It can be a relentless and wearing task, testing of the most loving of relationships.

If age didn't matter

Age and age-anxiety have come to matter in so many different ways in the complex weave of modern/postmodern life that it is hard to envisage a societal form where they would not matter. Despite the wilder prognostications of 'life extensionists', who see an eventual infinite lifespan, death remains one absolutely certainty. Moreover, life extension as an end in itself is vacuous unless why, or for what, living ever longer is addressed. The social and medical advances that have contributed to a longer lifespan circumvent existential questions about the meaningfulness of extending the process of living when a substantial proportion of that time amounts to prolonging the period of dying, and often difficult dying.

Suppressed age-anxiety permeates the Anglo-European slant on ageing and mortality, an emotional justification for spending time and money on protracting and 'rejuvenating' the lifespan. Conceivably, if the open expression of age-anxiety were not a cultural taboo, one major prop of the anti-ageing business would be weakened. Octavio Paz's perspective on the Mexican approach to mortality is illuminating in this respect:

The word death is not pronounced in New York, in Paris, in London, because it burns the lips. The Mexican, in contrast, is familiar with death, jokes about it, caresses it, sleeps with it, celebrates it; it is one of his toys and his most steadfast love. True, there is perhaps as much fear in his attitude as in that of others, but at least death is not hidden away: he looks at it face to face, with impatience, disdain, or irony.... Life and death are inseparable, and when the former lacks meaning, the latter becomes equally meaningless. Our contempt for death is not at odds with the cult we have made of it.

(Paz, 1985: 57–58)

Paz may be accused of somewhat over-caricaturing Mexican sentiments, missing the ambivalence—fascination and fear—that Mexicans can have towards death (Brandes, 2003). But Paz demonstrates that life and death can be culturally constructed as two sides of the same coin, mutually interdependent, and that ageing and death, accordingly, are demystified, less a demon to be beaten. And in doing so, it draws the sting from the narrative of decline: older age does not carry the constant comparison with 'the young', or 'being young'.

AGE INCLUSIVENESS

Age would matter less—or differently—if the shifting demographic contours were subjected to age-inclusive rather than age-exclusive social policies, locally and nationally. It is not necessary to create a spectre of conflicting generations in and beyond the workplace, or to imagine the prospect of a 'new solidarity' between the generations (AGE, 2009), to believe that age-blending could help facilitate mutual understanding and support for young and old alike. It also acknowledges that a vibrant, multi-generational workforce can be constructed around the different capacities, knowledge, and experiences of its members, regardless of age and its stereotypical associations.

Age inclusiveness would mean a radical shake up of long-standing polices and approaches to housing, transport, and families. Urban planning, dating from industrial boom-times for the active and car-driving population, make little sense for elderly or vulnerable citizens, or for younger people struggling to get onto the housing ladder. Developments with mixed, affordable designs and layouts, well integrated with accessible local transport, shopping, and social/health facilities would help keep a community intact. It would militate against the present fragmentation where old and young alike search for any suitable property to buy or rent, some retirees retreating to age-segregated residential homes or activity complexes.

Family polices aimed at 'married couple plus two children under one roof' are also well dated. Single parents, step-families, broken families, and cohabi-tees mix the ages, generations, and gender roles in ways unforeseen fifty years ago. There are some age inclusive, or intergenerational, programmes—governmental and voluntary—that have attempted to bridge separated generations. Many focus on younger and older people who have come to eye each other with bewilderment or suspicion while also feeling disempowered. The range and scope of such initiatives vary, but they can now be found in various part of the globe, especially in Europe, the Netherlands, the USA, Canada, Australia, and the UK. *Dixième famille* in France, for example, recruits nine families from different social backgrounds to pool their knowledge and skills to help a tenth—face-to-face and online—that is having difficulties. They provide homework help for children, job searches, support for the elderly, and assistance equipping the home.[6] Other intergenerational programmes include:[7]

- volunteers mentoring students in school
- older and younger people coming together to find ways of reducing fear of crime in their neighbourhood
- young volunteers providing services to older people: shopping, reading
- older volunteers supporting young parents
- toddlers visiting people with dementia in residential settings
- older people working with students on a school history project
- people from different generations working together to transform a waste area into a neighbourhood park

There is a dearth of independent evaluation studies on these initiatives, but the available few reveal promising outcomes (e.g. Hatton-Yeo, 2010).

~~~~~~~~~~~~~~~~

Age, we are told, 'is just a number'. In this book, I have attempted to convey that 'just' is an extravagant understatement. Age, the number, emerges as a potent lens through which to observe what can be loosely termed the 'human condition'. Through age, we track the present, the past, and the future. We both celebrate and fight age; it defines what we love and hate, accept and dread, eagerly anticipate and anxiously discard. We constantly 'work' at age, steering a path between our private experiences and public discourses—and dealing with the emotional residues, successfully or otherwise. In later years we may, or may not, wish to 'be as old as we feel', but our feelings are much shaped by how we look and how others judge our looks. Age, thus, becomes a serious game to play with others and a stopping-point for existential reflection. It is also an opportunity for commercial co-option: there is money to be made from age, from the business of beauty to the selling of pensions and annuities.

Age, though, is subject to postmodern slippage as time-worn categories which have pigeonholed 'child', 'youth', 'adult', and 'old' are challenged and their characteristics re-defined. It reminds us that, while chronologizing the lifespan remains, the meanings attributed to different bits or sections are subject to the politics and passions of the times. Much social and organizational policy flows from this, marooning some people, liberating others. It is here, especially, that the age theorist, the policy analyst, and the management practitioner need to be especially alert.

Notes

1. Why Age?

1. I. King, 'Business big shot: Richard Burrows, Former Bank of Ireland governor', *Timesonline* (17 August 2009), <http://business.timesonline.co.uk/tol/business/movers_and_shakers/article6798348.ece>, accessed 17 August 2010. © The Times, London, 17 August 2009.

   L. Hunt, 'No sympathy for drink-drive teenager', *Telegraph.co.uk* (15 September 2009), <http:// www.telegraph.co.uk/comment/columnists/lizhunt/6195362/No-sympathy-for-drink-drive-teenager.html>, accessed 3 September 2010. Permission granted by the Telegraph Media Group Limited 2009.

   'Couple enjoy same holiday for 50 years' (6 September 2009), *Telegraph.co.uk*, <http:// www.telegraph.co.uk/travel/travelnews/6146242/Couple-enjoy-same-holiday-for-50-years. html>, accessed 17 August 2010. Permission granted by Barcroft Media.

2. A. Meehan (1911). 'Parochial Registers', in C. G. Huberman (ed.), *The Catholic Encyclopedia*. New York: Robert Appleton Company.

3. D. Saint, 'Pulling the wool over dead eyes' (29th July 2008), *Northampton Chronicle & Echo* <http://www.northamptonchron.co.uk/david-saints-column/Pulling-the-wool-over-dead.4334233.jp>, accessed 17 August 2010.

4. 'Introduction: Apprenticeship', *Calendar of the Plea and Memoranda Rolls of the City of London, Volume 2: 1364–1381* (1929: 30–47), <http://www.british-history.ac.uk/report.aspx?compid=36671>, accessed 17 August 2010.

5. J. Burke (2010) 'India's censuswallahs go door to door to find 118bn people or maybe more', *Guardian*, 12 June: 19.

6. *Population Reference Bureau, World Population 2009* (August 2009) <http://www.prb.org/Datafinder/Topic/Bar.aspx?sort=v&order=d&variable=120>, accessed 17 August 2010.

7. 'Child protection', in *The State of the World's Children 2009*. York: UNICEF. <http://www.unicef.org/sowc09/docs/SOWC09_Table_9.pdf>, accessed 17 August 2010.

8. 'Call for concerted action to eliminate child labour in agriculture', *Global March Against Child Labour* (August 2009), <http://www.globalmarch.org/events/sarccla.php>, accessed 17 August 2010.

9. 'Fury as 12-year-old "model" fronts world fashion show', *MailOnline* (September 2007), <http://www.dailymail.co.uk/femail/article-482192/Fury-12-year-old-model-fronts-world-fashion-show.html##ixzz0wgi9PkYc>, accessed 15 August 2010.

10. Jeanne Grunert, 'Breaking into modeling', *LoveToKnowSeniors* (August 2010), <http://seniors.lovetoknow.com/Mature_Fashion_Models>, accessed 15 August 2010.

11. S. O'Connor, 'Models Direct: the rise of the mature model' (September 2009), <http://www.prlog.org/10346744-models-direct-the-rise-of-the-mature-model.html>, accessed 15 August 2010.

12. R. Simpson, 'The two faces of Twiggy at 59: how airbrushing in Olay ad hides truth of the skin she's in', *MailOnline* (July 2009), <http://www.dailymail.co.uk/tvshowbiz/article-1202399/Fury-faces-Twiggy-59-How-airbrushing-Olay-ad-hides-truth-skin-shes-in.html#ixzz0wgyhqUL3>, accessed 15 August 2010.

13. 'ASA Adjudication on Procter & Gamble (Health and Beauty Care) Ltd', *Advertising Standards Authority* (16 December 2009), <http://asa.org.uk/Complaints-and-ASA-action/Adjudications/2009/12/Procter-and-Gamble-%28Health-and-Beauty-Care%29-Ltd/TF_ADJ_47834.aspx>, accessed 31 August 2010.

14. Everton, 'Ashley qualls—17 year old dot com millionaire', *Connected Internet* (September 2007), <http://www.connectedinternet.co.uk/2007/09/03/ashley-qualls-17-year-old-dot-com-millionaire>, accessed 16 August 2010.

15. S. MacEntee, 'Irish teens become dot com millionaires', *smenon.com* (March 2008), <http://www.smemon.com/irish-teens-become-dot-com-millionaires/>, accessed 16 August 2010.

2. Age Work

1. 'How to Celebrate Birthdays of the Employees', *Marketing Profs* (July 2005), <http://www.marketingprofs.com/ea/qst_question.asp?qstID=8416>, accessed 13 March 2009.

2. 'How do I avoid workplace birthday celebrations?', *Workplace Doctors* (August 2010), <http://www.workplacedoctors.com/wpdocs/qdetail.asp?id=313>, accessed 17 August 2010.

3. 'Cuiva—sociopolitical organization', *Countries and their Cultures*, <http://www.everyculture.com/South-America/Cuiva-Sociopolitical-Organization.html>, accessed 17 August 2010.

4. 'Is 38 too old to get an I-banking job?', *BankersBall* (2008), <jobhttp://www.bankersball.com/pub/sidetawk/topic.php?id=40&page>, accessed 17 August 2010.

5. 'The age question', *AVC* (June 2007). <http://avc.blogs.com/a_vc/2007/06/the_age_questio.html>, accessed 17 August 2010.

6. 'Tua viso', *Tina Richards* (2010), <http://www.tinarichards.com/>, accessed 17 August 2010.

7. Personal communication.

8. Melanie was one of a mixed sample of employees who, in 2008, responded to my invitation to tell me about 'what it's like for you getting old in your organization'.

9. 'Dressing to look older', *Men'sFlair* (22 March 2007), <http://www.mensflair.com/style-advice/dressing-to-look-older.php>, accessed 17 August 2010.

10. 'Workplace fashion tips', *Lakx.com* (2007), <http://www.lakx.com/fashion/workplace-fashion-tips.shtml>, accessed 17 August 2010.

11. L. Armstrong, 'Dress for Your Age', *Timesonline* (9 January 2008), <http://women.timesonline.co.uk/tol/life_and_style/women/fashion/article3153313.ece>, accessed 17 August 2010.

12. L. Lyon, 'Corporate dressing: make your presence felt among peers', *ArticleSnatch.com* (2009), <http://www.articlesnatch.com/Article/Corporate-Dressing–Make-Your-Presence-Felt-Among-Peers/251297>, accessed 17 August 2010.

13. Publisher's description of Charla Krupp's 'How not to look your age', *Hatchette Book Group* (2010), <http://www.hachettebookgroup.com/books_9780446699976_Description.htm>, accessed 17 August 2010.

14. The Harley Group, 'Cosmetic surgery for men' (2008), <http://www.harleymedical.co.uk/cosmetic-surgery-for-men/?&gclid=CIi26ZKVg54CFQdl4wod21Ipqg>, accessed 16 August 2010.

3. Generations

1. 'Tips offered to close the generation gap in the workplace', *University of Wisconsin-Extension* (19 February 2001), <http://www.uwex.edu/news/read.cfm?id=258>, accessed 17 August 2010.

2. 'The younger generation', *Time* (5 November 1951), <http://www.time.com/time/printout/0,8816,856950,00.html>, accessed 17 August 2010.

3. 'Generation X reconsidered', *TimeArchive* (9 June 1997), <http://www.time.com/time/covers/0,16641,19970609,00.html>, accessed 17 August 2010.

4. P. Neate, 'Generation X: the slackers who changed the world', *Independent.co.uk* (18 February 2007), <http://www.independent.co.uk/news/uk/this-britain/generation-x-the-slackers-who-changed-the-world-436651.html>, accessed 17 August 2010.

5. CIPD, 'Gen UP. How the four generations work', Joint Survey Report (September 2008), <http://www.cipd.co.uk/NR/rdonlyres/25DA52DE-F120-4579-AFE3-564C8801425D/0/genuphowfourgenerationswork.pdf>, accessed 17 August 2010.

6. D. Fairhurst, 'Generations learn from each other', *Managementtoday.com* (1 October 2008), <http://www.managementtoday.co.uk/search/article/848121/generations-learn-other/>, accessed 17 August 2010.

7. D. Tobey, 'Boomers vs. Millennials: eliminating multi-generational friction in your workplace', *HRHero.com* (12 July 2007), <http://www.hrhero.com/audio/multi-generational1/>.

8. C. Marston (2008), 'Mixing four generations in the workplace' DVD, <http://www.enterprisemedia.com/product/00492/mixing_generations_workplace.html>, accessed 17 August 2010.

9. 'Bridging the generation gap at work', *Alliance Training and Consulting Inc.*, <http://www.alliancetac.com/index.html?PAGE_ID=2343>, accessed 17 August 2010.

10. 'Managing Multiple Generations in the Workplace', *KEYgroup*, <http://www.keygroupconsulting.com/lt-mmg.php>, accessed 17 August 2010.

11. 'Generation Clash!', *Monster*, <http://content.monster.ca/7371_en-CA_pf.asp>, accessed 17 August 2010.

12. 'Managing four generations in the workplace' (February 2009), *trainingABCdot.com*, <http://www.trainingabc.com/xcart/product.php?productid=18202&cat=325&page=1>, accessed 17 August 2010.

13. 'How interpersonal conflict hurts organizations', *CRMlearning*, <http://www.crmlearning.com/blog/?p=229>, accessed 17 August 2010.

14. M. Baker, 'Managing different generations in the workplace', *Insulation Outlook* (October 2009), <http://www.insulationoutlook.com/io/article.cfm?id=IO091004>, accessed 17 August 2010.

15. 'Managing the multigenerational workforce', *lakeshore*, <http://www.lakeshorestaffing.com/employers/resources/managing_the_multigenerational_workforce/>, accessed 17 August 2010.

16. 'Generational advertising strategy', *The Generational Imperative Inc*, <http://www.genimperative.com/AdvertisingStrategy.html>, accessed 17 August 2010.

17. Ann Fishman, 'Generation targeted marketing', <http://www.annfishman.com/downloads/GTM_Complete_Press_Kit.pdf>, accessed 17 August 2010.

18. '50-plus unemployed workers at risk of becoming a "lost generation"', *Age UK* (11 August 2010*)*, <http://www.ageuk.org.uk/latest-press/50-plus-unemployed-workers-lost-generation-risk/>, accessed 17 August 2010.

4. Ageism

1. A. Swenson, 'Age discrimination isn't just for Grandpa' (11 September 2009), *Wordpost.org*, <http://wordpost.org/2009/09/guest-post-age-discrimination/>, accessed 17 August 2010.

2. V. J. Roscigno et al. (2007). 'Age discrimination, social closure and employment', *Social Forces*, 86(1): 324.

3. ACAS (2006). *Age and the Workplace.* London: ACAS.

4. L. Peacock, 'Newcastle admin assistant wins "too young" age discrimination claim', *Personneltoday.com* (March 2008), <http://www.personneltoday.com/articles/2008/03/04/44684/newcastle-admin-assistant-wins-too-young-age-discrimination-claim.html>, accessed 16 August 2010.

5. C. Brooke, 'NHS manager wins £180,000 payout over age claim . . . a year after she pocketed almost £40,000', *MailOnline* (May 2010), <http://www.dailymail.co.uk/news/article-1279919/NHS-manager-wins-180-000-compensation-victimised-age.html?ito=feeds-news xml#ixzz0wlUQdB00>, accessed 16 August 2010.

6. G. Pitcher, 'Age discrimination claim costs bar owner £15,000 in compensation', *Personneltoday.com* (February 2008), <http://www.personneltoday.com/articles/article.aspx?liarticleid=44400&printerfriendly=true>, accessed 16 August 2010.

7. '*ius laboris*—Results of Age Discrimination Survey' (January 2006: 6), *lewissilkin,* <http://www.agediscrimination.info/international/Documents/1_Age_Disc_Survey.pdf>, accessed 17 August 2010.

8. 'Age discrimination in Employment Act—1997–2009', US Equal Employment Opportunity Commission, <http://www1.eeoc.gov//eeoc/statistics/enforcement/adea.cfm?renderforprint=1>, accessed 17 August 2010.

9. 'Annual Statistics 2007/08, 2008/09', *Tribunal Service*, <http://www.employmenttribunals.gov.uk/Publications/annualReports.htm>, accessed 17 August 2010.

10. C. Duncan and W. Loretto (2004). 'Never the right age? Gender and age-based discrimination in employment', *Gender, Work and Organization*, 11(1): 106.

11. 'Older workers "take less sickies"', *Health Insurance and Protection* (1 October 2007), <http://www.hi-mag.com/healthinsurance/article.do?articleid=20000101063>, accessed 17 August 2010.

12. D. Leaker (2008), 'Sickness absence from work in the UK Using the Labour Force Survey', *Economic & Labour Market Review*, 2(11): 18–22.

13. This phrase was originally coined by Yiannis Gabriel in 1991—'On organizational stories and myths: why it is easier to slay a dragon than to kill a myth', *International Sociology,* 6(4): 427–442. I borrow it with thanks.

14. 'Employing older workers: Introduction', *Department for Work and Pensions*, <http://www.businesslink.gov.uk>, accessed 17 August 2010.

15. R. Krys 'Eight reasons to employ a mixed aged workforce' (25 March 2003), *Personneltoday.com*, <http://www.personneltoday.com/articles/2003/03/25/18109/eight-reasons-to-employ-a-mixed-age-workforce.html> accessed 17 August 2010.

16. 'Environment and Ethics', *About B&Q*, <http://www.diy.com/diy/jsp/corporate/content/environment_ethics/ethics/respect.jsp>, accessed 17 August 2010.

17. 'Conditions of worker employment programme: example of leave provisions for fathers', *International Labour Organization*, <http://www.ilo.org/public/english/protection/condtrav/family/reconcilwf/specialleave.htm>, accessed 18 August 2010.

18. E. Saner, 'When women are too old to appear on TV', *guardian.co.uk* (4 February 2010), <http://www.guardian.co.uk/lifeandstyle/2010/feb/04/older-women-too-old-for-tv>, accessed 7 September 2010.

19. J. Plunkett, 'Director General tells BBC bosses to put more older women on screen', *guardian.co.uk* (24 September 2009), <http://www.guardian.co.uk/media/2009/sep/24/bbc-ageism-mark-thompson>, accessed 18 August 2010.

20. Comment from 'scrim' to *Guardian* article above (24 September 2009), <http://www.guardian.co.uk/media/2009/sep/24/bbc-ageism-mark-thompson#start-of-comments>, accessed 18 August 2010.

5. Capturing Age Cohorts

1. 'Officer hurt in youth jail riot', *BBC News* (2 October 2006), <http://news.bbc.co.uk/1/hi/england/shropshire/5398270.stm>, accessed 18 August 2010. Courtesy of BBC News Website.

2. 'Activities in the young offenders institute', *HM Prison Service*, <http://www.hmprisonservice.gov.uk/adviceandsupport/prison_life/youngoffenders/>, accessed 18 August 2010.

3. 'World Prison Brief', *Kings College London* (June 2010), <http://www.kcl.ac.uk/depsta/law/research/icps/worldbrief/>, accessed 18 August 2010.

4. J. Jamieson, G. McIvor, and C. Murray (1999), *Understanding Offending Among Young People: Social Work Research Findings No. 37*, <http://www.scotland.gov.uk/Publications/1999/11/9bb525fa-7c38-44a7-8835-a0540b9db328>, accessed 18 August 2010.

5. J. Lyon, C. Dennison, and A. Wilson (2000). *Tell Them So They Listen': Messages from Young People in Custody*. London: Home Office, Research Development and Statistics Directorate, 8, 10, 13, 16.

6. 'Campaign to end prison overcrowding', *The Howard League for Penal Reform* (2006), <http://www.howardleague.org/overcrowding/>, accessed 18 August 2010.

7. J. Lyon, C. Dennison, and A. Wilson (2000). *'Tell Them So They Listen': Messages from Young People in Custody*. London: Home Office, Research Development and Statistics Directorate. Quotes are located respectively on pages 30, 29, 32, 32, 33, 34, 36, 36, 37, 40, 40, 40, 41, 58 and 60.

8. 'Prison Officer', *HM Prison Service*, <http://www.hmprisonservice.gov.uk/careersandjobs/typeswork/prisonofficer/>, accessed 18 August 2010.

9. 'Turnkeys or professionals? A vision for the 21st century prison officer', *The Howard League for Penal Reform* (2009), <http://www.howardleague.org/fileadmin/howard_league/user/online_publications/Turnkeys_or_professionals_print_final.pdf>, accessed 18 August 2010.

10. 'Child labour resource guide—appendix 1 summary: international legal standards on child labour', *UNICEF*, <http://www.unicef.org.uk/publications/clrg/app1.asp>, accessed 18 August 2010.

11. 'ILO conventions on child labour', *International Labour Organization*, <http://www.ilo.org/ipec/facts/ILOconventionsonchildlabour/lang–en/>, accessed 18 August 2010.

12. 'Child protection from violence, exploitation and abuse', *UNICEF* (March 2008), <http://www.unicef.org/protection/index_childlabour.html>, accessed 18 August 2010.

13. 'The Cocoa Protocol: Success or Failure', *International Labor Rights Forum* (June 2008), <http://www.laborrights.org/stop-child-labor/cocoa-campaign/resources/10719>, accessed 18 August 2010.

14. 'Chocolate and slavery: child labor in Cote d'Ivoire', *TED Case Studies No. 664* (2002), <http//www1.american.edu/ted/chocolate-salve.htm>, accessed 18 August 2010.

15. Named *The Harkin-Engel Protocol* after Eliot Engel, US Representative, and American senator, Tom Harkin, both active in the movement to end child labour.

16. 'The cocoa protocol: success or failure', *International Labor Rights Forum* (June 2008), 2, <http://www.laborrights.org/stop-child-labor/cocoa-campaign/resources/10719>, accessed 18 August 2010.

17. 'Child Labour', *H&M* (June 2009), <http://www.hm.com/filearea/corporate/fileobjects/pdf/en/rm_download_responsibility_facts_pdf_childlabour_1245313551846.pdf>, accessed 18 August 2010.

18. 'Remarks by the president to the International Labor Organization Conference, Geneva' (6 June 1999), *The White House Office of the Press Secretary*, <http://clinton4.nara.gov/WH/New/html/19990616.html>, accessed 18 August 2010.

19. 'Causes of dementia, progression and drug treatments', *Alzheimer's Society*, <http://alzheimers.org.uk/factsheets>, accessed 18 August 2010.

20. 'World Health Report 2003—shaping the future', (2003), *World Health Organization, Geneva*, <http://www.who.int/whr/2003/en/>, accessed 18 August 2010.

21. M. Knapp et al. (2007). *Dementia UK*. Alzheimers Society: London.

22. *Living Well with Dementia: A National Dementia Strategy*. London: Department of Health, 2009.

23. Conclusion by Amyas Morse, head of the National Audit Office, on 14 January 2010, following publication of 'Improving dementia services in England—an interim report', *National Audit Office* (2010). See <http://www.nao.org.uk/publications/0910/improving_dementia_services.aspx>, accessed 18 August 2010.

24. 'Dementia patients "suffer stigma"', *BBC News* (6 October 2008), <http://news.bbc.co.uk/1/hi/health/7655066.stm>, accessed 18 August 2010.

25. 'Can Gerry Robinson fix dementia care homes: episode 2?', *BBC2* (Dec. 2009), <http://www.bbc.co.uk/programmes/b00phjk0#synopsis>, accessed 16 August 2010.

26. Comments on 'Can Gerry Robinson fix dementia care homes?', *Open2.net*. Respective postings: 8.12.09 (anonymous), 9.12.09 (Va S) and 11.12.09 (anonymous), <http://www.open2.net/dementia/freeleaflet.html#>, accessed 18 August 2010.

27. In H. Bowyers et al. (2009). *Older People's Vision of Long-Term Care*. York: Joseph Rowntree.

28. V. Cotrell and K. Hooker (2005). 'Possible selves of individuals with Alzheimer's disease', *Psychology and Aging*, 20: 285–294.

29. S. R. Sabat (2002). 'Epistemological issues in the study of insight in people with Alzheimer's disease', *Dementia*, 1(3): 279.

30. Clare, L. 2003. 'Managing threats to self: awareness in early stage Alzheimer's disease', *Social Science & Medicine*, 57(6): 1017–1029.

31. M. Van Dijkhuizen, L. Clare, and A. Pearce (2006). 'Striving for connection: appraisal and coping among women with early-stage Alzheimer's disease', *Dementia*, 5(1): 73.

32. L. Werezak and Stewart, N. 2009. 'Learning to live with early dementia', *Canadian Journal of Nursing Research*, 41(1): 366–384.

33. H. L. Menne, J. M. Kinney, and D. J. Morhardt (2002). 'Trying to continue to do as much as they can do': theoretical insights regarding continuity and meaning making in the face of dementia, *Dementia*, 1(3): 367.

34. David Shearn of *Dementia Care Matters Ltd* has been a prominent voice and featured on the *Can Gerry Robinson Fix Dementia Care* TV programmes, <http://www.dementiacarematters.com/>, accessed 8 September 2010.

35. *Living Well with Dementia: A National Dementia Strategy.* London: Department of Health, 2009: 58.

6. Retirement

1. P. Thane (2006). 'The "scandal" of women's pensions in Britain: how did it come about?' *History & Policy* (online journal). March: 1, <http://www.historyandpolicy.org/papers/policy-paper-42.html>, accessed 18 August 2010.

2 'Over 580 different jobs in Greece listed as "hazardous" = early retirement', *mina* (11 March 2010), <http://macedoniaonline.eu/content/view/13026/46/>, accessed 18 August 2010.

3. 'Guide to planning your money for retirement', *Directgov* (August 2010), <http://www.direct.gov.uk/en/Pensionsandretirementplanning/PlanningForRetirement/DG_10026792>, accessed 16 August 2010.

4. 'World Social Security Report 2010–2011' (2010), *International Labour Organization Geneva*, <http://www.socialsecurityextension.org/gimi/gess/ShowTheme.do?tid=1985>, accessed 18 August 2010.

5. P. Lally (2007). 'Identity and athletic retirement: a prospective study', *Psychology of Sport & Exercise*, 8(1): 85–100.

6. K. Warriner and D. Lavallee (2008). 'The retirement experiences of elite female gymnasts: self identity and the physical self', *Journal of Applied Sport Psychology*, 20(3): 307.

7. Ibid.,

8. R. S. Weiss (2005). *The Experience of Retirement.* Cornell: Cornell University Press, 75–6.

9. For example, see Bristol and District Retirement Council at <http://www.bristolretirement-council.co.uk/pages/aboutus.htm>, accessed 18 August 2010.

10. 'Passion & purpose: lifecrafting and legacy in the second half of life', *Third-Age LifeCrafting with Meg Newhouse*, <http://www.passionandpurpose.com/index.html>, accessed 8 September 2010.

11. 'The 3rd age', *Hirst Research and Marketing*, <http://www.hirst-research.co.uk/third_age.html>, accessed 18 August 2010.

12. 'Retired and loving it! Seniors share why they love their postwork lives', *AARP The magazine* (May/June 2010), <http://www.aarp.org/work/retirement-planning/info-04-2010/retired-and-loving-it.html>, accessed 18 August 2010.

13. A. S. W. Roper and S. Zapolsky, 'Baby boomers envision their retirement: an AARP segmentation analysis' (May 2004), *AARP Surveys and Statistics*, <http://www.aarp.org/work/retirement-planning/info-2004/aresearch-import-865.html>, accessed 19 August 2010.

14. 'The Retirement Show 2010—exhibitor brochure', <http://www.the-retirement-show.com/TRSbrochure2010.pdf>, 5, accessed 19 August 2010.

15. 'Bungalow retirement: older couples, independent on limited incomes living in a bungalow by the sea' (9 October 2006), *nomadplus*, <http://www.nottinghaminsight.org.uk/insight/asp/standardmetasearch.asp?st=5&tSearch=bungalow>, accessed 19 August 2010.

16. Kei-Homes, <http://www.kei-retirement.co.uk/index.php>, accessed 19 August 2010.

17. A particular problem facing gay and lesbian retirees in nursing homes or assisted-living centres. See J. Gross, 'Aging and Gay, and Facing Prejudice in Twilight', *New York Times* (9 October 2007), <http://www.nytimes.com/2007/10/09/us/09aged.html?_r=1>, accessed 19 August 2010. Also 'Homophobia in nursing homes, long-term care, assisted living, and home care', *Hospice and Nursing Home Blog* (21 February 2010), <http://hospiceandnursinghomes.blogspot.com/2010/02/homophobia-in-nursing-homes-long-term.html>, accessed 19 August 2010.

18. 'Welcome to Sun City Hilton Head—Bluffton, South Carolina', Del Webb (August 2010) <http://www.delwebb.com/communities/sc/bluffton/sun-city-hilton-head/index.aspx>, accessed 16 August 2010

19. 'Sun City Hilton Head, celebrates 10 years; enjoys booming sales', *Island Packet* (28 October 2005), <http://factfinder.census.gov/servlet/ADPTable?_bm=y&-geo_id=16000US0470320&-qr_name=ACS_2008_3YR_G00_DP3YR5&-ds_name=&-_lang=en&-redoLog=false>, accessed 19 August 2010.

20. 'Sun City CDP, Arizona (2006–2008)', *US Census Bureau*, <http://factfinder.census.gov/servlet/ADPTable?_bm=y&-geo_id=16000US0470320&-qr_name=ACS_2008_3YR_G00_DP3YR5&-ds_name=&-_lang=en&-redoLog=false>, accessed 19 August 2010.

21. '"Modern living": man on the cover: Del Webb', *Time*, 3 August 1962, <http://www.time.com/time/magazine/article/0,9171,896473-3,00.html>, accessed 19 August 2010.

22. 'About us', *The Villages*, <http://www.thevillages.com/AboutUs/aboutus.htm>, accessed 19 August 2010.

23. 'The Villages CDP. Florida (2006–2008)', *US Census Bureau*, <http://factfinder.census.gov/home/saff/main.html?_lang=en>, accessed 19 August 2010.

24. 'Recreation in The Villages', *The Villages*, <http://www.thevillages.com/recreation/recreation .asp>, accessed 19 August 2010.

25. 'Village center community development district, annual report for fiscal year ended 30 September 2009', *Village Center Community Development District* (3 September 2009), <http://districtgov.org/departments/finance/audits/VCCDD/2009%20Audit%20VCCDD.pdf>, accessed 19 August 2010.

26. The first three quotes are from K. E. McHugh and E. M. Larson-Keaghy (2005). 'These white walls: the dialectic of retirement communities', *Journal of Aging Studies*, 19: 246. The fourth is from A. D. Blechman (2008). *Leisureville*. New York: Atlantic Monthly Press, 22.

27. See, for example, the *Extra Care Charitable Trust*, <http://www.extracare.org.uk/aboutus>, accessed 19 August 2010.

28. 'Lark Hill Village Activities', *Lark Hill Village* (August 2010), <http://www.larkhillvillage.co.uk/>, accessed 16 August 2010

29. 'Retirement villages advice guide and information', *EAC HousingCare.org*, <http://www.housingcare.org/guides/item-retirement-villages.aspx>, accessed 19 August 2010.

30. A. D. Blechman (2008). *Leisureville*. New York: Atlantic Monthly Press: 168, 176.

7. A New Age?

1. 'Age discrimination filings jump during recession', *HRhero.com*, <http://employmentlaw-post.com/diversity/2009/08/16/age-discrimination-filings-jump-during-recession/>, accessed 19 August 2010.

2. 'Chocolate sales: a sweet spot in the recession' (11 April 2009), *Time*, <http://www.time.com/time/business/article/0,8599,1890565,00.html>, accessed 19 August 2010.

3. K. Allen, 'Hedge funds accused of gambling with lives of the poorest as food prices soar: commodity speculators push cocoa to 33-year high', *guardian.co.uk* (19 July 2010), <http://www.guardian.co.uk/business/2010/jul/19/speculators-commodities-food-price-rises>, accessed 19 August 2010.

4. N. Woolcock, 'Private school numbers stall as recession grips' (29 April 2009), *thetimes.co.uk*, <http://www.thetimes.co.uk/tto/public/sitesearch.do?querystring=recession±public±schools&sectionId=342&p=tto&pf=all>, accessed 19 August 2010.

5. 'Pensioners party home page', *Pensioners Party*, < http://www.thepensionersparty.org/index.html>, accessed 19 August 2010.

6. 'Tenth family network', *Association Dixieme Famille*, <http://www.dixiemefamille.com/index.php?version=en>, accessed 19 August 2010.

7. 'Building better communities for all ages between the generations', *Beth Johnson Foundation Centre for Intergenerational Practice*, <http://www.centreforip.org.uk>, accessed 19 August 2010.

References

AARP. 2005. *The State of 50+ America Research Report*. Washington: AARP Public Policy Institute.

——2008. *Investing in Training 50+ Workers: A Talent Management Survey*. Washington: American Association of Retired Persons.

Achenbaum, W. A. 1998. 'Perceptions of aging in America'. *National Forum*, 78(2): 30–34.

——2006. 'What is retirement for?' *The Wilson Quarterly*, 50 (Spring), 50–56.

Adams, K. B., Sanders, S., and Auth, E. A. 2004. 'Loneliness and depression in independent living retirement communities: risk and resilience factors'. *Aging & Mental Health*, 8(6): 475–485.

Adler, G., and Hilber, D. 2009. 'Industry hiring patterns of older workers'. *Research on Aging: A Quarterly of Social Gerontology and Adult Development*, 31(1): 69–88.

AGE. 2009. *A Plea for Greater Intergenerational Solidarity*. Brussels: European Older People's Platform.

Alwin, D. F., and Wray, L. A. 2005. 'A life-span developmental perspective on social status and health', *Gerontological Society of America*, 60: 7–14.

Ansello, E. F. 1978. 'Ageism: the subtle stereotype'. *Childhood Education*, 54(3): 118–123.

Aries, P. 1962. *Centuries of Childhood*. New York: Vintage Books.

Arulampalam, W., Booth, A. L., and Bryan, M. L. 2006. 'Is there a glass ceiling over Europe? Exploring the gender pay gap across the wage distribution'. *Industrial and Labor Relations Review*, 60(2): 163–186.

Ashton, T. S. 2006. *An Economic History of England: The Eighteenth Century*. London: Routledge.

Atchley, R. C. 1976. *The Sociology of Retirement*. New York: Wiley.

——1997. *Social Forces and Aging: An Introduction to Social Gerontology*. California: Wadsworth.

——1999. *Continuity and Adaptation in Aging: Creating Positive Experiences*. Baltimore: Johns Hopkins University Press.

Atkinson, M. 2008. 'Exploring Male Femininity in the "Crisis": Men and Cosmetic Surgery'. *Body & Society*, 14(1): 67–87.

Baily, C. 2009. 'Reverse intergenerational learning: A missed opportunity?' *AI & Society*, 23(1): 111–115.

Barak, B. 2009. 'Age identity: a cross-cultural global approach'. *International Journal of Behavioral Development*, 33(1): 2–11.

Barham, C., and Begum, N. 2007. *Sickness Absence from Work in the UK*. London: Labour Market Division, Office for National Statistics.

Barnett, R. C. 2004. 'Preface. Women and work: where are we, where did we come from, and where are we going?' *Journal of Social Issues*, 60(4): 667–674.

Bateson, M. C. 1990. *Composing a Life*. New York: Penguin.

Bauerlein, M. 2008. *The Dumbest Generation: How the Digital Age Stupefies Young Americans and Jeopardizes Our Future*. New York: Tarcher.

Becker, E. 1973. *The Denial of Death*. New York: Free Press.

Beehr, T. A., and Bennett, M. M. 2007. 'Examining retirement from a multi-level perspective'. In K. E. Shultz, and G. A. Adams (eds.), *Aging and Work in the 21st Century*. New York: Psychology Press.

Begum, N. 2004. 'Employment by occupation and industry'. *Labour Market Trends*, 112: 227–234.

Benjamin, K., and Wilson, S. 2005. *Facts and Misconceptions about Age, Health status and Employability*. Buxton: Health and Safety Laboratory.

Bennett, S., Maton, K., and Kervin, L. 2008. 'The "digital natives" debate: a critical review of the evidence'. *British Journal of Educational Technology*, 39(5): 775–786.

Bennett, T., and Holloway, K. 2004. 'Gang membership, drugs and crime in the UK'. *The British Journal of Criminology*, 44(3): 305–323.

Bennington, L., and Wein, R. 2002. 'Aiding and abetting employer discrimination: the job applicant's role'. *Employee Responsibilities and Rights Journal*, 14(1): 3–16.

Berg, M., and Hudson, P. 1992. 'Rehabilitating the industrial revolution'. *The Economic History Review*, 45(1): 24–50.

Bernard, M. et al. 2007. 'Housing and care for older people: life in an English purpose-built retirement village'. *Ageing and Society*, 27(4): 555–578.

Beroff, A., and Adams, T. R. 2000. *How to be a Teenage Millionaire*. Newburgh, NY: Entrepreneur Press.

Biddle, J. E., and Hamermesh, D. S. 1998. 'Beauty, productivity, and discrimination: lawyers' looks and lucre'. *Journal of Labor Economics*, 16(1): 172–201.

Biggs, S. 2004. 'New ageism. age imperialism, personal experience and ageing policy'. In S. O. Daatland, and S. Biggs (eds.), *Ageing and Diversity*. Bristol: The Policy Press.

——Bernard, M., Kingston, P., and Nettleton, H. 2001. 'Lifestyles of belief: narrative and culture in a retirement community'. *Ageing and Society*, 20(6): 649–672.

Blaikie, A. 1999. *Ageing and Popular Culture*. Cambridge: Cambridge University Press.

——2002. 'The secret world of subcultural aging: what unites and what divides?' In L. Andersson (ed.), *Cultural Gerontology*. Westport: Auburn House.

——2004. The search for ageing identities. In S. O. Daatland, and S. Biggs (eds.), *Ageing and Diversity*. Bristol: The Policy Press.

Blechman, A. D. 2008. *Leisureville*. New York: Atlantic Monthly Press.

Bøås, M., and Huser, A. 2006. 'Child labour and cocoa production in West Africa: the case of Cote d'Ivoire and Ghana'. Fafo Report No. 522.

Booth, A. L., Francesconi, M. and Frank, J. 2003. 'A sticky floor model of promotion, pay, and gender'. *European Economic Review*, 47(2): 295–322.

Borkenau, P., and Ostendorf, F. 2006. 'Fact and fiction in implicit personality theory'. *Journal of Personality*, 55(3): 415–443.

Bowers, A. H. et al. 2009. *Older People's Vision of Long-Term Care*. York: Joseph Rowntree.

Bradley, J. 1920. *Illuminated Manuscripts*. London: Bracken Books.

Brandes, S. 2003. 'Is There a Mexican view of death?' *Ethos*, 31(1): 127–144.

Bräuninger et al. 2010. 'Pensions in a post-crisis world'. *Deutsche Bank Research*, February 26.

Brewer, B. W. et al. 'Distancing oneself from a poor season: Divestment of athletic identity'. *Journal of Loss and Trauma*, 4(2): 149–162.

——2005. 'Dementia care mapping: a review of the research literature'. *Gerontologist*, 45 (supplement 1): 11.

—— 2008. 'Person centred care'. In R. Jacoby, C. Oppenheimer, T. Dening, and A. Thomas (eds.), *Oxford Textbook of Old Age Psychiatry*. Oxford: Oxford University Press.

Brosi, G., and Kleiner, B. H. 1999. 'Is age a handicap in finding employment?' *Equal Opportunities International*, 18(5): 100–104.

Burrow, J. A. 1986. *Ages of Man: A Study in Medieval Writing and Thought*. Oxford: Clarendon Press.

Butler, R. N. 1969. 'Age-ism: another form of bigotry'. *Gerontologist*, 9(4): 243–246.

——1989. 'Dispelling ageism: The cross-cutting intervention'. *The Annals of the American Academy of Political and Social Science*, 503: 138–147.

Calasanti, T. 2008. 'A feminist confronts ageism'. *Journal of Aging Studies*, 22(2): 152–157.

Callahan, J. J., and Lansperry, S. 1997. 'Density makes a difference: can we tap the power of NORCs?' *Perspective on Aging*, 26(1): 13–20.

CareCommission. 2009. *Remember, I'm Still Me*. Dundee: Mental Welfare Commission for Scotland.

Caroll, T. 2004. 'Masculine connections/feminist possibilities: women imagining "retirement"'. TASA Conference. Revisioning Institutions: Change in the 21st Century. La Trobe, Australia: Dec 8–11.

Carstensen, L. L. 1992. 'Social and emotional patterns in adulthood: support for socioemotional selectivity theory'. *Psychology and Aging*, 7(3): 331–338.

Chacko, P. M. 2005. *Tribal Communities and Social Change*. New Delhi: Sage Publications.

Chenoweth, L. et al. 2009. 'Caring for Aged Dementia Care Resident Study (CADRES) of person-centred care, dementia-care mapping, and usual care in dementia: a cluster-randomised trial'. *Lancet Neurology*, 8(4): 317–325.

Cheung, S., Ridout, F., Hackshaw, A., Sutton, S., Gannon, K., and Hutchison, I. 2009. 'Binge drinking amongst 8845 13–14-year-old English pupils and the harms they suffered'. *British Journal of Oral and Maxillofacial Surgery*, 47(7): 39–40.

Chodorow, N. 1979. *The Reproduction of Mothering: Psychoanalysis and the Sociology of Gender*. Berkeley, California: University of California Press.

Chudacoff, H. P. 1989. *How Old Are You? Age Consciousness in American Culture*. New Jersey: Princeton University Press.

Clarke, L. H., and Griffin, M. 2008. 'Visible and invisible ageing: beauty work as a response to ageism'. *Ageing and Society*, 28(5): 653–674.

Cohen-Mansfield, J., Dakheel-Ali, M., and Frank, J. K. 2010. 'The impact of a naturally occurring retirement communities service program in MD, USA'. *Health Promotion International*, 25(2): 210–220.

Cokayne, K. 2003. *Experiencing Old Age in Ancient Rome*. London: Routledge.

Coleman, L., and Cater, S. 2005. 'Underage "binge" drinking: a qualitative study into motivations and outcomes'. *Drugs: Education, Prevention, and Policy*, 12(2): 125–136.

Cotrell, V., and Schulz, R. 1993. 'The perspective of the patient with Alzheimer's disease: a neglected dimension of dementia research'. *Gerontologist*, 33(2): 205–211.

Coupland, C., Tempest, S., and Barnatt, C. 2008. 'What are the implications of the new UK age discrimination legislation for research and practice?' *Human Resource Management Journal*, 18(4): 423–431.

Coupland, D. 1991. *Generation X. Tales of an Accelerated Culture*. London: Abacus.

Covey, H. C. 1989. 'Old age portrayed by the ages-of-life models from the middle ages to the 16th century'. *Gerontologist*, 29(5): 692–698.

Croucher, K. 2006. *Making the Case for Retirement Villages*. York: Joseph Rowntree Foundation.

Crowe, E. P. 2008. *Genealogy Online*. New York: McGraw-Hill.

Cuddy, A. J. C., and Fiske, S. T. 2002. 'Doddering but dear: process, content, and function in stereotyping of older persons'. In T. D. Nelson (ed.), *Ageism: Stereotyping and Prejudice Against Older Persons*. Boston, Massachusetts: MIT Press.

Cullen, J. 2004. *The American Dream: A Short History of an Idea that Shaped a Nation*. Oxford: Oxford University Press.

Cullen, L. T., and Sachs, A. 2008. 'How not to look old on the job'. *Time*, 171(10): 55.

Daly, J. L. 2001. 'AIDS in Swaziland: the battle from within'. *African Studies Review*, 44(1): 21–35.

Davis, D. H. J. 2004. 'Dementia: Sociological and philosophical constructions'. *Social Science & Medicine*, 58(2): 369–378.

Davis, K. 2002. '"A dubious equality": men, women and cosmetic surgery'. *Body & Society*, 8(1): 49–65.

Davis, R. 1989. *My Journey into Alzheimer's Disease*. Amersham: Scripture Press.

de Beauvoir, S. 1972. *The Coming of Age*. New York: Putnam.

de Boer, M. E. et al. 2007. 'Suffering from dementia—the patient's perspective: a review of the literature'. *International Psychogeriatrics*, 19(6): 1021–1039.

Debroux, P. 2003. *Human Resource Management in Japan: Changes and Uncertainties: A New Human Resource Management System Fitting to the Global Economy*. Farnham: Ashgate Publishing.

DelCampo, R. G. et al. 2010. *Managing the Multi-Generational Workforce: From the GI Generation to the Millennials*. Farnham: Gower.

DOL. 2009. 'Notice of initial determination updating the list of products requiring federal contractor certification as to forced/indentured child labor pursuant to executive order 13126'. *Federal Register* 74(175): 46794–46796.

Dorsey, J. R. 2009. *Y-Size Your Business: How Gen Y Employees Can Save You Money and Grow Your Business*. Chichester: Wiley.

Dottridge, M., and Stuart, L. 2005. *Child Labour Today*. London: UNICEF.

Dove, M. 1986. *The Perfect Age of Man's Life*. Cambridge: Cambridge University Press.

Doward, J. 2009. 'Wealthy elderly turn backs on seaside havens'. *guardian.co.uk* (26 July 2009), <http://www.guardian.co.uk/world/2009/jul/26/wealthy-pensioners-cotswolds-kent-hampshire/print>, accessed 8 September 2010.

Down, S., and Reveley, J. 2004. 'Generational encounters and the social formation of entrepreneurial identity: "Young guns" and "old farts"'. *Organization*, 11(2): 233.

Duffy, B. et al. 2008. 'Closing the gaps-crime and public perceptions'. *International Review of Law, Computers and Technology*, 22(1–2): 17–44.

Duncan, C., and Loretto, W. 2004. 'Never the right age? Gender and age-based discrimination in employment'. *Gender, Work and Organization*, 11(1): 95–115.

Dupere, V. et al. 2007. 'Affiliation to youth gangs during adolescence: the interaction between childhood psychopathic tendencies and neighborhood disadvantage'. *Journal of Abnormal Child Psychology*, 35(6): 1035–1045.

Edmunds, J., and Turner, B. S. 2002. *Generational Consciousness, Narrative, and Politics*. Lanham, MD: Rowman & Littlefield.

————'Global generations: social change in the twentieth century'. *British Journal of Sociology*, 56(4): 559.

Ehrenberg, V. 1973. *From Solon to Socrates: Greek History and Civilization During the Sixth and Fifth Centuries BC*. London: Routledge.

Eisner, S. P. 2005. 'Managing generation Y'. *SAM Advanced Management Journal*, 70(4): 4–15.

Ekerdt, D. J. 1986. 'The busy ethic: moral continuity between work and retirement'. *Gerontologist*, 26: 239–244.

Elias, N. 1994. *The Civilising Process*. Oxford: Blackwell.

EOC. 2007. *Sex and Power: Who Runs Britain*. Manchester: Equal Opportunities Commission.

Erickson, T. 2008. *Plugged In: The Generation Y Guide to Thriving at Work*. Cambridge, Massachusetts: Harvard Business School Press.

Erikson, E. H. 1959. *Identity and the Life Cycle*. New York: Norton.

EUAFR. 2009. *Homophobia and Discrimination on Grounds of Sexual Orientation and Gender Identity in the EU Member States: Part II—The Social Situation*. Vienna: European Union Agency for Fundamental Rights.

Evans, S. 2009. '"That lot up there and us down here": social interaction and a sense of community in a mixed tenure UK retirement village', *Ageing and Society*, 29(2): 199–216.

Feagin, J. R., and Feagin, C. B. 1978. *Discrimination American Style: Institutional Racism and Sexism*. New York: Prentice Hall.

Feiertag, J., and Berge, Z. L. 2008. 'Training Generation N: how educators should approach the Net Generation'. *Education and Training*, 50(6): 457–464.

Feldman, D. 2007. 'Late-career and retirement issues'. In H. Gunz, and M. Peiperl (eds.), *Handbook of Career Studies*. Thousand Oaks: Sage Publications, Inc.

Fennis, B. M., and Pruyn, A. T. H. 2007. 'You are what you wear: brand personality influences on consumer impression formation'. *Journal of Business Research*, 60 (6): 634–639.

Ferrero, M. 2005. 'Radicalization as a reaction to failure: an economic model of Islamic extremism'. *Public Choice*, 122(1): 199–220.

Ferri, C. P. et al. 2005. 'Global prevalence of dementia: A Delphi consensus study'. *Lancet*, 366(9503): 2112–2117.

Fields, B. R. et al. 2007. *Millennial Leaders: Success Stories From Today's Most Brilliant Generation Y leaders*. Chambersburg, PA: Morgan James Publishing.

Filinson, R. 2008. 'Age discrimination legislation in the U.K.: a comparative and gerontological analysis'. *Journal of Cross-Cultural Gerontology*, 23(3): 225–237.

Fineman, S. 1983. *White Collar Unemployment: Impact and Stress*. Chichester: Wiley.

————2003. *Understanding Emotion at Work*. London: Sage.

————2009. '"When I'm sixty five": the shaping and shapers of retirement identity and experience'. In P. Hancock, and M. Tyler (eds.), *The Management of Everyday Life*. Houndmills, Basingtoke: Palgrave Macmillan.

—— Gabriel, Y., and Sims, D. 2010. *Organizing and Organizations*, 4th Edition. London: Sage.

Fink, B., Grammer, K., and Thornhill, R. 2001. 'Human (homo sapiens) facial attractiveness in relation to skin texture and color'. *Journal of Comparative Psychology*, 115(1): 92–100.

Flocker, M. 2003. *The Metrosexual Guide to Style: A Handbook for the Modern Man*. Cambridge, Mass: Da Capo Pr.

Foner, A. 1974. 'Age stratification and age conflict in political life'. *American Sociological Review*, 39(2): 187–196.

Frankish, C. J., Milligan, C. D., and Reid, C. 1998. 'A review of relationships between active living and determinants of health'. *Social Science and Medicine*, 47(3): 287–302.

Fraser, L. et al. 2009. 'Older workers: an exploration of the benefits, barriers and adaptations for older people in the workforce'. *Work: A Journal of Prevention, Assessment and Rehabilitation*, 33(3): 261–272.

French, H. 1996. 'For women in Ivory Coast, new fight for equality'. *New York Times*, 6 April.

Furnham, A., and Goletto-Tankel, M. P. 2002. 'Understanding savings, pensions and life assurance in 16–21-year-olds'. *Human Relations*, 55(5): 603.

Gabriel, Y. 2009. Reconciling an ethic of care with critical management pedagogy. *Management Learning*, 40(4): 379–385.

—— Gray, D. E., and Goregaokar, H. 2010. 'Temporary derailment or end of the line? Unemployed managers at 50'. *Organization Studies*, 31(12): 1687–712.

Gadassi, R., and Gati, I. 2009. 'The effect of gender stereotypes on explicit and implicit career preferences'. *Counseling Psychologist*, 37(6): 902–922.

Giancola, F. 2006. 'The generation gap: more myth than reality'. *Human Resource Planning*, 29(4): 32.

Gibson, K. J., Zerbe, W. J., and Franken, R. E. 1993. 'Employers' perceptions of the re-employment barriers faced by older job hunters'. *Relations Industrielles*, 48(2): 321–335.

Giddens, A. 1991. *Modernity and Self-Identity: Self and Society in the Late Modern Age*. Stanford, Ca.: Stanford University Press.

Giles, J. 1994. 'Generalization X'. *Newsweek*, 6 June: 62–72.

Gill, R., Henwood, K., and McLean, C. 2005. 'Body projects and the regulation of normative masculinity'. *Body & Society*, 11(1): 37–62.

Gilleard, C., and Higgs, P. 2005. *Contexts of Ageing: Class, Cohort and Community*. Polity Press: Cambridge.

————2007. 'The third age and the baby boomers: two approaches to the social structuring of later life'. *International Journal of Ageing and Later Life*, 2: 13–30.

————2009. 'The third age: field, habitus, or identity?' In I. R. Jones, P. Higgs, and D. J. Ekerdt (eds.), *Consumption & Generational Change: The Rise of Consumer Lifestyles*. New Brunswick: Transaction.

————2010. 'The power of the silver: age and identity politics in the 21st century'. *Journal of Aging & Social Policy*, 21: 277–295.

Gimlin, D. L. 2001. *Body Work: Beauty and Self-Image in American Culture*. California: University of California Press.

Glass, A. 2007. 'Understanding generational differences for competitive success'. *Industrial and Commercial Training*, 39(2): 98–103.

Glover, I., and Branine, M. 2001. '"Do not go gentle into that good night": some thoughts on paternalism, ageism, management and society'. In I. Glover, and M. Branine (eds.), *Ageism in Work and Employment*. Aldershot: Ashgate.

Goffman, E. 1963. *Stigma. Notes on the Management of Spoiled identity*. Englewood Cliffs, NJ: Prentice-Hall.

——1967. *Interaction Ritual*. New Jersey: Anchor Books.

Goldenberg, J. L. et al. 2000. 'Fleeing the body: a terror management perspective on the problem of human corporeality'. *Personality and Social Psychology Review*, 4(3): 200–218.

Goldin, C., and Sokoloff, K. 1982. 'Women, children, and industrialization in the early republic: evidence from the manufacturing censuses'. *The Journal of Economic History*, 42(4): 741–774.

Goldsmith, M. 1996. *Hearing the Voice of People with Dementia: Opportunities and Obstacles*. London: Jessica Kingsley Publishers.

Gorn Gerald, J., Jiang, Y., and Johar Gita, V. 2008. 'Babyfaces, trait inferences, and company evaluations in a public relations crisis'. *Journal of Consumer Research*, 35(1): 36–49.

Grace, R. E. 2010. *When Every Day is Saturday: The Retirement Guide for Boomers*. San Jose: Writer's Showcase.

Graham, V., and Tuffin, K. 2004. 'Retirement villages: companionship, privacy and security'. *Australasian Journal on Ageing*, 24(4): 184–188.

Granleese, J., and Sayer, G. 2006. 'Gendered ageism and 'lookism': a triple jeopardy for female academics'. *Women in Management Review*, 21(6): 500–517.

Grant, B. C. 2007. 'Retirement villages: more than enclaves for the aged'. *Activities, Adaptation & Aging*, 31(2): 37–55.

——2006. 'Retirement villages: an alternative form of housing on a ageing landscape'. *Social Policy Journal of New Zealand*, 27: 100–105.

Green, B. 2003. *Marketing to Leading-Edge Baby Boomers*. Lincoln: Writers Advantage Press.

Greer, G. 1991. *The Change*. Harmondsworth: Penguin.

Grier, B. 2004. 'Child labor and Africanist scholarship: a critical overview'. *African Studies Review*, 47(2): 1–25.

Griffin, J. 2010. *The Lonely Society*. London: Mental Health Foundation.

Griffiths, A. 2009. 'Healthy work for older workers: work design and management factors'. In W. Loretto, S. Vickerstaff, and K. M. White (eds.), *The Future of Older Workers: New Perspectives*. Bristol: The Policy Press.

Grogan, S. 2008. *Body Image: Understanding Body Dissatisfaction in Men, Women, and Children*. London: Routledge.

Gubrium, J. F. 1991. *The Mosaic of Care: Frail Elderly and their Families in the Real World*. New York: Springer.

——and Holstein, J. A. 1998. 'Narrative practice and the coherence of personal stories'. *Sociological Quarterly*, 39(1): 163–187.

Gullette, M. M. 2004. *Aged by Culture*. Chicago: University Of Chicago Press.

Hackett, P., and Hunter, P. 2010. *Who Governs Britain? A Profile of MPs in the New Parliament*. London: The Smith Institute.

Hagemann, F. et al. 2006. *Global Child Labour Trends 2000 to 2004*. Geneva: International Programme on the Elimination of Child Labour, International Labour Office.

Hamermesh, D. S., and Biddle, J. E. 1994. 'Beauty and the labor market'. *The American Economic Review*, 84(5): 1174–1194.

Hancock, P., and Tyler, M. 2001. *Work, Postmodernism and Organization: A Critical Introduction.* London: Sage.

Handy, J., and Davy, D. 2007. 'Gendered ageism: older women's experiences of employment agency practices'. *Asia Pacific Journal of Human Resources,* 45(1): 85–99.

Hanson, K., and Wapner, S. 1994. 'Transition to retirement: gender differences'. *International Journal of Aging & Human Development,* 39(3): 189–208.

Harwood, J., and Anderson, K. 2002. 'The presence and portrayal of social groups on prime-time television'. *Communication Reports,* 15(2): 81–98.

Hatton-Yeo, A. 2010. 'An introduction to intergenerational practice'. *Working with Older People,* 14(2): 4–11.

Hauari, H., and Hollingworth, K. 2009. *Understanding Fathering: Masculinity, Dversity and Change.* York: Joseph Rowntree Foundation.

HC. 2008. *Improving Services and Support for People with Dementia.* London: House of Commons, The Stationery Office.

——2009. *Role of the Prison Officer: House of Commons Justice Committee. Twelfth Report of Session 2008–09.* London: The Stationery Ofice.

Healey, T., and Ross, K. 2002. 'Growing old invisibly: older viewers talk television'. *Media, Culture & Society,* 24(1): 105.

Held, V. 2006. *The Ethics of Care: Personal, Political, and Global.* Oxford: Oxford University Press.

Henkens, C. J. I. M. 2005. 'Stereotyping older workers and retirement: the managers' point of view'. *Canadian Journal on Aging,* 24(4): 353–366.

Henrard, J. C. 1996. 'Cultural problems of ageing especially regarding gender and intergenerational equity'. *Social Science and Medicine,* 43(5): 667–680.

Hertogh, C. et al. 2007. 'Would we rather lose our life than lose our self? Lessons from the Dutch debate on euthanasia for patients with dementia'. *The American Journal of Bioethics,* 7(4): 48–56.

Hewlett, S. A., Sherbin, L., and Sumberg, K. 2009. 'How Gen Y and Boomers will reshape your agenda'. *Harvard Business Review,* (87) 7/8, Jul.-Aug.: 71–76.

Hills, J., Sefton, T., and Stewart, K. 2009. *Towards a More Equal Society? Poverty, Inequality and Policy Since 1997.* Bristol: Policy Press.

Hira, N. A. 2007. 'You raised them, now manage them'. *Fortune,* 155(9): 38–48.

Hise, D. T. 2004. *The War Against Men.* Oakland, CA: Elderberry Press.

Holden, R., and Harte, V. 2004. 'New graduate engagement with "professional development": A pilot study'. *Journal of European Industrial Training,* 28(2): 272–282.

Holliday, S. 2009. 'Life catching up with me'. *Bath Chronicle.* 5 November: 41.

Hornstein, Z. 2001. *Age Discrimination Legislation: Choices for the UK.* York: Joseph Rowntree Foundation.

Horrocks, R. 1994. *Masculinity in Crisis: Myths, Fantasies, and Realities.* New York: St. Martins.

Houseman, W. 1992. 'Heritage village revisited'. *New Choices for Living,* 31(1): 36–38.

Howard. 2009. *Turnkeys or Professionals? A Vision for the 21st Century Prison Officer.* London: Howard League for Penal Reform.

Howe, N., and Strauss, W. 2007. 'The next 20 years: how customer and workforce attitudes will evolve'. *Harvard Business Review,* 85(7/8): 41–52.

Hudson, 'Women less likely to aspire to top corporate positions'. *Hudson Highland Group* (6 March 2008), <http://us.hudson.com/node.asp?kwd=03–06–08-women-survey>, accessed 8 September 2010.

Hunt, M. E. et al. 1983. 'Retirement communities: an American original'. *Journal of Housing for the Elderly*, 1(3/4): 1–277.

——and Gunter-Hunt, G. 1986. 'Naturally occurring retirement communities'. *Journal of Housing for the Elderly*, 3(3): 3–22.

Hunt, S. 2005. *The Life Course: A Sociological Introduction*. Houndsmills: Palgrave Macmillan.

Hurd, C. L., Repta, R., and Griffin, M. 2007. 'Non-surgical cosmetic procedures: older women's perceptions and experiences'. *Journal of Women & Aging*, 19(3/4): 69.

Husselbee, D. 2000. 'NGOs as development partners to the corporates: child football stitchers in Pakistan'. *Development in Practice*, 10(3/4): 377–389.

IBR. 2007. 'Four in ten businesses worldwide have no women in senior management'. *Grant Thorton International Business Report* (March 2007), <http://wwwPress.gt.org.pl/-room/Press-archive/2007/women-in-management.asp>, accessed 8 September 2010.

IITA. 2002. *Child Labour in the Cocoa Sector of West Africa: A Synthesis of Findings in Cameroon, Cote d'Ivoire, Ghana and Nigeria*. Accra: IITA.

ILO. 2004. *Child Labour: A Textbook for University Students*. Geneva: ILO.

Innes, A. 2009. *Dementia Studies*. London: Sage.

Itzin, C., and Phillipson, C. 1995. 'Gendered ageism: a double jeopardy for women in organizations'. In C. Itzin, and J. Newman (eds.), *Gender, Culture and Organizational Change: Putting Theory into Practice*. London: Routledge.

James, J. B., Swanberg, J. E., and McKechnie, S. P. 2007. *Generational Differences in Perceptions of Older Workers' Capabilities*. Boston, MA: Center on Aging & Work/Workplace Flexibility at Boston College.

Jenkins, J. 2008. 'Strategies for managing talent in a multigenerational workforce'. *Employment Relations Today*, 34(4): 19–26.

Johnson, R. W., and Mommaerts, C. 2009. 'Unemployment rate hits all-time high for adults age 65 and older'. Urban Institute, Washington DC. <http://www.urban.org/retirement_policy/url.cfm>.

Jones, I. R, Leontowitsch, M., and Higgs, P. 2010. 'The experience of retirement in second modernity: generational habitus among retired senior managers'. *Sociology: The Journal of the British Sociological Association*, 44(1): 103–120.

Jonker, M. A. 2003. 'Estimation of life expectancy in the Middle Ages'. *Journal of the Royal Statistical Society*, 166(1): 105–117.

Jovic, E., Wallace, J. E., and Lemaire, J. 2006. 'The generation and gender shifts in medicine: an exploratory survey of internal medicine physicians'. *BMC Health Services Research*, 5(55): 1–10.

Kail, R. V., and Cavanaugh, J. C. 2008. *Human Development: A Life-Span View*. Belmont California: Wadsworth.

Kastenbaum, R. 1974. 'Gone tomorrow'. *Geriatrics*, 29(11): 127–134.

——1993. 'Encrusted elders: Arizona and the political spirit of postmodern aging'. In T. R. Cole et al. (eds.), *Voices and Visions of Aging: Toward a Critical Gerontology*. New York: Springer.

Katz, S. 2000. 'Busy bodies: activity, aging, and the management of everyday life'. *Journal of Aging Studies*, 14(2): 135–152.

Katz, S. and Marshall, B. 2003. 'New sex for old: lifestyle, consumerism, and the ethics of aging well'. *Journal of Aging Studies*, 17(1): 3–16.

Keene, J. 2006. 'Age discrimination'. In J. H. Greenhaus, and G. A. Callanan (eds.), *Encyclopedia of Career Development, Vol 1*. Thousand Oaks, CA: Sage.

Kennedy, G. E. et al. 2008. 'First year students' experiences with technology: are they really digital natives?' *Australasian Journal of Educational Technology*, 24(1): 108–122.

Kerr, G., and Dacyshyn, A. 2000. 'The retirement experiences of elite, female gymnasts'. *Journal of Applied Sport Psychology*, 12(2): 115–133.

Kertzer, D. I. 1983. 'Generation as a sociological problem'. *Annual Review of Sociology*, 9: 125–149.

Kessler, E. M., Rakoczy, K., and Staudinger, U. M. 2004. 'The portrayal of older people in prime time television series: the match with gerontological evidence'. *Ageing and society*, 24(04): 531–552.

Kestin, D., and Hoonaard, V. D. 2002. 'Life of the margins of a Florida retirement community: the experience of snowbirds, newcomers and widowed persons'. *Research on Aging*, 24(1): 50–66.

Khan, F. R., Munir, K. A., and Willmott, H. 2007. 'A dark side of institutional entrepreneurship: Soccer balls, child labour and postcolonial impoverishment'. *Organization Studies*, 28(7): 1055–1077.

Khan, F. R. 2007. 'Representational approaches matter'. *Journal of Business Ethics*, 73(1): 77–89.

King, Z. 2003. 'New or traditional careers? A study of UK graduates' preferences'. *Human Resource Management Journal*, 13(1): 5–26.

Kinsell, K., and He, W. 2009. *An Aging World: 2008*. Washington, DC: US Government Printing Office.

Kitwood, T. 1990. *Concern for Others*. London: Routledge.

Klepp, I. G., and Storm-Mathisen, A. 2005. 'Reading fashion as age: teenage girls' and grown women's accounts of clothing as body and social status'. *Fashion Theory: The Journal of Dress, Body & Culture*, 9(3): 323–342.

Kohli, M. 1986. 'The world we forgot: a historical review of the life course'. In V. Marshall (ed.), *Later Life*. Beverley Hills: Sage.

Kohli, M. 2000. 'Age integration through interest mediation: political parties and unions'. *Gerontologist*, 40(3): 279–282.

Kolk, A., and van Tulder, R. 2002. 'Child labor and multinational conduct: a comparison of international business and stakeholder codes'. *Journal of Business Ethics*, 36(3): 291–301.

Kozar, J. M., and Damhorst, M. L. 2008. 'Older women's responses to current fashion models'. *Management*, 12(3): 338–350.

Kreamer, A. 2007. *Going Gray*. London: Little, Brown and Co.

Krupp, C. 2009. *How Not to Look Old*. Boston: Springboard Press.

Kruse, D. L., and Mahony, D. 2000. 'Illegal child labor in the United States: prevalence and characteristics'. *Industrial and Labor Relations Review*, 54(1): 17–40.

Kubeck, J. E. et al. 1996. 'Does job-related training performance decline with age?' *Psychology and Aging*, 11(1): 92–107.

Lally, P. 2007. 'Identity and athletic retirement: a prospective study'. *Psychology of Sport & Exercise*, 8(1): 85–100.

Landy, F. J. 1996. 'Mandatory retirement and chronological age in public safety workers: testimony before the United States Senate Committee on Labor and Human Resources, American Psychological Association'. Washington, DC.

Langer, E. J. 2009. *Counterclockwise: Mindful Health and the Power of Possibility*. New York: Ballantine Books.

Laning, C. 2000. 'Faire names for English folk: late sixteenth century English names' (26 September 2000), <http://www.s-gabriel.org/names/christian/fairnames/>, accessed 8 September 2010.

Lashbrook, J. 2002. 'Age norms'. In *Encyclopedia of Aging*, <http://www.encyclopedia.com.>

Laslett, P. 1996. *A Fresh Map of Life: The Emergence of the Third Age*. Basingstoke: Macmillan.

Laurie, A. 1981. *The Languages of Clothes*. New York: Random House.

Lawrence, B. S. 1988. 'New wrinkles in the theory of age: demography, norms, and performance ratings'. *Academy of Management Journal*, 31 (2): 309–337.

——1996. 'Interest and indifference: the role of age in the organizational sciences'. *Research in Personnel and Human Resource Management*, 14: 1–60.

——2004. 'How old you are may depend on where you work'. In S. Chowdhury (ed.), *Next Generation Business Handbook*. NJ: Wiley.

Laws, G. 1995. 'Embodiment and emplacement: identities, representation and landscape in Sun City retirement communities'. *International Journal of Aging & Human Development*, 40(4): 253–280.

Laz, C. 1998. 'Act your age'. *Sociological Forum*, 13(1): 85–113.

Lerner, M. 1957. *America as a Civilization: Life and Thought in the United States Today*. New York: Simon and Schuster.

Levinson, D. 1979. *The Seasons of Man's Life*. New York: Ballantine.

Linstead, S. (ed.). 2004. *Organization Theory and Postmodern Thought*. London: Sage.

Loch, C. H. et al. 2010. 'How BMW is defusing the demographic time bomb'. *Harvard Business Review*, 88(3): 99–102.

Lockwood, N. R. 2009. *The Multigenerational Workforce: Opportunity for Competitive Success*. Alexandria, VA: The Society for Human Resource Management.

Loretto, W., Duncan, C., and White, P. J. 2000. 'Ageism and employment: controversies, ambiguities and younger people's perceptions'. *Ageing and Society*, 20(3): 279–302.

Loretto, W., and White, P. 2006. 'Work, more work and retirement: older workers' perspectives'. *Social Policy and Society*, 5(4): 495–506.

Louise, L. 1985. 'Bringing the family to work: women's culture on the shop floor'. *Feminist Studies*, 11(3): 519–540.

Lower, J. 2006. *A Practical Guide to Managing the Multigenerational Workforce: Skills for Nurse Managers*. Marblehead, MA: Hcpro Inc.

Luborsky, M. R., and LeBlanc, I. M. 2003. 'Cross-cultural perspectives on the concept of retirement: an analytic redefinition'. *Journal of Cross-Cultural Gerontology*, 18(4): 251–271.

Lucas, S. 2004. 'The images used to "sell" and represent retirement communities'. *Professional Geographer*, 56(4): 449–459.

Luria, A. R. 1985. 'Letter to Oliver Sacks', *The Man Who Mistook His Wife for a Hat*. London: Picador, 32.

Lynd, R. S., and Lynd, H. M. 1929. *Middletown: A Study in Contemporary American Culture*. New York: Harcourt Brace & Co.

Lyon, J., Dennison, C., and Wilson, A. 2000. *'Tell Them So They Listen': Messages from Young People in Custody*. London: Home Office, Research Development and Statistics Directorate.

Lyon, P., and Pollard, D. 1997. 'Perceptions of the older employee: Is anything really changing?' *Personnel Review*, 26(4): 245–257.

McCann, R., and Giles, H. 2002. 'Ageism in the workplace: a communication perspective'. In T. D. Nelson (ed.), *Ageism: Stereotyping and Prejudice Against Older Persons*. Massachusetts: MIT Press.

McConatha, J. T. et al. 2003. 'Attitudes toward aging: a comparative analysis of young adults from the United States and Germany'. *International Journal of Aging and Human Development*, 57(3): 203–215.

McCormack, B. 2004. 'Person-centredness in gerontological nursing: an overview of the literature'. *Journal of Clinical Nursing*, 13(s1): 31–38.

McDonagh, E. L. 1996. *Breaking the Abortion Deadlock: From Choice to Consent*. Oxford: Oxford University Press.

McHugh, K. E., and Larson-Keaghy, E. M. 2005. 'These white walls: the dialectic of retirement communities'. *Journal of Aging Studies*, 19: 241–256.

Mackenzie, J. 2006. 'Stigma and dementia: East European and South Asian family carers negotiating stigma in the UK'. *Dementia*, 5(2): 233–247.

McNair, S. 2006. 'How different is the older labour market? Attitudes to work and retirement among older people in Britain'. *Social Policy and Society*, 5(4): 485–494.

Macnicol, J. 2009. 'The American experience of age discrimination legislation'. In W. Loretto, S. Vickerstaff, and P. White (eds.), *The Future of Older Workers: New Perspectives*. Bristol: The Policy Press.

McQuaid, R., and Bond, S. 2004. *Gender Stereotyping In Career Choice*. Edinburgh: Employment Research Institute Napier University.

Magnuson, D. S., and Alexander, L. S. 2008. *Work With Me: A New Lens on Leading the Multigenerational Workforce*. Minneapolis: Personnel Decisions International.

Malul, M. 2009. 'Older workers' employment in dynamic technology changes'. *Journal of Socio-Economics*, 38(5): 809–813.

Mannheim, K. 1952. 'The problem of generations'. In K. Mannheim (ed.), *Essays on the Sociology of Knowledge*. London: RKP.

Marshall, E., and Hope, V. M. 2000. *Death and Disease in the Ancient City*. London: Routledge.

Marshall, V., and Taylor, P. 2005. 'Restructuring the lifecourse: work and retirement'. In M. L. Johnson (ed.), *The Cambridge Handbook of Age and Ageing*. Cambridge: Cambridge University Press.

Marston, C. 2007. *Motivating the 'What's In It For Me?' Workforce: Manage Across The Generational Divide and Increase Profits*. Chichester: Wiley.

Maruna, S., and King, A. 2009. 'Youth, crime and punitive public opinion: hopes and fears for the next generation'. In M. Barry, and F. McNeill (eds.), *Youth Offending and Youth Justice*. London: Jessica Kingsley.

Mellor, H. W. 1962. 'Retirement to the coast'. *The Town Planning Review*, 33(1): 40–48.

Moen, P., and Roehling, P. 2005. *The Career Mystique: Cracks in the American Dream*. Oxford: Rowman & Littlefield.

Mooney, H. 2009. 'Life expectancy in England between the rich and poor widens for both men and women'. *British Medical Journal*, 339(2): 2775.

Morgan, L. A., and Kunkel, S. R. 2007. *Aging, Society, and the Life Course.* New York: Springer.

Morgan, R. 2009. 'Children and young people: criminalisation and punishment'. In M. Barry, and F. McNeill (eds.), *Youth Offending and Youth Justice.* London: Jessica Kingsley.

Morin, R., and Taylor, P. 2009. *Different Age Groups, Different Recessions.* Washington: Pew Research Center.

Moschis, G. P., Euehun, L., and Mathur, A. 1997. 'Targeting the mature market: oppportunities and challenges'. *Journal of Consumer Marketing,* 14(4): 282–293.

Mowery, D. C., and Kamlet, M. S. 1993. 'New technologies and the aging work force'. In S. A. Bass, F. G. Caro, and Y. P. Chen (eds.), *Achieving a Productive Aging Society.* Westport, CT: Auburn House.

Mulvey, P. W., Ledford, G. E., and LeBlanc, P. V. 2000. 'Rewards of work: how they drive performance, retention and satisfaction'. *WorldatWork Journal,* 9(3): 6–18.

Muncie, J. 2009. *Youth and Crime.* London: Sage.

Munnell, A. H., Sass, S. A., and Soto, M. 2006. *Employer Attitudes Towards Older Workers: Survey Results.* Boston: Boston College, Center for Retirement Research.

Murji, K. 2007. 'Sociological engagements: institutional racism and beyond'. *Sociology,* 41(5): 843–855.

Murphy, S. A. 2007. *Leading a Multigenerational Workforce.* Washington, DC: AARP.

Murray, C. 2009. 'Typologies of young resisters and desisters'. *Youth Justice,* 9(2): 115–129.

Naegele, G., and Walker, A. 1999. 'Conclusion'. In A. Walker, and G. Naegele (eds.), *The Politics of Old Age in Europe.* Buckingham: Open University Press.

Nelson, T. D. 2005. 'Ageism: Prejudice against our feared future self'. *Journal of Social Issues,* 61(2): 207–221.

Neugarten, B. L., and Moore, J. W. 1965. 'Age norms, age constraints and adult socialization'. *American Journal of Sociology,* 70: 710–717.

Neumark, D. 2009. 'The Age Discrimination in Employment Act and the challenge of population aging'. *Research on Aging: A Quarterly Of Social Gerontology and Adult Development,* 31(1): 41–68.

Nolan, J., and Scott, J. 2009. 'Experiences of age and gender: narratives of progress and decline'. *International Journal of Aging and Human Development,* 69(2): 133–158.

O'Duffy, B. 2008. 'Radical atmosphere: explaining jihadist radicalization in the UK'. *Political Science and Politics,* 41(01): 37–42.

O'Hara. M. 2009. Animal magic. *Guardian,* London, 12 August.

O'Sullivan, A., and Sheffrin, S. M. 2003. *Economics: Principles in Action.* New Jersey: Prentice Hall.

Ogden, J., and Sherwood, F. 2008. 'Reducing the impact of media images'. *Health Education,* 108(6): 489–500.

Olsen, K. 1999. *Daily Life in 18th-Century England.* Santa Barbara: Greenwood Press.

Ortner, S. B. 1998. 'Generation X: anthropology in a media-saturated world'. *Cultural Anthropology,* 13(3): 414–440.

Panitt, M. 1993. 'You're playing too slowly'. *New Choices for Living,* March: 12.

Papson, S. 1986. From symbolic exchange to bureaucratic discourse: the Hallmark Greeting Card. *Theory Culture and Society,* 3(2): 99–111.

Parenti, C. 2008. 'Chocolate's bittersweet economy'. *CNNMoney.com*, (15 February 2008), <http://money.cnn.com/2008/01/24/news/international/chocolate_bittersweet.fortune/>, accessed 8 September 2010.

Parke, S. 2008. *Children and Young People in Custody 2006–2008*. London: HM Inspectorate of Prisons Youth Justice Board.

Parsons, E. 2007. 'Animating grandma: the indices of age and agency in contemporary children's films'. *Journal of Aging, Humanities, and the Arts*, 1(3): 221–229.

Paz, O. 1985. *The Labyrinth of Solitude: Life and Thought in Mexico*. New York: Grove Press.

PCIDT. 2009. *Oversight of Public and Private Initiatives to Eliminate the Worst Form of Child Labor in the Cocoa Sector on Cote d'Ivoire and Ghana*. Tulane: Payson Center for International Development Technology Transfer, Tulane University.

Pennington-Gray, L., and Lane, C. W. 2001. 'Profiling the silent generation—preferences for travel'. *Journal of Hospitality & Leisure Marketing*, 9(1): 73–95.

Perna, F. M., Ahlgren, R. L., and Zaichkowsky, L. 1999. 'The influence of career planning, race, and athletic injury on life satisfaction among recently retired collegiate male athletes'. *Sport Psychologist*, 13: 144–156.

Perrin, T. 2005. *The Business Case for Workers Age 50+: Planning for Tomorrow's Talent Needs in Today's Competitive Environment*. Washington, DC: AARP.

Pfann, G. A. et al. 2000. 'Business success and businesses' beauty capital'. *Economics Letters*, 67(2): 201–207.

Phakathi, M. 2009. 'Prevention is better than cure'. *Bulletin of the World Health Organization*, 87(5): 328–9.

Phillips, C. 2008. 'Negotiating identities: ethnicity and social relations in a young offenders' institution'. *Theoretical Criminology: An International Journal*, 12(3): 313–331.

Phillipson, C. 1990. 'The sociology of retirement'. In J. Bond, P. Coleman, and S. Pearce (eds.), *Ageing in Society: An Introduction to Social Gerontology*. London: Sage.

Pilcher, J. 1994. 'Mannheim's sociology of generations: an undervalued legacy'. *British Journal of Sociology*, 45(3): 481–495.

Pillay, H., Kelly, K., and Tones, M. 2006. 'Career aspirations of older workers: an Australian study'. *International Journal of Training & Development*, 10(4): 298–305.

Porter, S. 1951. 'Babies equal boom'. *New York Post*, 4 May.

Prensky, M. 2001. 'Digital natives, digital immigrants'. *On The Horizon*, 9(5): 1–6.

Price, C. A. 2000. 'Women and retirement: relinquishing professional identity'. *Journal of Aging Studies*, 14(1): 81–101.

Quadagno, J. S. 1982. *Aging in Early Industrial Society: Work, Family, and Social Policy in Nineteenth-Century England*. New York: Academic Press.

Raghavan, S., and Chatterjee, S. 2001. 'A taste of slavery: how your chocolate may be tainted'. *Knight Ridder Washington Bureau Newspapers* (24 June 2001), <http://www.rrojasdatabank.info/chocolate.pdf>, accessed 8 September 2010.

Reed, J., Stanley, D., and Clarke, C. 2004. *Health, Well-being and Older People*. Bristol: The Policy Press.

Reitzes, D. C., and Mutran, E. J. 2006. 'Lingering identities in retirement'. *Sociological Quarterly*, 47: 333–359.

Renfrow, D. G. 2004. 'A cartography of passing in everyday life'. *Symbolic Interaction*, 27(4): 485–506.

Rhodes, G. 2006. 'The evolutionary psychology of facial beauty'. *Annual Review of Psychology*, 57(1): 199–227.

Richmond, A. 1972. *A Long View from the Left*. New York: Delta.

Rivoli, P. 2005. *The Travels of a T-Shirt in the Global Economy: An Economist Examines the Markets, Power and Politics of World Trade*. Chichester: Wiley.

Rodgers, D. T. 1979. *The Work Ethic in Industrial America, 1850–1920*. Chicago: University of Chicago Press.

Romans, F. 2007. *The Transition of Women and Men from Work to Retirement*. Belgium: Eurostat, European Communities.

Roscigno, V. J. et al. 2007. 'Age discrimination, social closure and employment'. *Social Forces*, 86(1): 313–334.

Rose, M. B. 1989. 'Social policy and business: parish apprenticeship and the early factory system 1750–1834'. *Business History*, 31(4): 5–32.

Rose, N. 1996. 'The death of the social? Re-figuring the territory of government'. *Economy and Society*, 25(3): 327–356.

Rosnick, D., and Baker, D. 2010. 'The impact of the housing crash on the wealth of the baby boom cohorts'. *Journal of Aging & Social Policy*, 22(2): 117–128.

Sabat, S. R. 2002. 'Surviving manifestations of selfhood in Alzheimer's disease: a case study'. *Dementia*, 1(1): 25–36.

Sabat, S. R. 2006. 'Mind, meaning, and personhood in dementia: the effects of positioning'. In J. C. Hughes, S. J. Louw, and S. R. Sabat (eds.), *Dementia: Mind, Meaning and the Person*. Oxford: Oxford University Press.

Sabath, A. M. 2004. *Beyond Business Casual: What to Wear to Work If You Want to Get Ahead*. New York: ASJA Press.

Sacks, O. W. 2007. *Musicophilia*. New York: Random House.

Salthouse, T. A., and Maurer, T. J. 1996. 'Aging, job performance, and career development'. In J. E. Birren, and K. W. Schaie (eds.), *Handbook of the Psychology of Aging*. San Diego: Academic Press.

Savishinsky, J. 1995. 'The unbearable lightness of retirement: ritual and support in a modem life passage'. *Research on Aging*, 17(3): 243.

Scott, J. 2006. 'Family and gender roles: how attitudes are changing'. GeNet Working Paper No. 21, University of Cambridge.

Selmer, J. 2001. 'Human resource management in Japan—adjustment or transformation?' *International Journal of Manpower*, 22(3): 235–243.

Settersten, R. A. 2003. 'Age structuring and the rhythm of the life course'. In J. T. Mortimer and M. J. Shanahan (eds.), *Handbook of the Life Course*. New York: Plenum.

Settersten, R. A., Jr., and Hagestad, G. O. 1996. 'What's the latest? Cultural age deadlines for family transitions'. *Gerontologist*, 36(2): 178–188.

Shah, P., and Kleiner, B. 2005. 'New developments concerning age discrimination in the workplace'. *Equal Opportunities International*, 24(5/6): 15–23.

Shakespeare, W. 2000. *As You Like It*. New York: Penguin Books.

Shaw, S., and Fairhurst, D. 2008. 'Engaging a new generation of graduates'. *Education & Training*, 50(5): 366–378.

Shropshire, S., and McFarquhar, M. 2002. *Developing Multi-Agency Strategies to Address the Street Gang Culture and Reduce Gun Violence Among Young People. Briefing No. 4.* Manchester: Steve Shropshire and Michael McFarquhar Consultancy Group.

Sinclair, U. 1906. *The Jungle.* New York: Doubleday.

Snape, E., and Redman, T. 2003. 'Too old or too young? The impact of perceived age discrimination'. *Human Resource Management Journal,* 13(1): 78–89.

Soros, G. 2008. *The New Paradigm for Financial Markets. Public Affairs* New York: Perseus.

Stall, S. 1901. *What A Man of Forty-Five Ought to Know.* Philadelphia: The Vir Publishing.

Staller, A., and Petta, P. 2001. 'Introducing emotions into the computational study of social norms: a first evaluation'. *Journal of Artificial Societies and Social Simulation,* 4(1): 41.

Stevenson, M. C. et al. 2009. *Children as Victims, Witnesses and Offenders: Psychological Science and the Law.* New York: Guildford Press.

Strauss, W., and Howe, N. 1991. *Generations: The History of America's Future, 1584 to 2069.* New York: William Morrow and Company.

Streib, G. F., and Metsch, L. R. 2002. 'Conflict in retirement communities: applying an analytical framework'. *Research on Aging,* 24(1): 67–89.

Sturges, J., and Guest, D. 2001. 'Don't leave me this way! A qualitative study of influences on the organisational commitment and turnover intentions of graduates early in their career'. *British Journal of Guidance and Counselling,* 29(4): 447–462.

Swift, J. 2006. 'Justifying age discrimination'. *Industrial Law Journal,* 35(3): 228–244.

TAEN. 2009. *More Over-50s Redundant and Seen as 'Too Old'.* London: The Age and Employment Network. <http://taen.org.uk/media/view/55>.

Tapscott, D. 2008. *Grown Up Digital: How the Net Generation is Changing the World.* Maidenhead: McGraw-Hill Educational.

Taylor, P. et al. 2009a. *Different Age Groups, Different Recessions.* Washington, DC: Pew Research Center <http://pewsocialtrends.org/assets/pdf/recession-and-older-americans.pdf>.

Taylor, P. et al. 2009b. *Growing old in America: Expectations vs. reality.* Washington, DC: Pew Research Center.

Thomas, L. 2010. 'Patchwork pension plans adds to Greek debt woes'. *New York Times,* 11 March.

Thompson, J. K., and Heinberg, L. J. 1999. 'The media's influence on body image disturbance and eating disorders: we've reviled them, now can we rehabilitate them?' *Journal of Social Issues,* 55(2): 339–353.

Toppo, S. R. 2001. *Tribes in India.* New Delhi: Indian Publishers

Twigg, J. 2007. 'Clothing, age and the body: a critical review'. *Ageing and Society,* 27(2): 285–305.

UCDavis. 2008. 'UC Davis study of California women business leaders. A census of women directors and executive officers'. <www.gsm.ucdavis.edu/census>.

Van Solinge, H., and Henkens, K. 2008. 'Adjustment to and satisfaction with retirement: two of a kind'. *Psychology and Aging,* 23(2): 422–434.

Venkateswarlu, D. 2007. *Child Bondage Continues in Indian Cotton Supply Chain.* Hyderabad: Global Research and Consultancy Services.

Vickerstaff, S., and Cox, J. 2005. 'Retirement and risk: the individualisation of retirement experiences?' *Sociological Review,* 53(1): 77–95.

von Steinau-Steinrück, R. et al. 2009. *Age Discrimination Law in Europe*. New York: Wolters Kluwer.

Walker, H. et al. 2007. 'Women's experiences and perceptions of age discrimination in employment: implications for research and policy'. *Social Policy and Society*, 6(1): 37–48.

Wallis, P. 2008. 'Apprenticeship and training in premodern England'. *Journal of Economic History*, 68(03): 832–861.

Warhurst, C., and Nickson, D. 2007. 'Employee experience of aesthetic labour in retail and hospitality'. *Work Employment and Society*, 21(1): 103–120.

Warhurst, C. et al. 2009. 'Lookism: the new frontier of employment discrimination?' *Journal of Industrial Relations*, 51(1): 131–136.

Weiss, R. S. 2005. *The Experience of Retirement*. Cornell: Cornell University Press.

Weller, C. E. 2010. 'Introduction: retirement security in the Great Recession'. *Journal of Aging & Social Policy*, 22(2): 95–98.

Wellner, A. S. 2000. 'Generational divide'. *American Demographics*, 22(10): 52–58.

Westerman, J. W., and Yamamura, J. H. 2007. 'Generational preferences for work environment fit: effects on employee outcomes'. *Career Development International*, 12(2): 150–161.

Williams, A. et al. 1997. 'Talking about Generation X: Defining them as they define themselves'. *Journal of Language and Social Psychology*, 16(3): 251–277.

Williams, A., Ylanne, V., and Wadleigh, P. M. 2007. 'Selling the "elixir of life": images of the elderly in an Olivio advertising campaign'. *Journal of Aging Studies*, 21: 1–21.

Wilson, D., Sharp, C., and Patterson, A. 2006. *Young People and Crime: Findings from the 2005 Offending, Crime and Justice Survey*. London: Statistical Bulletin, Home Office Research Development and Statistics Directorate.

Winstanley, D., Clark, J., and Leeson, H. 2002. 'Approaches to child labour in the supply chain'. *Business Ethics: A European Review*, 11(3): 210–223.

Wolf, N. 1990. *The Beauty Myth*. London: Chatto and Windus.

Wolfe, I. 2009. 'Age discrimination charges spike: more fallout from Perfect Labor Storm' (17 March 2009), <http://hrblog.typepad.com/perfect_labor_storm/2009/03/age-discrimination-charges-spike-more-fallout-from-perfect-labor-storm-.html>, accessed 8 September 2010.

Wood, G., Harcourt, M., and Harcourt, S. 2004. 'The effects of age discrimination legislation on workplace practice: a New Zealand case study'. *Industrial Relations Journal*, 35(4): 359–371.

Wood, G., Wilkinson, A., and Harcourt, M. 2008. 'Age discrimination and working life: perspectives and contestations—a review of the contemporary literature'. *International Journal of Management Reviews*, 10(4): 425–442.

Woodall, J. 2007. 'Barriers to positive mental health in a Young Offenders Institution: a qualitative study'. *Health Education Journal*, 66(2): 132–140.

Zeisel, J. 2010. *I'm Still Here*. London: Piatkus Books.

Zeitzen, M. K. 2008. *Polygamy: A Cross-Cultural Analysis*. Oxford: Berg Publishers.

Ziyane, I. S., and Ehlers, V. J. 2007. Swazi men's contraceptive knowledge, attitudes, and practices. *Journal of Transcultural Nursing*, 18(1): 5–11.

Index

Boxes, figures and tables are indexed in bold.